THE NATIONAL INSTITUTE OF
ECONOMIC AND SOCIAL RESEARCH

Economic and Social Studies
XXXV

UNEMPLOYMENT: A PROBLEM OF POLICY

Analysis of British Experience and Prospects

UNEMPLOYMENT: A PROBLEM OF POLICY

Analysis of British Experience and Prospects

BY

G. D. N. WORSWICK

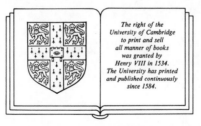

The right of the
University of Cambridge
to print and sell
all manner of books
was granted by
Henry VIII in 1534.
The University has printed
and published continuously
since 1584.

CAMBRIDGE UNIVERSITY PRESS

CAMBRIDGE

NEW YORK   PORT CHESTER

MELBOURNE   SYDNEY

Published by the Press Syndicate of the University of Cambridge
The Pitt Building, Trumpington Street, Cambridge CB2 1RP
40 West 20th Street, New York, NY 10011, USA
10 Stamford Road, Oakleigh, Melbourne 3166, Australia

First published 1991

Printed in Great Britain at
the University Press, Cambridge

British Library cataloguing in publication data

Worswick, G. D. N. (George David Norman)
Unemployment: a problem of policy: analysis of British
experience and prospects. (Economic and social studies): 35
1. Unemployment government policy Great Britain
I. Title   II. Series
331.13794

Library of Congress cataloguing in publication data

Worswick, G. D. N. (George David Norman)
Unemployment: a problem of policy: analysis of British
experience and prospects / by G. D. N. Worswick.
p.   cm. – (Economic and social studies: 35)
Includes bibliographical references.
ISBN 0 521 40034 1
1. Unemployed – Great Britain. 2. Unemployment – Great Britain.
3. Wages – Great Britain. 4. Great Britain – Economic policy – 1945–
HD5765.A6W69   1991
331.13'7941–dc20   90-44287

ISBN 0 521 40034 1 hardback

CONTENTS

PART 1   STRUCTURAL CHANGE

PART 2   THE WAGE QUESTION

PART 3   MACROECONOMIC POLICY

PART 4   INTERNATIONAL DIMENSION

LIST OF TABLES

SYMBOLS IN THE TABLES
... not available
– nil or negligible
n.a. not applicable

LIST OF CHARTS

PREFACE

Readers may recognise the provenance of the title of this book. To his study of *Unemployment*, published in 1909, W. H. Beveridge gave a sub-title, 'A Problem of Industry'. That work had a strong empirical foundation in trade union records of allowances paid to their members during unemployment, in the reports of Distress Committees, and in other sources. His principal recommendations were for the improved organisation of the labour market through Labour Exchanges to be established throughout the country and for the extension of unemployment insurance. The change of one word in the sub-title, from 'Industry' to 'Policy', denotes more than the minimum necessary to differentiate the product: it signifies that unemployment is here placed in a broader setting, which includes what is nowadays called macroeconomic policy, and which gives greater emphasis to the international dimension, recognising that British prospects for employment and unemployment are bound up with foreign trade and the movements of capital, as well as regional and worldwide institutions such as the European Economic Community and GATT. Beveridge himself had moved a long way in this direction when he published *Full Employment in a Free Society* in 1944. If there is a link with the 1909 Beveridge in the choice of title, there is another with the 1944 vintage, inasmuch as the present author is a survivor of the team of European economists in Oxford who wrote the *Economics of Full Employment*, which appeared almost simultaneously with the other study, and whose influence on his own thinking Beveridge generously acknowledged.

The change of standpoint between 1909 and 1944 can be summed up in two sentences. In 1909, Beveridge wrote: 'A rising demand for labour will be no cure for unemployment.' In 1944, we find: 'Adequate total demand for labour in an unplanned market economy cannot be taken for granted.' This reversal was brought about by the experience of the Great Depression and the theorising of J. M. Keynes. The debate which began among economists about Keynes's theory was overtaken by the war, and after the war it lay comparatively dormant because for a quarter of a century in most mature economies unemployment ceased to be much of a problem at all. However, its reappearance in the 1970s, and even more so in the 1980s, has reopened old questions, as well as bringing new ones, such as the persistence of inflation whether unemployment is high or low. But it has done so in a new context. The statistical recording of economic developments has been greatly extended in all mature economies, so that nowadays one can put hypotheses to the test of evidence in a far more systematic manner than was previously possible. There now exists a large and rapidly growing volume of empirical research bearing on various aspects of employment and unemployment. Much of it makes use of international comparisons, though our ultimate concern is with prospects in Britain. Empirical tests in economics, however, are rarely decisive, and important theoretical differences still remain. My object, in such cases, has not been to try to resolve them and 'advance the subject'. My purpose in this book is to explain the nature of theoretical differences in a manner intelligible to the educated non-specialist, and to bring to his or her attention the results of relevant empirical research and historical experience. I have not tried to hide my own opinions, but I have tried to be fair in presenting the opinions of others.

In writing this book, I have received help of many different kinds. My first obligation is to the Director, Andrew Britton, who encouraged me to take on a project at the National Institute. His invitation was a compliment which I very much appreciated, and I hope I have justified his confidence. The project could not have been undertaken without a generous grant from the Leverhulme Trust, for which I am very grateful. It enabled the Institute to appoint a research officer for three years, and I should like to thank the two holders of this post, Robert Gausden, who was especially helpful on the wage question, and Paul Gregg, who researched into many issues, statistical, structural and historical. They provided me with a great deal of material, but they are not responsible for the use I have made of it. Among colleagues who have commented on drafts, I must especially thank Michael Artis and John Bispham, not only for taking so much trouble over details, but for their efforts to put me right on important questions. I also thank Arthur Brown, Humphrey Cole, Peter Hart, David Mayes, Sig Prais and David Savage for comment at various stages. The views expressed, and errors which remain, are my responsibility alone. Kit Jones, Secretary, and the staff of the Institute were invariably helpful, notwithstanding my intermittent appearances. Fran Robinson took a great load off my shoulders in preparing the book for the Press, and in making the index. In Oxford, the Institute of Economics and Statistics kindly provided me with a place to work, and my wife gave much encouragement, particularly at times of dismay at the size of the job I had taken on.

June, 1990   G. D. N. Worswick

INTRODUCTION

The question I asked myself, in 1985, when work on this book began, was whether Britain had to have three million unemployed 'for ever'. Prior to the mid-1970s, a figure of one million unemployed had been considered by almost everyone as very high, and this view still prevailed at the time of the 1979 General Election, when 1.2 million was the basis of the famous 'Labour Isn't Working' electioneering slogan. But, from then on, unemployment rose in every year, going beyond three million in 1985 and, though output was once more growing quite strongly, there seemed little to suggest that unemployment would fall significantly. Medium-term projections by reputable teams of applied economists had unemployment staying at three million to 1990 and beyond. In the event, after a prolonged period during which the cumulation of person-years of unemployment was one and a quarter times that experienced in the 1930s (see Gregg and Worswick, 1988), unemployment fell fast after the end of 1986, and by the end of 1989 had fallen below 1.7 million. However, by the Spring of 1990, all the indications were that it was not going to go much further down, and might well start to rise again. If this should prove to be the case, this bottom turning point will be higher than the peak figure of the 1970s, and more than a million greater than the highest figure encountered before that.

Among the factors bringing about the swing from Conservative to Labour across the Second World War, many would give a high place to the fear of a return to the persistent unemployment of the interwar years – rarely less than 10 per cent, and rising beyond 20 per cent in the early 1930s. The wartime coalition government's white paper on *Employment Policy* recognised the responsibility of government to maintain a 'high and stable level of employment' after the war, but put no figure on this concept. In 1951, in answer to an enquiry from the United Nations Social and Economic Council as to what the British government considered to be 'full employment', it gave 3 per cent as the 'endurable maximum' of unemployment. In the event, for the next twenty years, actual unemployment was normally to run well below this. Not only that: it came to be accepted as an axiom of British politics that no government could survive any significant and sustained increase in unemployment. It is difficult to put precise figures on this statement, if only because the way unemployment is measured and percentage rates calculated changes over the years. But it is certainly the case that a suggestion made in the 1960s that such and such a policy risked causing three million unemployed was sufficient to reject it out of hand: no government could survive it, so it was said. The most significant political discovery of the 1980s was precisely that, not only can governments survive, but they can be re-elected with an increased majority, with unemployment approaching three million and still rising. Although much of the rise was the consequence of the government's own fiscal and monetary policies, one may doubt that it was intended when the policies were put in place. It is true that the Thatcher administration was the first since the Second World War explicitly to reject the idea that it could exercise direct control over the level of employment. At the same time, all the statements accompanying the 'monetarist' strategy being adopted indicated a belief that any 'transitional' increase in unemployment, during which the public, and especially trade unions, adapted their behaviour to the new regime, would be small. But, if not intended, the government was quick to appreciate that the very much higher unemployment was not nearly as electorally damaging as had been believed for so long, and felt under no obligation to follow such conventional policies as increased public expenditure which were being pressed upon it by many economists and by the opposition.

The practical demonstration of the invalidity of a long-held political doctrine prompts the idea that, perhaps, it may never have been true: it was constantly repeated, but had never been tested. Following this line of thought, more attention might have been paid to the General Election of 1935, in which the national government was returned with a majority of 247 seats when unemployment was still of the order of 2½ million. Alternatively, the doctrine could have been true in the social climate of the years of postwar reconstruction, but gradually lost its force as living standards rose, and memories of the Depression receded. If, notwith-standing high unemployment, the real incomes of the great majority of men and women who remain in work are seen to be rising steadily, as was the case in the 1980s, their interest in keeping things as they are might outweigh their concern for the less fortunate minority.

Whatever the reasons for its ultimate failure, the doctrine could only retain its force so long as the public believed that it was within the power of government to influence the levels of employment and unemployment. Perhaps the change in political attitudes reflected the public's recognition of the truth of the Thatcher government's assertion that it had no such power. As Nigel Lawson, then Chancellor of the Exchequer, told the Conservative Party Conference in 1984: 'You will not reduce unemploy-ment by increasing government spending or borrowing'. Did this imply that the principles of 'demand management', followed for more than a quarter of a century by Labour and Conservative governments alike, had always been wrong – so that full employment had come about, not because of but despite the efforts of government to achieve it? Or was it, perhaps, that changes had taken place in the structure or circumstances of the economy, so that policies once efficacious were no longer appropriate?

These changes in the perception of the electoral significance of unemployment, and of the power of government to do anything about it if it occurs, make this a good moment to review the prospects for employment and unemployment in Britain in the years ahead. To do this, we must obviously give consideration to the 'macroeconomic' questions of monetary and fiscal policy, because these are the ones which continue to receive most attention in public discussion. But the net has been cast more widely. There were those who pointed to the extraordinary advances taking place in computers and in the application of microelectronic technology in all forms of economic activity, with new equipment displacing workers, often in very large numbers. Before long, there would not be enough jobs to go round, and more and more people would have to learn to live without work. Casual enquiry among acquaintances not blessed with formal training in economics quickly produced a long list of additional candidates to explain three million unemployed. Apart from the last Labour government, and Mrs Thatcher, there were: the trade unions; unemployment benefit; New Commonwealth (that is, coloured) immigrants; the Common Market; competition from low wage countries, like Taiwan or Korea; competition from high wage (and productivity) countries like Germany. It seemed to me that it might make a good starting point not to reject any candidate out of hand, but to take it on its merits and seek, in books and, more especially, in recent journals, what evidence applied economists have been finding which bears on the various causes or explanations of employment and unemployment appearing on the list. This proved more Sisyphean than I had anticipated: no sooner was a section 'finished' than a new article, or quite often a book, appeared putting in serious question work hitherto considered definitive. I make no claim to have made a comprehensive survey: the list of journals I have not consulted is a lot longer than the list of those my colleague (one post - two persons) and I had time for. Still less do I claim to have been, for more than a fraction of the time, engaged in original research, as currently understood in the best economics departments. To borrow the phrase used by the *National Institute Economic Review*, I have written for those 'in business, and elsewhere, who need to take a view of the general economic situation and prospects'.

The evidence about the working of economies and of the effects of government policies is drawn from many countries, but when it comes to prospects the focus of interest is Britain. British prospects are, of course, closely tied to the rest of the world and especially to the Economic Community. But, as will be apparent, I think that national governments will continue to exercise considerable economic influence. The choice of policies depends partly on their intrinsic economic merits, and partly on their political feasibility. And there are times when the British two-party system seems to have rendered sensible economic policy virtually impossible. It is easier to bring out the interplay between politics and economics for a case with which I am familiar. French and German readers, should there prove to be any, will be able to make the necessary adjustments.

The late David Watt once asked me, in the early 1970s, when unemployment was still comparatively low, why I still worried about the unemployment consequences of different policies. If social security was adequate, why be bothered about employment as such? Having a job still is, in a society making ever increasing use of the division of labour, the only access to income for the majority of men and women. Adequate social security is an alternative source, but only partial. It provides no means for the recipient to increase his or her income. On the contrary many systems, including our own, may include 'poverty traps', discouraging self-help. Not all jobs permit increased earnings, but some do. Moreover, social security may have conditions attached, just as wealthy parents are no absolute income guarantee for their children. Besides income, a job gives status. Some jobs give more status than others, but even the most lowly employee can have a sense of belonging, of contributing to the common pool as well as taking out of it. Not everyone has a desire for status, or feels an obligation to contribute – but most do. I would not make work of this or that kind compulsory as, from time to time, the Chinese do. By full employment, I mean a state of affairs in which everyone who wants to work, can. Much work is arduous and repetitive, and it is not always easy to see it in the role of liberator. But can anyone doubt the role which the possibility of employment outside the home has played during this century in advancing the status and extending the freedom of women. Someone who is able and willing to work, but is unable to find a job, is being denied a basic human right in a civilised society.

If one could weigh in a balance different social and political objectives, on some absolute scale, the achievement of full employment in Britain might not come top of the list. The averting of ecological disaster for the planet, or the elimination of the terrible poverty in Africa may seem more important. On that scale, Britain's employment problems may seem little local matters. But they are of interest precisely because full employment has turned out to be so difficult. Thirty years ago most economists would have said that 'the problem of unemployment has been solved'. But, before our eyes it has been unsolved. How did that happen? What has gone wrong? If we are to speculate about future employment prospects, we must give answers to those sorts of question.

Before we come to analysis, we must get a grip on concepts and numbers. Who is 'employed', 'self-employed' or 'unemployed'? How are these categories defined, how do the definitions change and what are the numbers involved? The next chapter deals with such questions, and inevitably brings in a lot of statistics, which many readers will be tempted to pass by. But I would urge them not to skip the section on the relation between employment and unemployment. In ordinary discourse, there is a tendency to speak of a rise in employment and a fall in unemployment as two sides of the same coin. It comes as a surprise to find employment and unemployment rising together: yet this paradoxical behaviour is quite common. If there is an upward trend in employment, such as has been apparent in the United States for a long time, it requires only a slowing down in the rate of increase for unemployment to rise. Another reason is a change in definition, of which there have been many for unemployment in recent years in Britain. In theoretical discussion one is apt to put these reservations at the back of one's mind, and to speak of employment and unemployment changes as mirror images. It is as well to start off with a strong antidote.

The main body of the work is grouped in four parts, as follows: 1) Structural Change; 2) Real Wages, Nominal Wages and Employment; 3) Macroeconomic Policy; 4) The International Dimension. The last three parts, in the main, approach the determinants of employment and unemployment in macroeconomic terms. They deal with aggregate concepts, such as total employment and unemployment, exports and imports, national income and output, and rates of inflation. This is the approach to be found in textbooks and in articles in quality newspapers. Implicitly, this approach treats labour and capital, or exports and imports, as though they were totals of homogeneous units. In the structuralist approach the emphasis is on the heterogeneity of the components of demand and supply. Men and women are employed, full-time or part-time, in particular firms in particular industries in particular places. If there is a spontaneous change in the pattern of demand, or if new products or new processes are introduced, firms must adapt to the change, and so must workers. In some sectors, shortages of labour will appear, while in others there will be surpluses. For the gaps to close again, workers displaced from declining firms and industries must find out where the new jobs are. They may need retraining, or to move their homes, which takes time; meanwhile they may be unemployed. The structuralist approach attempts to identify the various types of imbalance or mismatch between occupations, industries and locations.

The structuralist and macroeconomic approaches to employment and unemployment are not mutually exclusive; they are complementary. Nevertheless, far more attention has in fact been paid to the macro-economic approach in the past fifty years and more, and the structuralists have not had much of a showing. Structuralist explanations of the Depression of the 1930s did not catch on. The idea appeared again in the early 1960s in the United States, when unemployment was high, and was used in argument against expansionist fiscal and monetary policy. It received a magisterial dismissal from Robert Solow in the Wicksell Lecture in Stockholm in 1964 (Solow, 1964). But that was a quarter of a century ago. Times have changed. In Britain in the 1980s, demand management has been under a cloud, and the emphasis put on the 'supply side'. This is a somewhat ambiguous expression, but it certainly includes the ideas of the importance of change, and the removal of obstacles which might stand in its way. It seems appropriate, therefore, to start with the structuralist approach.

PART I.   STRUCTURAL CHANGE

In the macroeconomics of output and employment, the 'state of the arts' is implicitly taken as given. In the longer run, however, it is clear that changes in 'the state of the arts', that is, innovation in productive processes and in goods and services, have a powerful influence on the pattern and volume of employment. In this part we explore various aspects of the impact of change on employment. The most continuing source of structural change in industry is new technology, which is the subject of the first chapter. A brief review indicates that economic theory recognises the possibility of lasting technological unemployment. *A priori* one would expect any speeding up of technical change to give rise to higher unemployment. However, the slowdown of productivity growth which has occurred since 1973 in the Western world puts a question mark against this thesis. In a parenthesis, however, we consider whether a 'productivity miracle' occurred in Britain during the 1980s. It can be argued that, whatever the economic performance so far, the full effects of information technology (IT) have yet to be felt and a separate chapter is devoted to a number of surveys of current and expected use of IT.

Technical change is the main factor causing the initial displacement of workers, although we should not exclude spontaneous changes in tastes. When unemployment rises, it could be because of such displacements, or because of a deficiency in demand. A number of statistical analyses have attempted to distinguish between 'structural' and 'demand deficiency' unemployment, and some of them are briefly reviewed. The results are ambiguous, but there is one mismatch, namely that between different regions of the British economy, which has been so enduring that it is pursued in much greater detail. Besides describing past developments we consider whether policies exist which might lead to more balanced employment and to lower unemployment.

Common to the amelioration of almost every kind of mismatch is the need for training and retraining of men and women, for first employment, and for subsequent re-employment following the disappearance of old jobs. Who should provide this training, how should it be financed? In the final chapter of this part we ask who will provide the jobs in the future. There has lately been a notable growth of self-employment: nevertheless, most men and women will continue to be employees, of private firms or of a variety of employers in the public sector. How should we expect these different forms to develop in the future? In the private sector, will it be, as many believe, the small firms which will provide the jobs, or will large firms remain the employers for most workers? And is there a role for the public sector, especially in the provision of services?

PART 2. THE WAGE QUESTION

Of the many links between wages and employment, two have been most prominent at different times. In classical models of the economy, the level of employment is determined by the level of real wages. In this approach, 'involuntary unemployment' does not occur. In the real world wages are normally contracted and paid in money, and the 'real wage' then depends on how prices subsequently behave. The first chapter of this part explores, with the aid of statistical evidence and international comparisons, the complex relationships between nominal wages, real wages and employment. The conclusion is that for most of the postwar period, the significant wage 'problem' for Britain has been not excessive real wages, but the tendency for nominal wage increases (wage inflation) to be somewhat too big, whether there is full employment, or unemployment. As a result, governments have increasingly resorted to policies whose consequence is higher unemployment, in the hope of curbing the wage inflation. The following three chapters explore policy alternatives which have been suggested to overcome the tendency.

Wage subsidies have been proposed as a means of increasing employment in a number of contexts, among them the idea that the objectives of devaluation might be achieved without provoking the knock-on effects on nominal wage claims. Profit sharing has a long and, until recently, undistinguished history but has come into fashion again, partly as a result of Weitzman's vigorous argument that it would be a powerful antidote to stagflation. The last chapter in this part reviews the theoretical status, as well as the experience in many countries, of incomes policies. They have been very much out of fashion in Britain in the 1980s, but, since the alternative solution to the problem they were invented to solve has so far, in Britain at any rate, proved no more efficacious, it is possible that future governments may find themselves embarking once more on this difficult road.

PART 3. MACROECONOMIC POLICY

For a quarter of a century after the war, the doctrine that fiscal policy should aim to balance the economy, and not just the budget, was generally accepted by British economists and governments alike. The new orthodoxy of demand management was challenged in the later 1970s both by the speeding up of inflation and the doctrine of monetarism, which, for a brief spell, dictated policy in the early 1980s. The extent to which, if at all, governments can determine the level of employment, became a matter of acute controversy. This is the first of two difficulties confronting anyone attempting an objective analysis. The other difficulty is that the British economy is not self-contained. Government policies aimed at promoting employment in Britain may have favourable, or unfavourable, effects on employment in other countries, just as the policies of other countries will have effects on employment here. The difficulty has been compounded by the fact that the 'openness' of the British economy has not been constant, and the institutional framework within which it works is also changing. Under the Bretton Woods system, exchange rates were fixed, but could be altered in certain circumstances. That system had crumbled by the early 1970s, since when exchange rates have floated, or have been fixed with respect to some currencies and floating with respect to others, as in the European Exchange Rate Mechanism (ERM). It seems likely too that British employment will be increasingly influenced in a variety of ways by the policies of the European Community.

We shall try to overcome the second difficulty of openness by means of the conventional, if unsatisfactory, device of first analysing the scope for government employment policy as though the British economy were self-contained, or 'closed', and then considering in a fourth part the extent to which conclusions reached for a closed economy have to be modified, or even reversed, by openness. Clumsy though it is, this device has one advantage. Much of the theoretical debate has related to an imaginary closed economy. Whether this has been because of analytical convenience, or because many of the arguments originated in the United States, which in the past has been less open than, say, Britain or France or

Germany, it is interesting to speculate. But with a closed economy, it is easier to bring to the surface the nature of the issues which have divided economists in the last twenty years. The first chapter of Part 3 is theoretical and discusses two basic types of model of the economy – 'classical' and 'Keynesian'. The former, which includes various forms of monetarism, has the central property that, if upset by a shock of some kind, the economy will find its way back to an 'equilibrium' position, including, *inter alia*, full employment of labour. 'Keynesian' models, on the other hand, allow for the possibility that disturbances will not be self-correcting: the equilibrating mechanism can get stuck, or, to change the metaphor, the gears may fail to mesh. Consequently unemployment may be persistent. This theoretical excursion indicates the kind of evidence needed to decide which kind of model best represents actual economies. First comes a survey of evidence of a general nature, and in the following chapter there is an historical sketch of some important policy episodes in different countries at different times. The general conclusion of this chapter is that demand management still 'works' in the way one would expect, and the argument that it is ineffective is not borne out. In many cases, it was the objectives of policy which changed, moving away from the maintenance of employment to the containment of inflation. We had already noted in Part 2 the proneness of the British economy to nominal wage inflation which is too high for comfort in international competition. The relation between economic behaviour and policy objectives is one of the themes taken up in the final chapter of this part. Also discussed is the 'electoral' cycle, sometimes called the 'political business cycle'. This leads on to a broader discussion of the interaction between economics and politics in the British context and to the extent to which policies which economists think feasible can be translated into political action. The conclusions reached here about employment policy have to be subject to the constraints which may be imposed by openness on the one hand, and international commitments, notably to the European Community on the other. These form the subject of Part 4.

PART 4. THE INTERNATIONAL DIMENSION

'Openness' involves migration of people, trade in goods and services and the movement of capital. The significance of 'openness' for the economy is examined in the context of the successive stages of deregulation, both domestic and international, since the war, and of the different international regimes from Bretton Woods to the latest stage of internationally managed floating. There follows an analysis of the situations in which the international dimension helps, or hinders, domestic employment policy.

Particular attention is given to capital movements and the exchange rate. The discussion is conducted in general terms, and then narrowed to the European dimension, especially the EMS and the exchange rate mechanism, the single market, and the possibility of a European government with significant budgetary leverage. The obvious conclusion is reached that British employment prospects are affected by international competitiveness. Since this conclusion will be reached by every other country as well, the scope for improved competitiveness depends as much on international cooperation as it does on nationalistic competition.

For much of the postwar period the doctrine prevailed that a sustained deficit in the balance of payments on current account constituted a constraint on domestic expansion. In the last few years contrary arguments have been put forward and it is important to understand them. If a deficit has to be reduced, the key is a reduction in the real exchange rate. What is the scope for this in a world of free capital movements? How far can one country achieve it acting alone? Would it be helped by international cooperation and, if so, what is the scope for this? In a final chapter of this part we shall look at some aspects of the European Economic Community, in particular the single market, the exchange rate mechanism of the European Monetary System and the implications of a common currency.

We shall attempt, in a concluding chapter, to draw together the different strands and to state what we believe to be the most likely prospects for employment, indicating the most important factors which will improve or worsen these prospects.

2

CONCEPTS AND MEASUREMENTS

Employment, in the sense in which we use the word in this book, is 'paid work'. A man paints his own house; that is work, but not employment. Another does the painting, for which money is paid; the work becomes employment. If the money is paid to a firm, which, in turn, pays a wage to the painter, he is employed, pure and simple. If there is no firm, and the money goes into his own pocket, he is self-employed. Our interest in employment is primarily as a means of livelihood. In an economy with extensive division of labour and specialisation, the possibility for most men or women being able to fend entirely for themselves and independently of others is virtually nil. To ensure a livelihood, it is not necessary to keep the same employment, but to have some employment. The appropriate income unit is a household, which may be a single person, but also includes a group of people who live at the same address. Employment and self-employment are not the only sources of income. There is income from property, in the form of rent, interest and dividends. Some 'private incomes' provide sufficient for the recipient not to need employment. In 1989 one fifth of the adult population owned some shares, which means that four fifths had none. The main source of income for those seeking employment, but unable to find it, is social security. The dominant importance of income from employment and self-employment is shown for some recent years in table 2.1. The table excludes some miscellaneous items which total less than 3 per cent.

Table 2.1. *Percentage distribution of household incomes (United Kingdom)*

	1971	1981	1985	1988
Wages and salaries	68	64	60	60
Income from self-employment	9	8	9	10
Rent, dividends and interest	6	6	7	8
Private pensions, annuities	5	6	8	8
Social Security benefits	10	13	13	12

Source: *Social Trends 20*, HMSO, 1990.

THE LABOUR FORCE

On the whole the various concepts relating to employment have not been particularly contentious, although there are some problems in the treatment of part-time employees; double jobs, that is, jobs separately counted but done by one person; and 'discouraged workers', that is people of working age who dropped out of the working population because they did not look for jobs simply because they believed there were none to find, and were not qualified for unemployment benefit. The principal British source of information about employment is the Labour Force Survey, whose purpose is to identify the level and structure of employment and unemployment in the United Kingdom in a manner which is harmonised and synchronised with similar surveys in all European Community countries. It was based in 1989 on a responding sample of over 60,000 households. It provides annual data.[1]

In 1971, as many as 30 per cent of men aged 65–9, and 29 per cent of women aged 60–4 were in, or searching for, employment. These activity rates had fallen by 1988 to 12 and 20 per cent respectively: but, though these are not negligible numbers, they are not included in the conventional population of working age, which is 16–64 for men, and 16–59 for women, 65 and 60 being the ages when statutory pensions become available (subject to deductions for those who stay in employment). The *population of working age* (Great Britain),[2] 26.6 million in 1987, had risen by two million in the previous decade, but is expected to grow by only a further half a million in the next decade. The *economically active*, or the labour force, consist of those in employment, *plus* the unemployed, as measured nowadays according to ILO/OECD definitions.[3] Take away from this total the armed forces, and we arrive at the *civilian labour force*. The *economically inactive* are those who have retired, are keeping house, or are permanently unable to work. The civilian labour force (Great Britain) in 1971 was just below 25 million and, by 1980, it had risen by 1.5 million, only to lose nearly half a million in the next two years. From 1983 onwards, it rose quite strongly to reach 28 million in mid-1989. This implied an average annual increase over the whole eighteen year period of 166,000. The Department of Employment projects, on the assumption of a constant pressure of demand for labour at the level of January 1990, that the civilian labour force would rise by a further 0.8 million by the year 2001, implying an average annual rate of increase of 67,000. The growth of the total is, therefore, much slower than it was in the past two decades, and most of the increase is women, who are expected to make up 45 per cent of the labour force in 2001.

Table 2.2. *Estimates and projections of civilian activity rates in Great Britain*
per cent

	1971	1976	1981	1986	1991	1996	2001
Males							
Working age	90.7	90.5	89.1	86.4	87.2	87.1	86.7
All ages	80.5	78.9	76.5	73.9	74.2	73.5	72.9
Females							
Working age	56.7	62.2	64.0	67.5	72.1	73.8	74.8
All ages	43.9	46.8	47.6	49.9	53.3	54.6	55.4

Sources: *Employment Gazette*, May 1987 and April 1990.

ACTIVITY RATES

Beneath the comparatively placid slow climb of the labour force there have been some significant changes in composition in the past two decades. Table 2.2 shows activity rates for males and females in selected years since 1971, extended to include the Department of Employment's projections.

The activity rate for males of working age – over 90 per cent in the 1970s – dropped nearly 4 percentage points in the recession, but rebounded, though not fully in the subsequent recovery. The apparent stability in the projection period reflects mainly the method of calculation which assumes a constant pressure of demand for labour. The difference between the activity rate for 'all ages' and 'working age' starts at 10 per cent in 1971 and widens to 14 per cent in 2001, reflecting a tendency for a diminishing proportion of men in the higher age groups to remain economically active. The activity rate for females of working age rose strongly in the 1970s: it did fall in the recession, but only by less than one percentage point, whereupon it resumed its upward march. This is continued in the projection period so that, at the turn of the century, nearly three women of working age out of every four will be economically active. As with men, the activity rates drop off in the highest age groups, though not by much. The rising trend of the female activity rate outweighs the decline in the male rate: activity for men and women of working age taken together, which was 74.5 per cent in 1971, will be over 80 per cent at the end of the century.

EMPLOYMENT

By definition, the Civilian Labour Force is the sum of Employees in jobs *plus* Self-employed *plus* People on Government Work Training Schemes

Table 2.3. *Male and female employees in employment: Great Britain (millions)*

	1971	1979	1983	1989
Male	13.4	13.2	11.9	11.7
Female	8.2	9.5	8.9	10.2

Sources: *Annual Abstracts of Statistics; Employment Gazette.*

plus Unemployed. It would be convenient if the labour force were exogenous, but we have seen that it varies with the demand for labour. In booms, employment rises, not only by drawing from the unemployed, but by bringing into the economically active men and, particularly, women who had previously been inactive. There is no point in searching for jobs when they are not to be found: when jobs become more plentiful, more people will join the search. Similarly, in recession, some men who lose jobs will not even register at job centres: this may apply especially to older workers. And some, especially part-time female employees, will not seek jobs which are not there, or they may not be eligible for unemployment benefit. During the 1980s recession, the male activity rate fell sharply, and did not subsequently fully recover. Some of these men may well have entered the 'black economy'.[4]

In chart 8.1 on page 83 we show the course of employment in the United Kingdom since the 1950s. On the scale to which it is drawn, the overall impression is one of flatness. Looking closer, we can see a climb to a peak in 1966, an uneven plateau until 1979, and then a distinct drop at the beginning of the 1980s, followed by some recovery. This drop was the most definite movement either way over a short period in the whole postwar period, and here we look more closely at the developments since the early 1970s.

Table 2.3 shows male and female employment in Great Britain for selected years since 1971. Male employment fell throughout the period until 1989: by 2 per cent in the 1970s, by 9.5 per cent from 1979 to 1983, and by a further 2 per cent up to 1989. By contrast, female employment rose by 15 per cent in the 1970s, fell back by 6 per cent from 1979 to 1983, and then rose again by a further 15 per cent to 1989. In these figures, an employee counts as one, whether part-time or full-time. 4.1 per cent of male employees were part-time in 1971, and 7.7 per cent in 1989, and the fall in employment over the period was entirely of full-timers. In the case of women, both part-time and full-time numbers rose over the whole period, with part-timers, who constituted 33.5 per cent of the total in 1971 and 41.8 per cent in 1989, rising the faster. The fall in full-time male employment was associated with the course of manufacturing industries.

Between 1971 and 1979, employment in these industries fell from 7.9 to 7.1 million, that is, about 1 per cent a year. Then from 1979 to 1983 there was a steep drop from 7.1 to 5.4 million, a fall of 24 per cent. From 1983 to 1989 the fall continued, from 5.4 to 5.1 million, at much the same rate of decline as in the 1970s.

SELF-EMPLOYMENT

The number of self-employed, which had been rising prior to 1971 to a figure of 1.9 million, fell back a little (by 1.2 per cent) in the 1970s. Whereas employees in employment fell by 2.1 million in the recession from 1979 to 1983, the number of self-employed rose by 318,000, divided roughly equally between men and women. From 1983 until 1989, both male and female self-employment continued to rise, the former by 518,000 and the latter by 213,000. Overall the numbers of self-employed rose from 1979 to 1989 by 1.3 million, from under two million to over three million. This is an extraordinary change, and there are two principal explanations. Firstly, a shift to self-employment is a phenomenon which has been observed before in recessions in Britain and elsewhere. When jobs disappear, perforce men and women set up for themselves. What is significant about the 1980s recession is that in terms of employment it was so prolonged. Adding employees in employment and self-employed together, the total had fallen between 1979 and 1983 by 1.75 million, or 7 per cent. It was not until 1988 that the 1979 total was reached again and surpassed: in every year between it had been below the starting level. The second factor is a product of the 'enterprise culture', the encouragement given by the government, in the form of tax reliefs and other measures, to small enterprises, whose heads will appear, in many cases, in the self-employed category. That the growth of self employment is not exclusively accounted for by the recession is indicated by the growth of self-employment of women, side by side with the growth of employees in employment. Adding employees in employment and self-employment together, we find that the total for males fell by 4 per cent between 1979 and 1989, but the percentage in self-employment rose from 10 to 17 per cent. For women, the total rose by 15 per cent, and the share of self-employment rose from 3.5 to 6.7 per cent. The fact that the percentage share of self-employment in the total of males increased by more than twice that of females, suggests that the recession itself played a significant part.

UNEMPLOYMENT

Current estimates of unemployment are derived from two distinct sources. First, there is the Labour Force Survey (LFS) described above, and from which we drew figures for employment and self-employment. The LFS defines unemployment in terms of seeking for work (see note 3 to this chapter). The second source comes from the administration of unemployment insurance, which dates back to 1911, and which, since the Second World War, has been incorporated in the comprehensive national insurance. This source provides the monthly figures of unemployment, which receive full media coverage. There have been changes, from time to time, of the way in which the numbers unemployed are counted, particularly in the 1980s, of which more a little later. But they do not disguise the large changes which have occurred since the Second World War. In the 21 years 1948–68 inclusive, the highest number of persons wholly unemployed in Great Britain was 550,000 (in 1968), and in only three years did it exceed 500,000. The average over the whole period was 350,000. The highest percentage rate was 2.3. In the 1970s, average unemployment fell just short of one million, with figures well beyond that mark in the later half. In the 1980s, the level of unemployment has been higher in every year than in any previous year since the war, exceeding three million in the mid-1980s, falling back to 1.7 million at the end of 1989. Some commentators in 1989 were suggesting that the economy was 'overheating', with the implication that it might be desirable if unemployment were to stop falling. It is worth emphasising that 1.7 million is still nearly 700,000 higher than it was in 1979 on the same definition, and well over four times as high as the average of the 1950s and 1960s. To find unemployment experience comparable to the 1980s, it is necessary to go back to the 1930s (Gregg and Worswick, 1988). In these long distance comparisons we have only made rough mental allowance for changes in definition: for instance, in prewar unemployment rates the denominator, 'insured workers' did not cover all employees. But, if a consistent series could be constructed throughout, it would not alter the broad picture. Unfortunately, the same cannot be said with such confidence for the 1980s.

Our concern is primarily with the official figures published monthly by the Department of Employment. Most of the discussion has referred to the estimates for the United Kingdom and, accordingly, we switch from the Great Britain basis which we have used so far. In 1974, job centres were separated from social security benefit offices and thereafter the number of unemployed was based on registrations at job centres. In 1982, this registration became voluntary, and the new criterion for unemployment became the number of claims for, and receipts of, unemployment or supplementary benefit. The effect of the switch was to reduce the numbers unemployed in October, 1982, by 190,000. The benefit criterion is easy to measure monthly but, according to Johnson (1988), there is only a two-thirds overlap between the claimant count and the Labour

Force Survey measure which is used for international comparisons. In the spring of 1986, it excluded 800,000 persons who were not entitled to benefit, but were seeking work, but it included 860,000 persons who were claiming benefit, but had not, in fact, looked for work in the past four weeks. Johnson argued that if one counted all those caught in the claimant net and all those caught in the Labour Force Survey net, the number unemployed must have been nearer four million than the official 3.2 million.

Let us put the Labour Force Survey aside, and return to the official figures. In October, 1979, a decision to pay benefits fortnightly had the effect of increasing the numbers unemployed by 20,000. But after that date, every redefinition of the official statistics (and they went into double figures) had the effect of reducing the official estimate. Johnson has a table listing changes between 1979 and 1986 which add up to 458,000, the two largest being the switch from registration to claiming benefit and, in 1985, a new treatment of men of sixty and over, which had the effect of their leaving the definition, though not the substance of unemployment. These changes were not the only way in which the official estimates were reduced; the other way was by 'Special Measures' which, by March 1987, had, according to Johnson, reduced the unemployed by nearly 400,000. Together with redefinition, this would have raised the official count to over four million in 1986. Not all those on special employment programmes, such as the Community Programme, would necessarily have been unemployed, if they had not been involved: just as likely, they would have been 'economically inactive'. The Department of Employment only began to publish figures for 'work-related training'[5] in 1983. These are in the first row in table 2.4. In the second row are the estimates made by Trinder (1988) for the number covered by special employment and training schemes of all kinds. He enumerates eight programmes in all, of which the Youth Opportunities Programme (YOP), followed by Youth Training Schemes and Community Programmes were the largest, with Job Release and Enterprise allowance contributing significant numbers. There is general agreement that YOP was a hastily contrived cosmetic

Table 2.4. *Special employment measures and training schemes (Great Britain)*

	1981	1982	1983	1984	1985	1986	1987	1988	1989
Dept of Employment	–	–	8	168	168	218	303	335	456
Trinder	318	503	643	651	660	722	776	–	–

Sources: *Employment Gazette*; Trinder (1988).

device, to keep young people off the unemployment register, but it also seems that the genuine training, or employment, element in these schemes has been gradually increasing.

Apart from lowering the average level of unemployment, the changes to official figures had effects on the changes in level, by understating the increase between 1979 and 1983, and then disguising an improvement which was taking place between 1983 and 1986. But, since the official figure began its long drop from 3.1 million at the end of 1986 to less than 1.7 million at the end of 1989, it has been overstating the improvement. This was because a series of moves, in particular the introduction of Restart interviews with the long-term unemployed, discouraged people from claiming benefit who would otherwise have been counted as unemployed.

Gregg (1990) has studied the usefulness of the official monthly unemployment count, which is based on claims for benefit, as an indicator of excess labour supply. He set up a model to estimate the relationship between employment and claimant unemployment, and then added in additional factors such as Special Employment Measures, and variations in the administration of the benefit system. He found that typical labour-supply variables such as post-tax real wages add nothing by way of explanation. Claimant unemployment is a function of eligibility to claim benefit of those not in work, rather than a measure of excess labour supply. He found, for instance, that the effect of Restart interviews was to reduce the claimant count of unemployed by half a million at the beginning of 1988.[6] In studying unemployment over time, or in different countries, it is more common to compare rates than absolute numbers. When unemployment insurance was first introduced in Britain workers had cards which were held and stamped by employers when they were in work, and lodged in labour exchanges when they were out of work. The unemployment rate for a particular industry was the number of cards in the labour exchanges on a certain day divided by the total of cards issued for workers in that industry. In that system the rate of unemployment was unemployed/(unemployed *plus* employed). That ratio remained the basis of the rate until 1986, except that the method for estimating employment changed in a number of ways. In that year it was decided to bring into the denominator the self-employed and HM forces. The economic logic of this was not clear, but the practical effect was to reduce the unemployment rate by 1.4 per cent. Johnson quotes a calculation showing that had the method of counting of 1979 been unchanged, unemployment in September 1986 would have been 3.6 million, and the unemployment rate 14.2 per cent. However, as a result of the changes in the count, and the new way of measuring the rate, the official figures were 3.2 million, and 11.6 per cent.

Table 2.5. *Working population, employment and unemployment, etc. in the United Kingdom and Great Britain (thousands)[a]*

	1971		1988	
	UK	GB	UK	GB
Working population	25,123	24,545	28,211	27,516
Unemployed	724	687	2,341	2,225
Self-employed	1,909	1,842	2,986	2,926
Employees in employment	22,122	21,648	22,226	21,714
Work-related training programmes	–	–	343	335

Source: *Annual Abstract.*
Note: [a]Figures do not add because of exclusion of HM Forces – 368,000 for both the United Kingdom and Great Britain in 1971 and 316,000 in 1988.

It would obviously be helpful to the reader if throughout this book we stuck consistently to one statistical concept of Britain, either the 'United Kingdom', or 'Great Britain'. Unfortunately not all figures are regularly available for the United Kingdom; some are for Great Britain only. Before we leave this preliminary inspection of the statistical picture and turn to the question of full employment, this may therefore be a convenient place to include a table showing the principal magnitudes we have discussed so far for the two areas in recent years.

FULL EMPLOYMENT

In *Full Employment in a Free Society* (1944), William Beveridge referred to one definition of full employment as being, 'a state of affairs in which the number of unfilled vacancies is not appreciably below the number of unemployed persons ...'. He chose himself to define full employment as having more vacant jobs than unemployed persons, rather than slightly fewer, and he added that jobs should be at 'fair wages'. The labour market should always be a seller's market, rather than a buyer's market. Is it possible to interpret such concepts in terms of the kind of number we have just been describing?

Beveridge himself ventured a figure of 3 per cent for Britain. This was not just a guess. It was built up from 1 per cent for frictional unemployment, 1 per cent for seasonal and 1 per cent to allow for fluctuations of exports in an international trading system – and he gave evidence in support of each estimate. But, of course, in 1944 there had not been anything like full employment in peacetime since before 1914. Was it possible, in the years after the Second World War, to make more thoroughgoing estimates from actual data than Beveridge could do? There have been three principal statistical approaches, all of which we shall examine later in this book. The first starts from a postulated inverse relationship between unemployment (U) and unfilled vacancies (V). If there is a well-defined UV curve, the point on it where $U=V$ would make a good starting point. Whether, for full employment, vacancies should be a little less, or rather more, is a gloss to be added later. The second was the Phillips curve (1958) relating wage inflation to unemployment. In this case one could either choose for full employment the level of unemployment which delivered zero wage inflation, or the (lower) level which delivered zero price inflation; or one could choose some even lower level of unemployment which would deliver steady, but still just acceptable, inflation. The third approach, of Friedman (1968), begins by rejecting Phillips in the long run, asserting instead that there is a unique 'natural rate' of unemployment below which there would be accelerating inflation and above which inflation would be decelerating. If this were true, there would be little point in aiming at any level of unemployment below the natural rate, nor, for that matter, above it.

Had any one of the empirical relationships proved strong and stable, it might have provided a bridge from observed data to the desired objective of full employment. But, in the event, neither UV nor Phillips which had initially looked promising, survived the accumulation of new data as time passed. In our view, the evidence for a 'natural rate' of unemployment was the weakest of all. However, the failure to distil operational targets from the data does not leave us exactly where we were before. In the course of research prompted by the original hypotheses, each approach has thrown up ideas of possible consequences of expanding employment and reducing unemployment. Looking back to the mid-1970s, we know that at no time has Britain had full employment. That tells us the direction of the path we want to tread, even though we may not know, until we are some way along it, just how far it will be safe to go.

PART 1

STRUCTURAL CHANGE

3

TECHNOLOGY AND EMPLOYMENT

Many people believe that unemployment has risen to such high levels because technology, especially the revolution in information technology (IT), has destroyed jobs. It is recognised that there is a growing demand for highly trained men and women to construct and to operate computers, microprocessors and manufacturing processes based upon them. But the rising demand for electronic engineers, programmers and the like is far outweighed by the fall in demand for men and women – less skilled workers – whose tasks can now be performed by computer-controlled machinery. In the manufacture of cars, there may still be an assembly line, but there are few men and women adding and fixing component parts: the bulk of the tasks are performed by robots.

Confronted with such fears, we might first refer to history, and observe that technical change which 'saves labour' is neither new nor harmful. Without going as far back as the discovery of fire and the invention of the wheel, we might restrict ourselves to the changes of the past two hundred years since the industrial revolution began in Britain. In this short span of time, succeeding generations have seen remarkable changes in agriculture, in industry and in services, which have brought to the majority of people in the developed world standards of life which, before the eighteenth century, were the lot of only a small minority. The steam engine enormously enhanced the productive powers of workers in industry and in transport on sea and land, so that 'output per worker' was many times that of the handicraft workers and ostlers and coachmen who preceded them. When big advances in technology occurred, there were, it is true, often pools of unemployment left behind among the users of the old methods. Where work had been concentrated in particular areas and no alternative employments were available, such unemployment could cause great hardship. But such 'technological unemployment' would not be permanent. The new advances were accompanied by increasing output and by rising total employment. Not only did workers share in the gains of rising output per worker of goods and services, but there were gains from the reduction of much drudgery and in shorter hours of work.

THE CONTRIBUTION OF ECONOMIC THEORY

The appeal to historical experience will satisfy some, but others will urge that the appeal is unduly complacent. Does economic theory provide us with a clear guidance for the future? If one believes that 'classical' economics gives a good account of economic reality, there is really no problem to examine. The introduction of a new technology may have the immediate effect of putting a number of workers using the older methods out of work, but, if prices and wages are flexible, unemployment cannot persist. Flexible prices will ensure that the adjustment of demands to the new pattern of supply will take place, and flexible wages will ensure that the labour market clears, so that 'full employment' or the 'natural rate of unemployment', according to terminological preference, will be restored. But not all economists accept this optimistic scenario. The equilibrating mechanisms may not function in the prescribed manner to eliminate 'involuntary' unemployment. That was the message of Keynes's *General Theory*. It happens that, in the early presentations of that theory, whether by Keynes himself, or in the Hicksian IS/LM model so much used in American textbooks, 'technology' was implicitly assumed to remain unchanged. But it is possible to link that model with a production function in which technical change of different kinds can be represented by changes in the appropriate coefficients. This has been done by Sinclair (1981). His model is of a closed economy, in which total output, Q, is produced by amounts of homogeneous labour, L, and homogeneous capital, K. The particular form of function he chooses to represent Q, as being determined by K and L, has the property that the elasticity of substitution of labour and capital, which is a measure of the ease with which one factor of production can be substituted for the other, while keeping output unchanged, is constant, irrespective of the relative magnitudes of wages and the rate of interest. This function also contains three coefficients which represent technology, changes in one or the other of which will represent technical change which saves labour, capital or both.[1]

Sinclair is primarily concerned with short-period changes in the economy, in which L may vary, but K is taken to be constant. The supply function we have just described is linked to a set of equations determining aggregate demand. Real income, or expenditure, depends on the rate of interest and the level of real money balances; the demand for nominal money depends on real income, prices and the interest rate; the supply of money depends on the interest rate; and the money market clears. On the demand side, this is a slight modification of the familiar IS/LM representation of a closed economy. By making aggregate demand equal to total supply, Q, the model can be reduced to a single equation in which Q is a function of the price level, P, and the coefficients which appear in the equations for expenditure, the demand for money and the supply of money. Four sub-models are developed, according to four different assumptions about wage behaviour. Each of these sub-models is solved for L, total employment, and the effects of a change in any one of the three 'technology' coefficients are worked out. It turns out that, depending on the values of the various coefficients in the model, the level of employment may rise, or fall. A fall is more likely when the money-wage rate is taken as fixed.

Notwithstanding its apparent sophistication, the assumptions behind this model are highly restrictive. In particular, the capital stock is taken as fixed, which means that technical change is 'disembodied': it is as though a magic wand were passed over all the existing capital stock, which at once becomes more productive. Yet much new technology has to be embodied in new plant or equipment which takes time to produce.

The Sinclair analysis employs the conventional theoretical model which represents production as being undertaken by homogeneous factors, labour and capital, which can be combined in any proportion. A completely different approach, which has the merit of highlighting the importance of investment in new equipment, makes use of the idea of fixed coefficients between the inputs, labour and equipment, and output. In this model, the economy consists initially of a stock of machines, owned by a Planner and operated by labour to produce a consumer good, which goes to pay the wages of workers operating machines or building new ones. The machines are, in the first instance, made by hand in one year and last for a period of years. Any surplus of consumer goods over and above the wages of the two sets of workers accrues to the Planner. There is an indefinite supply of labour willing to work at whatever wage is fixed, and raw materials are plentiful and free. With a given technology, the Planner's surplus will be bigger the bigger the stock of machines and the smaller the wage. So many workers are needed to work a machine to make consumer goods, and so many to build one machine. A change in technology can be represented by a change in one or both of these numbers.[2]

Starting with an initial stock of machines of the same technology, the Planner must assign a number of workers to build new machines to replace those which will be withdrawn at the end of the year, and the right number to work the stock to make consumer goods. According to the wage, w, that will determine his own surplus, S. When a new technology is invented, the old machines have to remain in use initially, in order to go on producing consumer goods: but the workers in the 'investment' sector can now build machines of the new type, which will gradually replace the old ones. According to the nature of new technology (does it require more or less workers to operate a new machine, and more or less workers to build one?) the final number of machines will be larger or smaller than the original stock, in order to deliver a given surplus to the Planner. It is intuitively obvious, for instance, that if the 'new' machine requires fewer workers to build it, but has the same output as the old, then fewer workers will be needed to yield the same surplus to the Planner as were required with the old machines.[3] It is possible to work out the consequences of other kinds of technical change, many of which will entail an increase in employment, but some a reduction. The merit of this particular type of model is that it brings out into the open the role of investment in 'embodying' the new technology, and that it takes time for the full effects of a technical change to work themselves through: at any date, the capital stock will contain a certain number of machines of the old technology and a certain number of the new. The former number will decline and the latter increase, until eventually the whole stock consists only of new technology machines.

The substantial point which comes out of the Sinclair model, and this fixed coefficient model, is that, according to its nature, a technical change can lead to an increase in employment, if labour is available, but it may also lead to a lasting fall in employment. These results are suggestive. Nevertheless the models remain very abstract. In both cases they refer to the impact of a single technical change on employment. In a few cases, this may seem apposite. The prolonged misery of the hand-loom weavers seemed to stem directly from the introduction of the power loom, and one suspects that the microelectronic computer may have similarly far-reaching consequences. But, in most cases, technical changes do not come in large discrete jumps, lifting the entire productive system from one level of performance to another. Breakthroughs undoubtedly occur, but they are then exploited by a succession of further changes and modifications, which, between them, raise productivity by many times the improvement initially achieved. It may, therefore, be nearer to reality to visualise technical change as a continuous stream of innovations, larger and smaller, with shorter and longer time intervals between them. This perception of the problem was the basis of Salter's (1960) remarkable study of *Productivity and Technical Change*.[4] A flow of new knowledge leads to a continuous change in the production function for each commodity. The common characteristic of these new functions is that they are superior to those already in use, in the sense that less of one, or more, factors of production is needed to produce a given output, the inputs of the other factors remaining the same. Whether a new method will in fact be adopted will depend on many things, including the relative prices of the different factors of production. A newly constructed plant will embody the 'best-practice' currently available and, it may be supposed, is more profitable than would be any plant embodying an earlier technology. We can visualise an industry as the steps of a moving staircase, in which the lowest step just starting off corresponds to the most recent plant, with the best-practice and lowest costs (and highest profits), while the step at the top has the highest costs, and is about to go out of business altogether.

As Salter pointed out, besides labour productivity there are, in principle, as many 'productivity' ratios as there are distinguishable inputs required to achieve a given output. Of these other ratios, the one most frequently encountered in the literature is that of capital. Economic theorists stress that when capital is substituted for labour, there may often be a rise in the productivity of labour, but a fall in the productivity of capital. For this reason, some go further and argue that the proper thing to measure is the 'total factor productivity', which is the weighted average of the separate factor productivities. Salter stresses that one must distinguish between the *measurement* of productivity, and the interpretation of any change in the measure being observed. When it comes to measurement, there is far more extensive statistical information about labour productivity for different economies, industries and periods, than there is for any of the other concepts.[5]

The empirical data which Salter studied were figures for production industries, mostly manufacturing, for the United Kingdom for 1924–50 and the United States, 1923–50. Changes in output in each industry can be compared with changes in such variables as prices, wage costs and employment. Salter considered various possible explanations for the growth of productivity. The hypothesis that it originated in greater personal effort and efficiency of workers was rejected, because of lack of association between movements of labour productivity and earnings. The view that it was the result of factor substitution – notably capital – is unsatisfactory, since labour and non-labour costs are positively associated, which is the opposite of what the hypothesis requires. The results he found are consistent with uneven technical advance between industries, when these advances are of a type saving labour, capital and materials. Economies of scale may reinforce differences in productivity movements originating in technical advance.

Salter had remarked at the beginning of his study that the then growing interest in productivity was partly the consequence of widespread full employment, so that it is not surprising that he had nothing to say about the impact of technical advance on total employment and unemployment. Thus economic theory does not appear to give us very firm guidance about what to expect from technical change. The first two models we examined certainly indicated the possibility of lasting technological unemployment: unfortunately, they were confined to a single, albeit pervasive, change in technology. Salter's dynamic model is much more realistic in this respect: unfortunately, it is not addressed to the employment question. However, his study does make clear the importance of the link between technical advance and productivity growth, and this suggests a possible test of whether the increase in unemployment since the mid-1970s can be attributed to an acceleration of technical change.

TECHNICAL ADVANCE AND PRODUCTIVITY

It is certainly widely believed that technical change has been speeding up since the Second World War. To begin with, there was a backlog of ideas and methods developed for war which could be applied to peaceful purposes. Then there were spectacular advances in industrial chemistry, including the creation of a host of new materials. From 1960 onwards, the new microelectronic technologies, notably the computer, became increasingly important. All this would lead one to expect that productivity – output per person employed – would increase, possibly at an accelerating rate. And this, for many countries is what we find. Jones (1976) published figures for the annual average rate of increase in output per person employed for the whole economy and for manufacturing for successive periods, 1955–60, 1960–4, 1964–9, and 1969–73. For the first three of these periods there is an acceleration in productivity growth for the European Big Five (that is, the original EEC members, France, Germany, Italy, Belgium and the Netherlands) as well as Austria and the United Kingdom, for both total output and for manufacturing. The acceleration continued into the fourth period, 1969–73, for the United Kingdom in both series, and in Austria for total output per person employed, but there was a dip in both series for the Big Five, and in manufacturing for Austria. By contrast, the United States showed quite a different profile of productivity growth in the postwar period up to the early 1970s. Denison (1985) has made estimates of actual national income per person employed (at constant prices), and of potential income per person employed, a concept designed to get rid of short-period, cyclical, changes in productivity. In the five years 1948–53, both these productivity growth measures were more than double the equivalent annual rates for 1929–41, but, in the next two decades, 1953–64 and 1964–73, both rates fell, although still remaining above the prewar levels, and they went on falling in 1973–9 and again in 1979–82, when they were, in fact, negative.

From the late 1940s into the early 1970s, unemployment in most European countries remained extremely low by previous and subsequent historical standards. In the United States, however, unemployment was not, on average and by its own standards, exceptionally low. But these developments give no support at all to the idea of accelerating technical change being a cause of higher unemployment. In those European countries where labour productivity was accelerating, unemployment remained low, whereas in the United States, the beginning of a rise in unemployment more or less coincided with the beginning of a slowdown in productivity growth.

Big rises in unemployment were not apparent in most advanced countries until after 1973, and especially after 1979 or 1980. Had the rate of increase in productivity continued high or growing in the 1970s, as in the 1960s, one might still argue for technical change being a causal factor in unemployment, but operating with a time lag of several years. But we have already observed that the speed-up of productivity growth had begun to falter in a number of countries at the end of the 1960s, and after 1973 the trend in productivity growth fell in virtually every advanced country. From then, until the end of the decade, the average annual rate of increase in productivity in most countries was halved, and that included the United States, where, as we have seen, productivity growth had already started to fall. The proportionate fall in total factor productivity was even sharper. Once again, the message of the data after 1973 is hostile to the argument that technical change causes unemployment. Since the recession of the 1980s, two countries have experienced considerable falls in unemployment. The earlier case was the United States, where unemployment fell back after 1983 from over $9\frac{1}{2}$ per cent to less than $5\frac{1}{2}$ per cent in 1988, not far from the United States full employment 'norm'. In Britain unemployment stayed high until 1986, after which it began to fall sharply. In both countries productivity growth has moved above the rates of the 1970s, and in Britain productivity growth in manufacturing is back to the rates of the late 1960s. This experience still does not support the idea of technical change causing unemployment – if anything, apparently, the reverse.

Is that, then, all that there is to it; namely that, whatever brought about the rise in unemployment in the 1970s and 1980s, it was not any speeding up of technical change. But there is more to be said.

Is there any evidence, first of all, that, contrary to popular belief, there was a slowing down in the flow of new technology? Denison (1985, page 41), who declared himself baffled by the scale of the productivity slowdown, drew attention to the view of Mansfield, 'as informed and judicious observer of this scene as can be found', who reported (1982): 'Many of the available bits and scraps of data point to a slackening in the pace of innovation in the United States. But the data are so crude and incomplete that it would be foolish to put too much weight on them'. More recently, Griliches (1988) has examined the 'possible exhaustion of the well springs of technological change'. Griliches stresses the pervasive character of the slowdown, by country (he quotes data from twelve countries) and by sector (he quotes data for total factor productivity by industrial sector in the United States). The latter showed falls in most sectors between 1967–73 and 1974–85, but not in all. There were rises in agriculture, construction, finance and insurance and other services; but there are doubts about the ability of economists to measure inputs and outputs unambiguously in service industries. For instance, asks Griliches, is it credible that in the United States there was no rise whatever in the productivity in financial and other services in the whole period since the Second World War? He also, rightly, places a question mark over the statistical significance of some of the observed changes in trend. Depending on the *a priori* date chosen for the break in trend, one can find strong changes between the average growth rate for periods of years before and after the break. In the United States these changes are not statistically significant for manufacturing, although they are for more economy-wide measures of productivity growth.

There was a decline in the 1960s in R&D expenditures in United States industry, as measured by the ratio of R&D to sales (ROS) and of basic research as a per cent of total R&D expenditures (PBSC) and, given the time lags normally associated with the impact of R&D on productivity, this looks a good candidate. But there are difficulties. The R&D slowdown was less pronounced in other Western countries and Japan, notwithstanding larger falls in productivity growth rates in those countries. Griliches' conclusion is that, while there is a link between R&D falls and declines in productivity growth, it can only account for a small part of the slowdown.

The Mansfield 'scraps' of evidence and Griliches' calculations were for the United States. Even if these factors could account for the slowdown there, could they do so as well elsewhere? There is no reason why not, in principle. But one widely held view of the faster growth of productivity elsewhere after the Second World War than in the United States, is that other countries were 'catching up' with the more advanced *level* of American technology. But, if that were the case, and it has been questioned,[6] why should a slowing down in the United States be transferred to other countries, so long as the absolute gap in productivity levels still remained?

Another supply-side candidate to explain the slowdown was a postulated effect on productivity of the sharp increases in energy costs brought about by OPEC 1 and OPEC 2, in 1973–4 and 1979. This suggestion was examined in detail by Berndt and Wood (1986). They doubted whether energy conservation could be the medium, on the grounds that the own-price elasticity of demand for energy is probably less than one tenth of the figure the hypothesis would call for. A similar objection can be made against the suggestion that the sharp rise in raw material prices, which occurred a little before OPEC 1, was responsible. Berndt and Wood, however, did think that the adjustment made by firms in the utilisation of capital in response to the jump in energy costs might have contributed something to the slowdown. So we have a number of supply-side candidates – fewer innovations, lower R&D ratios, adjustment of capital utilisation – each contributing small amounts in different countries, but even together not accounting for any substantial part of the slowdown.

The remaining candidate is the clash between the existing stance of fiscal and monetary policy and the extra cost inflation induced by the energy price rise.[7] For importing countries, these cost increases were similar in their effects to increases in indirect taxes, and the decision not to accommodate them, for example, by reducing VAT rates, was tantamount to deflationary fiscal policy. Since labour productivity is normally pro-cyclical, this alone would have sufficed to reduce the average productivity growth rate until full output recovery became possible. If the recession were prolonged, causing a more than normal falling off in investment, this might have longer-lasting effects on the productivity trend.

A DIGRESSION ON THE THATCHER 'MIRACLE'

The argument so far has been that one cannot make an acceleration of technical change responsible for the higher unemployment in the developed world since the mid-1970s, because in fact there has been notable slowdown in productivity growth throughout the western world, which has not yet been reversed. But there is a twist in the story in the British case, inasmuch as there have been claims that a 'productivity miracle' took place in the 1980s. So far as the thesis under examination is concerned, such a miracle, if it occurred, would be unhelpful, since a significant *fall* in unemployment began after 1986, which continued through 1989.[8] However, the 'productivity miracle' has played an important role in the debate about demand management, which we discuss more fully in Part 3. By rejecting conventional demand management, and in particular by introducing a deflationary budget in 1981, when the rules of the old game would have indicated reflation, the government succeeded in launching the longest period of steady growth since the war, during which productivity growth outstripped that of earlier periods. This was an achievement of the 'supply side'.

So far as GDP per person employed is concerned, the average annual rate of increase was unduly low between 1973 and 1979, and in the 1980s has reverted to something like the rates experienced before 1973. But not more than that. In the past, there was a tendency for productivity growth to rise in booms, as output increases ran ahead of employment, with the opposite tendency in recessions, with output dropping off faster than firms could shed labour. It was also common for firms to hoard labour in recessions in the confident expectation of early recovery. Thus, it is important to separate 'cycle' from 'trend', which is especially difficult for the 1980s, since the recession from 1979 to 1981 was the deepest since the war. 1979 was a peak year, and if we measure from that starting year we find an annual average rate of productivity growth 1979–88 of 2.1 per cent, which is well below the rates of the 1960s. If we start from the trough, in 1980, say, the average rate 1980–8 comes up to 2.6 per cent, which is the same as the rate for 1959–69. Insofar as there has been a perception of improvement relative to France or Germany, this arises more from deterioration there than improvement here.

More attention has been paid to productivity in manufacturing than elsewhere, no doubt because there is less ambiguity about the concept and measurement of productivity than in other sectors, such as financial ser-vices, for example, and because of the availability of data. Darby and Wren-Lewis (1989) used the employment equation of the National Insti-tute's econometric model, which incorporates a constant 'underlying' growth of productivity of 3 per cent per annum, to determine what produc-tivity should be in 1988, according to the normal factors used in the equa-tion.[9] They found that, of an increase in productivity of 39 per cent, 38 per cent could be accounted for by the equation, with only one percentage point for the 'miracle'. They drew attention to the many reports from firms of improved working practices in the 1980s, but these, they believed, were the consequence of the exceptional shake-out of labour which occurred during the recession, when firms realised that, this time, there was going to be no quick recovery. It is, of course, not excluded that some firms may indeed have moved onto a faster and lasting productivity growth track, with other firms improving less than average. Lasting improvements need to be embodied in new equipment, but investment in manufacturing was below the 1979 level in every one of the eight following years, being little more than two thirds in 1981–4. Only in 1988 was the 1979 level reached, and surpassed thereafter. If those higher levels could be sustained for a number of years, a lasting improvement in the productivity rate might be achieved, but that lies in the future.

CONCLUSION

To return to the main theme: we do not think that the rise in unemploy-ment since the mid-1970s can be explained by the speeding up of technical change. Nevertheless, there are many who say that the full effects of IT have yet to be seen, and this will be the subject of the next chapter.

4

THE IMPACT OF INFORMATION TECHNOLOGY

Most of the evidence concerning technical change, which we have considered up to now, has been indirect, as well as aggregative, being statistics for labour productivity or total factor productivity, for the whole economy, or substantial sectors of it such as manufacturing. We concluded that the rise in unemployment in the advanced countries in the 1970s and 1980s could not be laid at the door of any speeding up of technical change, but we admit to being uneasy that we may have missed something, somewhere. After all, individual cases of spectacular replacements of labour by computers and computer controlled machinery seem to be reported in the newspapers almost daily. The social scientist should, of course, be wary of anecdotal evidence – but when there are so many anecdotes one begins to wonder. Moreover, as Leontief has remarked, even on the assumption of an accelerated introduction of computers, the information technology (IT) revolution will still be in its early stages at the turn of the century, at the level say of 1820 in the history of the industrial revolution.

Direct information about the speed with which IT is being introduced, and the effect it is having on employment and unemployment in particular cases can be obtained from surveys of firms – and a variety of such surveys have been undertaken in recent years. They have included questions, not only about the extent of IT introduction already reached, but about plans for the future, as well as questions on the attitude of the workers directly affected by the new methods. In this chapter we shall try to indicate what additional light these surveys throw on the prospects for employment.

The most comprehensive study of this type was published by Leontief and Duchin (1986). It was Leontief who invented the input–output model of an economy, which records the outputs of all the other sectors which flow, as inputs, into a particular sector, and which, together with labour of various kinds employed in that sector, produce its output. Given the final demand in the economy, for consumption and investment, private and public, and for net exports, and given the various 'technical coefficients' relating specific inputs into a sector to its output, one can work out the labour employment and the output of each sector. The methodology of the Leontief–Duchin study is to use a dynamic input–

output model of the United States. It is dynamic in the sense that it allows for the growth of final demand, so that the inputs into each sector include, besides the requirements for current output and the replacement of capital, the additional requirements for the expansion of capital: it is also dynamic in the sense that the technical coefficients relating inputs to outputs do not remain fixed, but change from year to year in accordance with the technical changes taking place in the past, and as postulated for the future.

The state of the United States economy over the years 1963 to 2000 is described in terms of commodity flows among 89 producing sectors, and the labour inputs absorbed by each of them in terms of 53 occupations. The data are organised for each year in four matrices: A matrix – input requirements on current account; B matrix – capital expansion require-ments; R matrix – capital replacement requirements; L matrix – labour inputs of each sector, with respect to current output, capital replacement and expansion. There are sector studies of the use of computers to automate production and office operation, as well as education and health care. The dynamic input–output model is then used to generate the sectoral outputs and investment and labour requirements of the United States economy under alternative assumptions about technologi-cal change.

Altogether four scenarios are studied. S_1 is the reference scenario: in it the years 1963–80 simply represent the actual technical change which took place in those years. For the remainder of the period 1980–2000, it is assumed that the technology of 1980 is frozen, in terms of the numbers of computers, robots, NC machine tools and so on of that year, and there are no new technological changes until the end of the century: however, final demand is allowed to continue to grow. S_2 and S_3 are the same as scenario S_1 up to 1980, but thereafter project increasing use of computers in all sectors, S_3 adopting them at a faster rate than S_2. The growth of final demand is kept the same in all three scenarios, so that differences between sectors thereafter are attributable entirely to the different assumptions being made about technical change. Obviously S_2 will require less labour (5 per cent in fact) in the year 2000 than S_1, and S_3 less still. In these initial runs, no effort was made to square the total labour requirements with the labour force likely to be available, particularly that represented by the projections made by the Bureau of Labor Statistics (BLS), and the S_4 scenario scaled down the labour requirements of S_3 to fit. As we shall argue more fully a little later, we doubt whether big models of this kind have much to tell us about the likely effects of IT on total employment: it is in the changes in the relative sizes of different occupations where the interest lies.

We report the more striking results emerging from a comparison of the proportional distribution of employment in the year 2000, between the fast IT introduction scenario S_3 and the reference scenario S_1, in which technical change stopped at the level reached in 1980. The biggest proportionate rise is in Professionals, who would constitute 14.5 per cent of the total in S_1, but 19.8 per cent in S_3. No other group gains proportionately on this scale, but there are perceptible gains for Craftsmen and Service workers, and small gains for Operatives and Labourers. The big losers are Managers, down from 10.8 per cent to 7.2 per cent, and Clerical workers, down from 18.4 to 11.4 per cent. Clerical workers figure on almost everyone's list of potential losers from IT. The Managerial group is perhaps, at first sight, a little more unexpected. It arises mainly from the arrival and spread of the desk-top computer terminal, which has revolutionised information retrieval for managers, hitherto having to rely on document assembly and analysis by sub-managers, but now able to do both from their desks, provided, of course, that they have acquired the necessary expertise with the computer. These relative changes are, of course, dependent for their achievement on a great expansion in educational and retraining facilities. At the 'anecdotal' level, conventional typewriters disappear in S_3 in 1985, and in that scenario also, human draughtsmen are wholly replaced by computers by the year 2000.

Estimates of the impact of IT on employment in the United Kingdom, using broadly similar methods, have been made over a period of years by Whitley and Wilson of Warwick University, and they summarised their work in a paper for OECD (1987). Their model is a dynamic version of the Cambridge Growth Project model, which has a Keynesian structure incorporating an input–output system. It has half as many sectors as the Leontief–Duchin model of the United States, and their projection of the future impact of IT has less empirical underpinning. Their principal assumptions are that IT will lead to the restoration of overall productivity growth to the rates achieved in the 1950s and 1960s, that is, about 2 per cent per annum for the whole economy: but certain sectoral trends are 'bent' upwards for the years 1985–95. With these assumptions the model yields a growth of GDP at an average rate of 2 per cent, with a small PSBR, and near zero current account balance. On this basis there would be little rise in employment, so that unemployment stays around the three million which was the figure at the time the projection was made. It will be noticed that, since then, the British economy was already moving 'off line', with output growing at over 4 per cent a year, and unemployment falling below two million. However, the balance of payments also moved into a record deficit of over 4 per cent of GDP, which many consider unsustainable, and correcting which may require a much slower growth of GDP. But the Whitley–Wilson projection was not intended primarily as a forecast, and, as with the Leontief–Duchin projection, the interest lies less in what they say about total employment than in the impact of IT on sectors. In the Whitley–Wilson simulation, manufacturing output grows at 2 per cent a year, with an annual fall in employment of 1.7 per cent. Service output grows at 3.1 per cent, which requires an annual *rise* in employment of 1.5 per cent. This continuing shift in the balance of employment towards services is familiar enough. Nevertheless, one cannot be too confident about it. Suppose, say Whitley and Wilson, there was an additional adoption of IT, beyond what they had been assuming. If it occurred in manufacturing, while the impact effect would be to reduce employment, the secondary effects, especially those arising from increased foreign demand derived from improved competitiveness, would more than offset the initial effect, and employment would rise. On the other hand, if the extra IT was concentrated in services, the overall consequence would be more likely a fall in employment. This conclusion echoes the observation by Leontief and Duchin that equipment per worker in offices in the early 1980s was a mere $2,000 on average, compared with the $25,000 backing the factory worker. This refers to equipment of all kinds, and not just IT. But the further use of IT in offices probably calls for more drastic changes in organisation before it can become fully effective, than would be the case in factories. There is the hint in these two studies that 'office employment' may not provide a rapidly expanding sector to absorb unemployment.

Notwithstanding the detailed study of particular sectors, the projections from these models are still arithmetical calculations, behind which lie many practical problems. Of these, the most important is the required investment in human capital. It is not just a matter of replacing an old conventional machine tool with a new, numerically controlled, one. There have also to be complementary operatives who have learned how to set and maintain the NC tool. This was fully recognised by Leontief and Duchin, who emphasised the demands which will be placed on the education system not only to train workers, but also additional teachers, and their growth scenarios postulated big increases in the numbers in education. It is here, as much as anywhere, that the question whether IT will release workers for better jobs, or else release them into unemployment, will be answered. In a survey of some 1,200 establishments, representative of the full range of manufacturing in the United Kingdom, Northcott (1986) enquired from 'microelectronic user' firms what had been the main difficulties in adopting microelectronic methods. By far the largest disadvantage cited was 'lack of people with microelectronic expertise'. In 1985 nearly half of firms claimed this, a fraction which had been growing slowly over previous years. Though other factors were of some importance, such as high costs, lack of finance and the general economic situation, none outranked the shortage of expertise.

With memories of the Battle of Wapping still fresh, it comes as something of a surprise that 'opposition from shopfloor or union' comes very low in the list of obstacles to IT adoption. This view, however, was endorsed not only by another Policy Studies Institute report a year later (Daniel, 1987), but also by a survey of Scottish firms undertaken by the Fraser of Allander Institute (Simpson *et al.*, 1986). Workers are not unaware that IT may eliminate jobs, but, at the same time, they see the willingness of the firm to invest in new technology as a sign of confidence. And, while there is a sense in which IT may deskill a particular operation, it may also increase the range of operations which can come under the *control* of a worker, even though he no longer performs any of the separate operations himself. After all, it requires skill to light a fire by rubbing two sticks together, and hardly any to switch on an electric fire. But, with the switch, many other operations can be controlled as well. However, it is possible that survey results may be biased to the extent that questions about IT are put to workers still in employment, and not to people who lost their jobs in the wake of some earlier technical advance.

With technical advance there is, as a rule, an overall saving of labour in the production of any particular good or service. Very frequently, there is a small increase in the number of skilled workers, offset by a larger fall in unskilled workers. Time and again advances have been made by devising machines to perform tasks previously performed by human hands or, in the case of calculations, by human brains. The machines required skilled workers to operate and maintain them, and shortage of skills of one kind or another has frequently been a brake on expansion. We saw that 'lack of people with microelectronic expertise' was constraining some firms in the mid-1980s; reports of shortages continue.

It is difficult to find figures to show that IT is leading to the automation of unskilled jobs to a disproportionate degree. Take the case of banking. It is a matter of common observation that the cash dispenser has very much reduced the provision of cash by human tellers, but such has been the growth of customers and, equally important, the range of services provided by banks, that up to now employment in banking has been drifting upward. But, in 1989, the Midland Bank announced a reorganisation which will involve the loss of employment over a period of years. Whether this will be followed by other banks remains to be seen. In any case, this may not be an ideal example, since tellers were never unskilled, in the sense we are considering here. So let us, simply for the sake of argument, suppose that the process we have described is occurring and that there is an excess supply of unskilled workers. One market solution is for wages of the unskilled to fall, relative to the average wage. Such falls will sooner or later bring wages down to the 'floor' provided by social security. If, by then, there is still a surplus of unskilled, some economists recommend lowering the floor. However, this is only one half of the story. It amounts to shifting the supply curve of unskilled labour, which in the nature of this example, will be fairly flat, bodily downwards. But, whether or not this will lead to any increase in employment depends on the demand for unskilled labour, and the presumption is that it will be low. So far as firms are concerned, to take on cheaper labour entails giving up the new technology whose introduction took over the jobs of the unskilled workers in the first place. And such technical regress is rarely seen. The position of the public sector is somewhat different. For the public sector is already committed to paying social security to the unemployed, and so has an interest in eliciting any value-added from the worker, however exiguous, and even if it falls short of the social security payment.

The second line of advance is to increase the volume of training so that the unskilled can cross the threshold of expertise which will render them employable once more in the normal way. The inadequacy of vocational training in Britain, by comparison with other countries, has been the subject of adverse comment since the last century, and more recently, Prais and his colleagues at the National Institute of Economic and Social Research (1990) have shown that Britain continues to lag behind other countries in Europe and North America and Japan. During the 1980s the government embarked on a number of schemes. The early Youth Training Scheme was hastily cobbled together, with considerable weight being given simply to reducing the number of young people on the unemployment register. Other schemes followed, and at the end of 1988, the government announced an entirely new scheme, which it was hoped would be established in the 1990s (Department of Employment, 1988).

It is not our intention to comment in any detail either on past schemes or on the new proposals: we shall confine ourselves to a few points of principle. The government envisages that in the next three or four years, a hundred or so Training and Enterprise Councils will come into being in different localities, which will take on the responsibility for training and retraining, and for the promotion of small businesses and self-employment in their areas. Each Council will consist of about a dozen members of whom two thirds will be drawn from business. At the beginning there will be a National Training Task Force, to advise the Secretary of State for Employment on setting up the TECs. While the government will provide some funds through placing contracts with the TECs, it hopes that the latter will become the driving force in providing and financing training: ' ... the Government hope to place "ownership" of the training and enterprise system where it belongs – with employers' (*loc.cit.* para. 5.7). Justifying this aim, the White Paper argues that: 'By promoting training arrangements that are closely linked to business success, TECs will generate more private investment in training. As employers recognise the economic necessity to train and the returns available, they will be encouraged to make a larger investment in training' (*loc.cit.* para. 5.19). Just why, in the 1990s, British employers should recognise an 'economic necessity', which, for the most part, they have conspicuously failed to recognise in the past hundred years and more is not explained.

Expanding firms seeking additional trained workers have two options. They can take on additional untrained workers and provide the training themselves, or pay others to do it. Or they can entice already trained workers from other firms, by offering better pay or conditions. This is the well-known problem of the free rider, which is inherent in many competitive situations. If firms belong to a fairly well recognised 'industry', which has been in existence for some time, though competing with one another, they may also see the advantage of cooperation in meeting a common need, in this case for more trained workers. Such 'industrial' arrangements have existed for a long time, in recent decades in the form of Industrial Training Boards, which have been financed by compulsory levies raised on firms in the 'industry'. (The remaining handful of such boards are to be phased out.) There are good economic reasons why the 'industrial' approach may be becoming less appropriate. The structure of production is becoming more fluid as new technology crosses hitherto traditional boundaries; and this process is speeded up in an atmosphere of deregulation. In the financial sector we are seeing building societies becoming banks, and banks becoming building societies. From this point of view the basis of TECs on localities and not industries is sensible. Even so, the free rider problem remains.

All firms have *some* interest in the training of school leavers, although there is evidence that firms in declining industries and many firms in recession put cuts in training programmes high on their priority list of economies. But, in the modern world fewer and fewer entrants to industry and commerce can expect to follow a 'linear' occupational progression throughout their working lives. Skills which were still sought after in coalmining, steelmaking and shipbuilding only twenty years ago, no longer have a market in Britain. The need for the retraining of skilled workers is likely to increase in importance. It is hard to imagine individual firms responding to the 'economic necessity' of retraining workers made redundant in declining industries. The firms in those industries are doubtless aware of the problem, but have little incentive to do anything about it, and in any case are likely to lack the resources. Firms in new, expanding, industries, have greater incentive perhaps, but why should they single out the 'retreads', when youngsters straight from school are available? Why should the firms establishing superstores, leisure complexes and the like in the West Midlands be particularly concerned with ex-skilled workers from the automobile industry and the many small manufacturing firms which used to supply it with bits and pieces of all kinds?

Training, like education, is not a good which can be classified as either private or public, simply from first economic principles. There are plenty of examples, in Britain and elsewhere, of private markets in some kinds of education, in which fee-paying schools and other institutions can be run at a profit, just as can the training of people to drive cars or use word-processors. But, in the widest sense, training and education are more instances of market failure than of success. In every advanced country, at one time or another, the State has had to come in to extend basic education to all children, irrespective of their parents' ability to pay. As for training, what history tells us is that private firms in many industries have done less in this respect in Britain than in many other countries. It is incumbent on the government to take responsibility for remedying the deficiencies. What is needed is a comprehensive programme for training the young, closely related to the provision which already exists for those going on to higher education. And only government is likely to grasp the scale of retraining which will increasingly be required and be in a position to respond. To suppose that what is needed can emerge from local TECs is wishful thinking.

5

STRUCTURAL UNEMPLOYMENT

INTRODUCTION

Changes in technology are likely to be found at the root of many instances where workers are no longer required in some older, declining, industry, while there are vacancies in new industries, requiring different skills, or located in different places. But there are other possible sources of industrial change. As real income rises, there is a tendency in advanced countries for shifts to occur, from agriculture to manufacturing, and from manufacturing to services. No doubt the very increase in real income originates in technical progress in some sectors, but some derived changes in the pattern of demand may not have a technological base. Another, and recent, industrial change was brought about by the discovery of reserves of oil under the North Sea. Exploration and development were already under way in the early 1970s, and when, at the end of 1973, OPEC – the Organisation of Petroleum Exporting Countries – succeeded in quadrupling the world price of oil, rapid expansion became extremely profitable. The first oil came on stream in 1975 and within five years Britain, starting from a position in which virtually all its oil was imported, had reached self-sufficiency and was about to begin a spell as a net exporter. Prior to the North Sea oil, British oil imports had to be paid for by exports of manufactures or of services, such as shipping, banking or insurance. North Sea oil meant that fewer such exports were needed to achieve any given balance in the current account. In terms of GDP, this meant that there could be a *relative* shift out of manufacturing and some services to make room for the proportion of output coming from the extraction and production of oil. Whether or not this entailed an absolute reduction in manufacturing and other service output depended on what happened to GDP. Had it been possible to engineer an increase in GDP, over and above what it would otherwise have been, no absolute fall might have been needed. Even then, some fall in employment might have followed because, once oil was flowing, the industry used less labour than the manufacturing and service industries making way for it. As it was, the arrival of self-sufficiency coincided with the deepest recession since the war, itself partly precipitated by OPEC 2. Consequently, there was a very large absolute fall in manufacturing employment, and a corresponding increase in unemployment. In a case like this, can one distinguish between any extra unemployment necessitated by the change in industrial structure and the loss consequent upon a general recession?

Historians of unemployment have often distinguished four categories: seasonal, frictional, structural and cyclical unemployment. Seasonal is self-explanatory, and we put it aside. Frictional and structural both require the coexistence of unemployment and unfilled vacancies. One distinction is that it is frictional if the unemployment and vacancies exist in the same industry, or occupation, and structural if in different industries or occupations, implying greater obstacles, for example, retraining, to be overcome in matching unemployed to jobs. Cyclical encapsulates the idea that some industries alternate between periods of high and low activity, with the unemployment of the latter 'cyclical'. In his study of regional economics in Britain, Brown (1972) offered a different fourth category, namely 'demand deficiency' unemployment, which exists when unemployment exceeds vacancies of all kinds in a region. There are, as we noted in Chapter 2, ambiguities in the measurement of unemployment, and the same is true of vacancies, but, for the moment, let us overlook these ambiguities. Besides ignoring seasonal, let us drop frictional as well, or else lump it in with structural, leaving us with just two categories, structural and demand deficiency. Is it possible to distinguish between them?

UV ANALYSIS

One method is UV analysis – U for unemployment and V for (unfilled) vacancies. During the 1950s and 1960s it was observed in Britain that there seemed to be a good statistical relationship between U and V. Plotting pairs of observations of U and V, they traced out a curve, convex to the origin. The relationship appeared to become less clear in the late 1960s, but it was suggested that it might be possible to distinguish between movements along a UV curve, and bodily shifts of the whole curve, using the amount of the shift as an indicator of structural unemployment.

Let us begin with the essential theory of the UV curve. We assume that methods of production do not change, the only thing which does change being the level of total demand, which rises and falls. There are L workers, all alike; there is perfect information about jobs, and perfect mobility. Initially, there is no demand for labour, so that unfilled vacancies are zero, and unemployment U, measured along the x-axis, is equal to L. Now let the demand for labour, which is derived from the demand for goods, rise. As it does so, it creates vacancies, which are

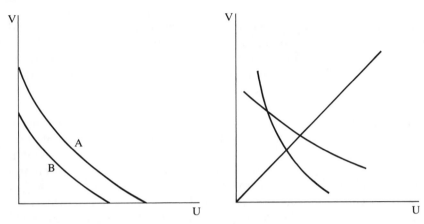

Chart 5.1 *Unemployment and vacancies*

instantly filled. So, unfilled vacancies remain zero, but U falls as D, the demand for labour, rises. When D reaches L, unemployment will have fallen to zero, while V, unfilled vacancies, is still zero. But, if D continues to rise beyond L, it can only create unfilled vacancies, one for one: but now, unemployment remains at zero. In other words, in this world of perfect information and mobility, when there is unemployment, we have zero vacancies; and when there are unfilled vacancies, there is zero unemployment. The UV curve, tracing out pairs of observations, consists of the two axes of reference (chart 5.1).

What happens if we introduce a little imperfection? Once more, as D rises from zero, U will fall, one for one: but beyond a certain point the imperfection begins to tell, and as D rises by one, unemployment falls by less than one, by $(1-s)$, say, leaving an unfilled vacancy of s. As D continues to rise, the frictions or imperfections get a bit stronger, so that the reduction of unemployment gets less and less and the fraction, s, of unfilled vacancies gets larger. This time, the UV curve is not running straight back along the x-axis, but rising gradually away from it. Consider now the point where this backwardly rising UV curve cuts the 45 degree line drawn from the origin. At this point, unemployment will equal vacancies. At this point, of course, D already exceeds L. As D continues to rise, there will be further reductions in unemployment, but more and more of the extra demand will turn up in unfilled vacancies, until a point is reached when all workers are in employment, and U has fallen to zero. Since a freehand draftsman is likely to make a UV curve look symmetrical about the 45 degree line, it should be mentioned that there is no reason why it should be. But, it is likely, for the reasons given, to be convex to the origin.

If we have two economies, with the same sized labour force, and the UV curve of economy A stays above that of B throughout its length, we would have little hesitation in saying that the labour market in economy A was less perfect than in B. (The extreme of perfection is, of course, the axes of reference.) But what if the curves were to cross? How could we then compare the degree of market imperfection in the two economies? The best answer seems to be to compare them where $U=V$. That is to say, we draw the 45 degree line from the origin, and the higher of the two curves cutting this line denotes the economy with the greater labour market imperfection. The reason for choosing the points where unemployment and vacancies are equal, is that they represent the points of zero demand deficiency. If someone is still unemployed at the point where $U=V$, it must be because: he has not yet found a vacancy in his own trade (frictional); or, he is in the wrong place to accept a vacancy (locational); or, there is a vacancy, but it is in another industry or occupation (structural). One can make shorter, or longer, lists of the specific mismatches which prevent a particular vacancy being filled immediately by a particular unemployed worker, but the essential aspect of all these types of unemployment is that they are ascribable to market imperfection and not to any excess of numerical supply over numerical demand for labour. It also seems reasonable to characterise the level of unemployment where $U=V$ as corresponding to 'full employment', since it can be argued that, if unemployment is greater than this, there must be demand deficiency.

The analysis just described can be used to compare different economies at the same date, or the same economy at different dates. It was extensively developed by Brown and his colleagues when they were studying the regional economics of the United Kingdom at the end of the 1960s.[1] The analysis supported the important conclusion that the main reason for differences in unemployment in different regions of the United Kingdom arose from differences in the pressure of demand for labour, and not differences in the experience and quality of the supply.

More recently, in his study of world inflation, Brown (1985) applied the analysis to compare different economies at different dates. UV charts were provided for the United States, the United Kingdom, Japan, Germany and France, covering a period from the mid-1950s to the 1980s. Using the $U=V$ criterion of full employment, corrected where necessary for divergence between recorded and 'true' values, the conclusion was that there had been little change in labour market imperfection in Germany and Japan (less than half of 1 per cent), whereas in the United States, the United Kingdom and France, market imperfection could account for rises of the order of 2 per cent in the 'full employment' level of unemployment. In Britain, much of the rise up to 1976 could be put down to this, and to an increased propensity to register, but most of the rise since 1979 was attributable to demand deficiency. It is tempting to link the rise up to 1976 with industrial change, but there could have been other causes. For instance, Brown himself has suggested that in the years of persistent labour shortage after the war, employers got into the habit of hoarding labour in downturns, in anticipation of rapid recovery. If, as appeared to be the case in 1966, they believe that a normal recovery is not on the way, they may shed labour. This may well have happened after 1979, and would accord with the conclusions of Darby and Wren-Lewis about labour shedding in the 1980s recession, which we noted earlier (see page 32). If reserves of labour hitherto held inside the firm are 'externalised' in this way, the *UV* curve would shift upwards.

For the *UV* analysis to work, we have to hypothesise an underlying curve, which shifts up or down according to the strengthening or weakening of structural factors, or labour market imperfections, whatever label is being used. It *was* plausible to discern a curve beneath the *UV* scatter diagram for the 1950s and up to 1966. There was little trend in unemployment and the charts of unemployment and vacancies mirror one another quite neatly. But, thereafter, there was an upward trend in unemployment, and also the economy experienced a number of shocks – the 1967 devaluation, OPEC 1 and OPEC 2. It is doubtful whether, in this period, one can decompose movements of the economy into a trend and cyclical fluctuations, and one is bound to treat the results of *UV* analysis for the 1970s with some reserve. There is additional reason for caution when we come to the 1980s, to which we will return after outlining an alternative approach to the measurement of structural unemployment.

AN ALTERNATIVE APPROACH

The alternative starts from the proposition that structural unemployment exists when there is a mismatch between vacant jobs and unemployed workers such that, if the latter were available with different skills, and/or in different places, the level of unemployment would fall. The idea is then to calculate the number of workers in the 'wrong' occupations, industries or places in this sense. Jackman and Roper (1987) calculated a number of indexes of this kind for Britain as well as for some other countries. The basic ingredients of four of the indexes are u_i and v_i, which are the ratios of unemployment and vacancies in the i'th sector to total unemployment and vacancies respectively. The simplest index is $\frac{1}{2}\Sigma|u_i-v_i|$, which is half the sum of the absolute differences between the unemployment and vacancy ratios in each sector (occupation, industry or region), and represents the proportion of the unemployed who are in the 'wrong' sector.[2] Three other indexes make use of the same ingredients, while the fifth index is based, not on unemployment and vacancies, but on sectoral employment growth rates.

Their conclusion for Britain was: '... that there has not been much change in structural imbalance over the past twenty years, with the exception of a sharp increase in industrial imbalance after 1979'. There are some differences between Brown's results and those of Jackman and Roper. Brown attributes virtually all the rise after 1979 to demand deficiency, while Jackman and Roper think structural change might have contributed. This is not the end of the story, however. The Jackman and Roper paper was subjected to careful scrutiny by Wood (1988) and in a reply by Jackman and Kan (1988) it was conceded that the earlier conclusion that there was no evidence of any increase in structural imbalance in the United Kingdom was becoming increasingly difficult to accept. A study of regional differences in wages and in house prices convinced them that two kinds of structural unemployment had emerged, in the long-term unemployed and in regional differences. They also noticed the interesting fact that the normal inverse relationship between unemployment and vacancies had disappeared in 1986, when a small positive association was indicated. This takes us back to the *UV* analysis.

A key element of that approach is reversibility in response to demand changes. With a fall in demand, we slide down the curve: when demand recovers, we slide up again. This latter presupposes sufficient idle capacity of plant and equipment to be available to re-employ labour. But, while output began to recover after 1981, and employment after 1983, in the last recession unemployment continued to rise until 1986, seven years after the previous peak of activity. Meanwhile, much plant in manufacturing had been dismantled, whole factories being razed to the ground, and new investment in manufacturing ran over 30 per cent below the 1979 level for three years in the trough. When, in the last stage of the recovery, there was a very strong rise in aggregate demand, it was accompanied by a huge surge in imports of manufactures, suggesting that domestic productive capacity had already been reached in the production of tradeables, while unemployment was still far higher than it had been in 1979, when it was about 1.2 million. The most recent 'cycle', if such it may be described, from 1979 to 1988, is twice as long as any previous postwar cycle. Whereas most of the increase in unemployment in the recession at the beginning could properly be categorised as demand deficiency, the prolongation of high unemployment may have gradually transformed it to structural. In the nature of the case, such a change will not show up in *UV* charts for some years after the end of the recovery. But, we think there is a *prima facie* case that there is a regional imbalance, and we examine this question in greater depth in the next chapter.

6

THE REGIONAL PROBLEM

In a world in which industries rise and fall in response to new technologies and changing tastes, it would not be surprising to find disparities in employment opportunities and rates of unemployment in different locations at different times. But if the disparities are large, and even more if they are persistent, that would call for explanation. What we have seen in Britain since the end of the First World War is a pattern of relative unemployment rates in different parts of the country which has been remarkably persistent, albeit there have been changes which we shall note, and in two periods, the 1930s and 1980s, the differences have been very large. The areas of greatest growth (or smallest decline) in employment have, in the main, been in the South East and, until the 1970s, the Midlands, whereas the employment growth has been slower (or decline greater) and unemployment higher in the northern parts of England, Wales, Scotland and Northern Ireland. There has, of course, been some net migration of jobs and of people from the less to the more prosperous regions, although not, so far, on a scale sufficient to eliminate the differences. Besides the movements between larger regions of the country, there have also been more localised movements, such as those from city centres to suburbs and beyond. And there has been a tendency for immigrants from different parts of the New Commonwealth to settle in particular towns and cities.

The best systematic analysis of the regional problem is that which Brown (1972) and his colleagues provided nearly twenty years ago. As things were to turn out, that research was conducted towards the end of what is now seen, from the vantage point of 1990, as a quite exceptional episode in British employment and, more especially, unemployment experience. After the interruption of the Second World War, the upward trend in the labour force was resumed, albeit at a somewhat slower rate than that of the interwar years, and with larger fluctuations.

Some further slowing down in the trend is expected by the end of the century. Until the end of the 1960s, total employment stayed close to the labour force, and unemployment rates were exceptionally low by historical standards, with national average rates normally within the range of 1 to 3 per cent. Thereafter, employment begins to part company with the labour force: if there is any trend after 1966, it is flat, being at times

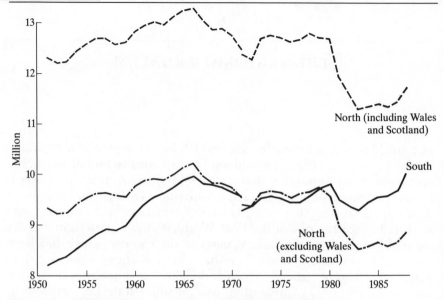

Chart 6.1 *GB, employment in north and south, 1951–88*
Source: *Employment Gazette* and *British Labour Statistics: Historical Abstract,* 1971

well below the 1966 level, and unemployment rises to heights not seen since the 1930s.

We begin our discussion with a brief review of developments since the Second World War, concentrating especially on the period since 1971, for which there exist unbroken series on a consistent basis for the main labour market variables. We then examine how far the post-1971 experience, and recent research, strengthen or weaken the conclusions which Brown had reached. We must then take a view about whether the regional disparities which still exist are likely to disappear as the result of the normal working of market forces, or whether special measures of 'regional policy' are needed and, if so, of what kinds.

DEVELOPMENTS IN EMPLOYMENT AND UNEMPLOYMENT

Employment
We can see the broad outlines of the employment problem by dividing Great Britain into a North and a South, separated by a line running roughly from the Bristol Channel to the Wash. The South includes the standard regions of East Anglia, the South-East and the South-West, while the North consists of the remaining five English regions plus Wales and Scotland.[1] Northern Ireland, the region of the United Kingdom with the lowest income per head and the highest unemployment rates, is

excluded. This exclusion could be defended on the grounds of the special political problems of the province, but there is also a practical reason, namely that the consistent statistical series since 1971, on which we shall draw heavily, are for the standard regions of Great Britain only. These series run back as far as 1971, but it is possible to go further back and get a general impression of the course of regional employment since 1951, by using the data recorded in the *Historical Abstract* and *Yearbooks of Labour Statistics* (discontinued in 1976) which are based on insurance cards. There were changes in the definition of this series between 1951 and 1971, but they were not such as to require detailed attention in the present context. On the other hand, there was a difference between the figures for 1971 on the old basis and the new, and we show this as a discontinuity in chart 6.1. We have drawn two variants of the North, one including and the other excluding Wales and Scotland. From 1951, there was a steady rise in employment in the South and in the North, on both measures. 1966 is seen to have constituted a sharp postwar peak in employment. From 1951 to 1971, the South had been steadily overtaking the North, and this is brought out in chart 6.2, which shows the *difference* in employment in North and South. The annual average change in the difference between the North (including Wales and Scotland) and the South was about 60,000 a year. Then there was a lull until the later 1970s, when the

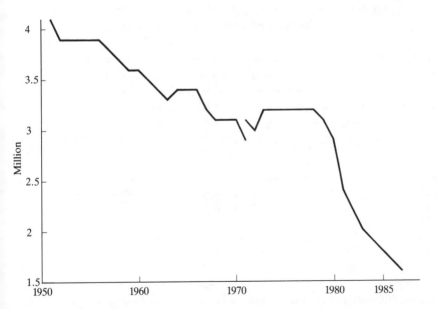

Chart 6.2 *GB difference in employment between north and south, 1951–88*
Source: *Employment Gazette* and *British Labour Statistics: Historical Abstract,* 1971

difference started to fall again, nearly three times as fast as earlier on, until 1983, when it begins to slow down again.

The background to this persistent relative shift in employment between North and South has varied considerably. Between 1951 and 1971, there was first a strong rise in employment in both North and South, followed, after 1966, by an almost equally sharp rate of fall. During all this time unemployment rates were low. In the 1970s there was some recovery in employment in both North and South, albeit average unemployment was now somewhat higher. Then came the 1979 recession, with a steep plunge in the South, and an even steeper one in the North. Throughout this last period, unemployment was much higher than it had been before 1979. Thus, except for the lull in the 1970s, the relative shift in employment from North to South seems to have continued irrespective of whether employment was growing or declining, and unemployment was low or high.[2] We will return later to the pause of the 1970s.

Unemployment

In table 6.1 we record five-year averages of the unemployment percentages for Great Britain, and the five-year averages of the *difference* between regional rates and the national rate (all figures for the month of May up to

Table 6.1. *Five-year averages of difference between regional rates of unemployment and national rate: 1950 to 1988*

per cent

	1950–4	1955–9	1960–4	1965–9	1970–4	1975–9	1980–4	1985–8
GB rate	1.54	1.56	1.72	1.88	2.38	3.90	8.46	10.02
Span[a]	2.14	2.00	2.58	2.22	3.08	2.42	6.06	6.77
S.East	−0.46	−0.54	−0.64	−0.62	−0.70	−1.10	−2.50	−2.72
E.Anglia				0.26	−0.22	−0.60	−1.94	−2.92
S.West	−0.20	0.02	−0.22	0.24	0.40	0.36	−1.26	−1.50
W.Mid.	−0.80	−0.38	−0.54	−0.56	0.02	−0.08	1.88	1.32
E.Mid.	−0.50	−0.44	−0.44	−0.52	−0.02	−0.62	−0.82	−0.85
Y&H				−0.20	0.70	−0.12	0.84	1.47
N.West	0.74	0.46	0.52	0.08	1.06	1.14	2.66	3.07
North	0.88	0.48	1.60	1.60	2.38	1.32	3.56	3.87
Wales	1.34	1.22	0.94	1.44	1.44	1.30	2.44	2.85
Scotland	1.30	1.46	1.94	1.36	2.36	1.30	1.98	2.67

Sources: *Historical Abstract* and *Yearbooks of Labour Statistics. Economic Trends*: 1989 Supplement.

[a] Difference between highest and lowest regional rate.

1964, and for the second quarter thereafter). The second line shows the span, or range, between the highest and lowest regional rates. Up to 1965, figures were derived from the *Historical Abstract of British Labour Statistics*, and for the years since, from the 1989 Supplement to *Economic Trends*. There have been changes in the definition of unemployment, which have been especially frequent since 1979, and their net effect was quite substantial. For example, the 1989 *Trends* Supplement gives a figure of 10.8 per cent for 1985 which corresponds to well over 13 per cent on the definition prevailing in 1979.[3] When definitional changes are made, revised figures are usually published for earlier years, but the revisions never go further back than 1971. It could well be that the effect of a revision is sometimes larger in some regions than in others. But there is a reasonable presumption that the direction of change in each case was the same in each region, so that the comparative differences from the national rate would be less affected.

The South-East is the one region which has had lower than average unemployment throughout the period. The two other members of our South-East Anglia and the South-West – fared about average until the 1970s but, since 1975, have both shown considerable improvement. Among the seven regions of our North, there are four – North-West, North, Wales and Scotland – which had above-average unemployment throughout, a divergence which was already apparent in the interwar years. The North-West region did not do too badly until the 1960s, but by the 1980s had much higher unemployment relative to the average. The remaining regions of our North have had mixed fortunes. Until the late 1960s, all three had below-average unemployment; but the recession of the 1980s brought a remarkable deterioration in the position of the West Midlands, and to a lesser extent of Yorkshire and Humberside. The level of unemployment in the East Midlands, of course, rose in the recession, but it remained below the national average. If one wished to dramatise the North–South divide, one might confine attention to the four regions whose unemployment exceeds the national rate by more than $2\frac{1}{2}$ per cent in the later 1980s and the South-East and East Anglia, where it is more than $2\frac{1}{2}$ per cent less. However, we will persist with our simple geographical divide between all ten regions.

In general, it appears that the rise in unemployment is greater in regions where unemployment is already above average, but the range, or span, between the highest and lowest regional rates does not rise in proportion to an increase in the national rate. Egginton (1988) points out that to use the span leaves out of account the performance of eight of the ten regions, and he calculates the coefficient of variation (standard deviation divided by the mean) of the regional rates for the years since 1970. He finds the coefficient falling from the order of 50 per cent in the

early 1970s to around 30 per cent in the 1980s, showing that the spread
has increased less than the national rate itself.

How does one explain the disparities of the past? Will they persist?
Should steps be taken to reduce them? In analysing these questions, we
follow the lines set out by Brown (1972) amplifying or qualifying his
argument in the light of more recent experience and research. Brown
argued that a case for regional policy would exist if:

1.   Population and industry are in the wrong places in relation to natural
resources and physical features, or that their distribution is moving in the
wrong direction, or in the right direction, but too slowly.

2.   Population and industry are in the wrong places in relation to each
other, or their distribution is getting worse, or getting better too slowly, so
that they are too congested or too scattered.

3.   Labour and capital are in the wrong places in relation to each other,
giving rise to differences in the level of personal incomes, or to labour
shortages in some areas and labour surpluses in others. Market forces
should come into play to reduce such differences, but they may not
eliminate them altogether. A steady state may be reached of flows of
labour in one direction, and of enterprises in the other, but with persistent
differences remaining in levels of personal income and unemployment.

4.   In some circumstances, market forces might even work perversely,
intensifying and not narrowing differences in income and unemployment.

5.   Even when population is moving in the right direction, the movement itself might impose psychic costs, such as the rapid break-up of
communities, and other costs such as the duplication of social capital.

How far do any of these conditions apply in Britain today? In the early
days of the industrial revolution, natural resources played a large part in
determining industrial location. Agriculture and coalmining are obvious
instances, but other industries, such as shipbuilding, iron and steel,
brickmaking and other industries where raw materials were bulky, were
drawn to particular sites. However, already by the 1960s, the proportion
of industry whose location was tied down by natural factors was probably
as little as 10 per cent. Since then, the main resource-based industry to
emerge has been the extraction of natural gas and oil from the North Sea.
The location of the gas and oil fields dictates the location of platforms,
and where terminals should be sited and pipelines laid. The development
of the industry generated employment, particularly in Scotland, but once
the capital was installed, the number of workers involved was not very
large. Some cities, such as Aberdeen, expanded very rapidly, but already
the peak of employment has been passed. Natural resources exert no

stronger pull today than they did twenty years ago. This does not mean that location of jobs has become purely a matter of chance, but rather that other factors can exercise a more decisive influence.

Among such factors is the relation of industrial concentrations to one another. Brown found that 'potential' – a general measure of the accessibility of each place from all units of population in the country – has some association with the prosperity of that place, but there were important exceptions. Another view was that there were advantages to be gained from the regional assemblage of firms in the same, or related, industries, but again the evidence was not strong. A new 'concentration' factor has emerged in recent years in the tendency of high-technology firms to be established in the South. The primary pull, in a number of cases, has been close proximity to research laboratories of universities, as witnessed by the creation of Science Parks in Cambridge and elsewhere. Efforts were made to build up a group of high-tech industries in the Scottish lowlands, but the stronger growth appears to have been in the South, notably in a belt either side of the M4 motorway. These firms are near several universities, as well as Harwell and Heathrow, and it may well be that they generate external economies of scale, such as a pool of highly trained workers, as the number of firms grows. This may qualify somewhat Brown's judgement that the pull of regional agglomerations is not strong: in any case, if there is a pull, it intensifies the North–South divide.

Brown argued that the kernel of the regional problem was the maladjustment between the location of people and of jobs, which the interregional flow of labour had been insufficient to remove. There was, as we saw earlier, a temporary halt to the migration of jobs from North to South during the 1970s, and though the average unemployment rate rose, the disparity between the highest and the lowest hardly increased. However, in the 1980s, the national unemployment rate rose sharply, the gap between the highest and the lowest also increased, and the relative North–South flow of jobs was resumed, leaving one with the impression that in 1988 the regional problem was as intense as when Brown wrote, if not more so.

In Brown's research, it appeared that the dominant factor explaining the differences in regional unemployment rates was the 'composition effect', whereby in some regions there was a disproportionate share of employment in old, declining industries, and a smaller than average share in new, growing, ones. Has such an effect continued? The post-1971 employment data, to which we referred earlier, gave figures for employees in employment in each of twelve industrial groups[4] for the month of June each year from 1971 to 1988. Seven of these groups registered a fall in employment over the whole period, and of these seven, only one –

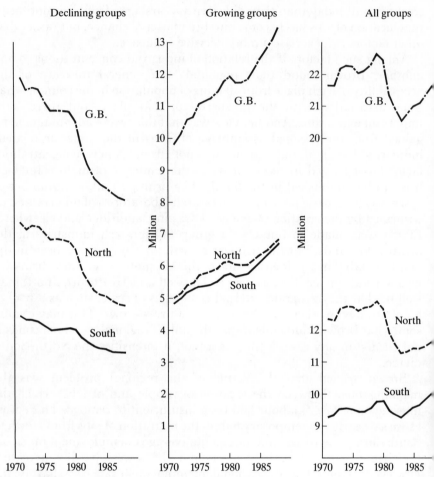

Chart 6.3 *GB, employees in employment, 1971–88*
Source: *Employment Gazette*
Note: The central scale refers to both Declining and Growing groups.

transport and communication – could be regarded as a service industry:
the rest, which includes manufacturing, would be classified as goods. The
five growing groups would all be classed as services.

Employment in the declining groups fell throughout the period in both
North and South, faster in the former than in the latter, with a pause
before the recession (chart 6.3). The five expanding service groups grew
throughout, this time with a pause during the recession: the rate of
growth in the North was virtually the same as in the South. The
composition effect is apparent. At the beginning of the period, the North

had substantially greater employment in industries about to decline than in those about to expand. The South, on the other hand, began with slightly more employed in the potential growth sector. By 1988 the South had over 600,000 more in employment than in 1971, while the North still had over 600,000 less. The composition effect is, of course, ultimately self-extinguishing, except to the extent that new industries start up larger in one region than in others. Already the North has more employment in the growing groups than in the declining groups. But the disparity in the South is much greater, so that, even if, from now on, there were level pegging in the growth rates of the expanding sector on both sides of the frontier, the growth of employment in the South would be faster for many years to come.

Since the Second World War, the trend has been for employment opportunities in the South to grow faster (or, on occasion, to decline more slowly) than in the North. (Although, as we have seen, the regions of our North and South are by no means homogeneous, we will continue these names, as shorthand for more complex statements about all ten regions.) In the main, these trends are the consequence of changes in the pattern of demand and in techniques of production. Some centres of employment are uniquely determined by physical factors and some are the product of government decisions, while many older firms are where they are simply because they always have been. New firms mostly have to weigh up the relative importance of a variety of factors, such as proximity to market, access to motorways and railways or airports, availability of suitable labour supply, and so on. In making their choices, they have not been responding exclusively to market forces. Since the mid-1930s, there has been some element of 'regional policy' in place, stronger at some times than at others, and it must be supposed that this too has exerted an influence. To go into detail why some regions have witnessed greater growth in employment opportunities than others would take us too far afield. What does require explanation is the persistence over such long periods of large disparities in unemployment rates. Why are they not eliminated by mobility of factors of production – labour moving from high unemployment regions to those where employment prospects appear better, and capital moving from regions where labour is relatively scarce to those where it is more abundant? And why do wages not fall in regions of high unemployment relative to those elsewhere? It should not be thought that there are no differences at all in average earnings: there are. Nevertheless the evidence which Brown examined (mainly from 1959 to 1969) led him to conclude that wage increases in any industry in areas of high demand spread, through national wage agreements and otherwise, to other regions. Why earnings in a particular firm were what they were depended more on the industry it was in than on the region. Using data from 1970 to 1987, Egginton (1988) found that, after allowing for differences in hours worked and industrial structure, the dispersion of earnings across regions was exceedingly small compared with the variation in unemployment. The implication of such findings is that deficiency of demand in a region expresses itself more in higher unemployment than in relatively lower wages.

Brown estimated that, if wage differences were fully reflected in price differences, it might take an additional 10 per cent relative difference in earnings to eliminate the $1\frac{3}{4}$ per cent difference in demand deficiency unemployment which existed at the time between the high and low unemployment regions, the already existing wage differential being of the same order. However, just as wages were related within industries across regions, so to some extent prices were standardised. If the advantage of lower wages were taken in higher profits, any improvement in unemployment would have to await the shift of production from other regions to the new lower cost region.

Present government policy is to break down national collective bargaining agreements, and to scrap minimum wage legislation. Presumably, national agreements would be replaced by regional or local agreements, or even, as some economists seem to suggest, be limited to agreements with individual employers. It should not, however, be too readily assumed that the abolition of formal national agreements will break the link between wages in the same industry, or occupation, across regions. Ideas about the 'rate for the job' are widely held, and relativity can arouse strong feelings. And there are practical problems. Is it feasible to pay train drivers who live in Edinburgh 10 or 20 per cent less than their opposite numbers living in London, who drive the same train and work the same number of hours?

Differential wages are primarily advocated as a means of attracting capital to move from high to low wage regions. The other form of mobility is of labour moving from areas of high to low unemployment. Whether lowering wages in the North, with the effect of reducing unemployment there, would increase or decrease the total number of people from the North seeking employment in the South is anybody's guess. Here a different set of problems is encountered, namely the availability of housing and the cost of moving. The evidence seems to be that non-manual workers are more mobile than manual, and it seems fairly clear that council house tenancies and high house prices in the South have deterred migration.[5]

PROSPECTS UNDER ALTERNATIVE POLICIES

The first alternative is to continue as now, and not to introduce any additional measures specifically aimed at increasing employment in the

North. The developments of employment and unemployment which we have described are not the outcome of pure market forces: there has been some regional policy in place for more than half a century, and there still remain powers to make grants to firms setting up in certain regions, such as Nissan in the North-East. Unemployment in the North rises and falls with the national average, and the North has shared in the general fall after 1986. However, there is no sign of any relative improvement occurring. When unemployment reached two million in 1981,[6] the percentage of the total in the North was 69: it fell a little, to 67 per cent of the peak total of three million in 1986, but when the total reached two million again in 1988 on the way down, the percentage in the North was 69 once more. The point can be made in a different way. In the first quarter of 1990, when the unemployment rate for Great Britain was 5.4 per cent, the span between the highest and lowest regional rates was 5.3 per cent. The last time there was a Great Britain rate of this order was in the third quarter of 1980, when it was 5.2 per cent. At that time the span between the highest and lowest regional rates was 4.6 per cent. The divide remains.

If nothing is done, employment opportunities will continue to grow faster in the South than in the North. One may hazard a guess that, in the absence of fast direct rail links from the North to the Channel tunnel, the balance of employment may tilt more towards the South. Eventually, of course, the composition effect will extinguish itself, but it may have several decades of life in it yet. There are, so far as one can judge, no physical obstacles to further industrial and commercial development in the South. At one time, if agricultural land was 'good', that sufficed to keep development out. But with modern methods of production there is a surplus of agricultural land, and even more organic farming is unlikely to use it all up. There is often intense local opposition to further development in particular places, but there is no way of testing the strength of opinion about further development of the South as a whole. Individual families cheerfully put more and more cars on the road, while deploring the ever increasing traffic congestion, and the further motorway and by-pass building it necessitates. Slowing down, or stopping, the relative shift of jobs from North to South would not make a spectacular difference in this regard, but it might be welcome, and southerners might be prepared to pay some price to tilt the employment balance back to the North.

Such an element does not turn up in the market price of things people buy, but requires the intervention of public finance. In fact, of course, the South already pays a price for higher unemployment in the North through social security and the tax system. In 1988, 46 per cent of employees in employment were in the South, but 67 per cent of unemployed were in the

North. In the absence of any social security, can one doubt that the movement from North to South would have been much greater than it was? This almost invisible, but nevertheless substantial form of interregional transfer should not be overlooked in any assessment of the costs and benefits of regional policy. Possible benefits to the South in tilting the balance of employment towards the North should not be overlooked either, but it is those employment prospects which are our main concern.

REGIONAL POLICY

It is sometimes said that regional policy does not work, or alternatively that it has been tried and failed. It clearly has not succeeded in equalising unemployment rates, for instance. But the imbalance would have been greater still in its absence.[7] Since its inception, regional policy has taken many forms. In the early postwar period, when there was a great excess demand for investment of all kinds, it was possible, simply by giving government approvals more freely, to steer nearly one half of all new factory building into development areas. In the 1950s the control of new factory development by means of Industrial Development Certificates (IDCs), which had replaced building licences, was exercised with a lighter and lighter touch. Then, from 1960 until the later 1970s, the trend was towards a more and more active policy. There were many changes in the definition of localities within which the government's special powers could be exercised. Initially, the broader development areas were abandoned in favour of a large number of more narrowly defined districts, only to be replaced again in 1966 with new development areas, to which were added in 1970, intermediate areas.[8] At that time more than half the geographical area of the United Kingdom, containing 35 per cent of the working population, was eligible to receive some degree of government assistance. Besides the 'negative' control of IDCs, which reached a peak in 1966, falling back thereafter until their abandonment in 1982, there was a wide and varying array of measures of financial assistance to firms in development areas. Initially, investment incentives took the form of differential allowances, but when tax allowances generally were abolished in 1970 in favour of direct investment grants, the regional investment incentives took the form of grants paid at different rates according to the type of area. These investment grants became the largest single item of regional aid. Another important, though short-lived, item was the Regional Employment Premium, a payroll subsidy to manufacturing firms in the development areas. Moore, Rhodes and Tyler (1986) have provided constant price estimates of the total cost to the Exchequer of all forms of regional aid. From small beginnings in the early 1960s, the cost rose tenfold to a peak in the early 1970s, dropped back, from 1976 to 1983, to a plateau one third below the peak and then fell again to below half. The peak of expenditure coincides with the halting during the 1970s of the steady shift of jobs from North to South which we observed in chart 6.2 had occurred in every year since 1950, and was to resume at twice the rate in the early 1980s.

Government can influence the distribution of employment in a number of ways. It is a large employer, and can choose to locate establishments in areas of high unemployment. It can undertake, directly or indirectly, development expenditure, such as the clearance of derelict sites, or the construction of trading estates. It can discourage enterprise, whether private or public, from locating in particular areas. Equally it can offer financial inducements to enterprises to come in to particular areas or regions. All these forms have been used, at one time or another, in the past half century. There may well be good arguments for direct expenditures in particular cases, but we will confine our comments to general incentives, working through the market. The economically 'neutral' device would be to have lower rates of VAT in the North than in the South: this might, one imagines, be administratively complicated, especially if one had more than a single 'divide'. Policy in the 1950s and 1960s rested heavily on differential incentives to capital investment. Some thought that direct cash grants would be more effective than equivalent reliefs from taxation, but the stronger objection was that such incentives would encourage capital intensive production methods in areas where it was labour that was in surplus. There was evidence that this had been happening. The Regional Employment Premium was introduced in 1967, which partially, though not wholly, offset the bias in favour of capital of the existing measures. Unfortunately, the Regional Employment Premium was not persisted with. If, with substantial unemployment still in the North, one had to choose a single instrument, this would be the one to choose. It offers the same incentive to firms to set up in the North as would be achieved if the wage level in the North fell, with the difference that any cost would be borne by the taxpayers in both South and North, and not exclusively by the wage-earners of the North. The objection that one should not pay a premium to firms already established in the North, has no more validity than that firms already established should not take advantage of any wage cuts. If the sole object was to redistribute employment from South to North, without altering the total, one could reduce the employer's contribution to national insurance in the North and raise it in the South, not necessarily by equal amounts, since the elasticities of employment with respect to costs might not be identical in the two regions. But, if unemployment is high in both South and North, there is no need to limit policy to redistribution. Nor is there any obligation to use one instrument only.

CONCLUSION

In our statistical presentation of the problem, we drew a line from the Bristol Channel to the Wash, and contrasted the employment and unemployment fortunes of those to the North and South of it. This North–South divide stands for a more varied differentiation between smaller areas of the country in which employment opportunities grow at various rates, and others experiencing decline. There are some growth areas in the geographical North, as well as depressed areas in the South. Both North and South have inner cities with high rates of unemployment. Again, for largely statistical convenience, we excluded Northern Ireland, which has the highest unemployment of all the standard regions of the United Kingdom. In any policy of giving public financial preference, in one form or another, to particular areas or regions of the country the question arises of the degree of targeting which is best. The smaller are the target areas which qualify for preferential treatment, the further, on the face of it, will any given net expenditure go in job creation. But there are disadvantages. Even if the initial allocation of funds was optimal, the processes of economic change, which are going on all the time, mean that some areas may take off and appear to be no longer in need of help, while other, previously prosperous, areas fall on bad times. The smaller the areas, the more frequently is their status likely to change. The arrival or departure of a single large enterprise might suffice to alter the entitlement to aid of a small town, for instance. There would be uncertainty about the continuity of aid. Anomalies might occur quite often, in which of two neighbouring small areas one might just fall within and the other just without the criteria of eligibility for assistance. It is true that with very large regions, some aid will be wasted, in the sense that many firms benefiting from aid would have prospered anyway. We think that the balance of the argument is in favour of very large regions, to receive different amounts of aid. If the decision were to be taken to intensify regional policy, we would have to go into the targeting question more fully. Nevertheless, in order to bring out the points of principle, we stay with the stylised North–South divide.

Present government policy is to allow the greatest freedom possible to market forces, allowing aggregate outcomes to emerge from the optimising decisions of hundreds of firms and thousands of consumers. In the North–South context, the emphasis is on achieving greater wage flexibility, for example by breaking down national wage agreements. This may have some success in attracting capital to the North. The other leg of flexibility is for labour to migrate from the areas of high to those of low unemployment. This calls for the South to grow faster. In particular, it calls for more housing of the kind which the incoming families can afford.

Jobs are increasing, and new building of houses and factories and other installations is taking place in the South, with consequences of increasing congestion on the roads and pressure on public transport, which meet with increasing resistance from those who already live there. The population of the South might be willing to pay some price to steer more of the new development to the North, but there is no way in which such preferences can find expression in market prices, as ordinarily determined. This is a 'public good' issue, and its resolution requires the intervention of public finance in one form or another.

Employment opportunities in the North will continue to lag behind those of the South for many years, probably into the next century, unless regional policy is revived on a scale not currently contemplated. If it is, there would still remain the question of the relation of British regional policy to the parallel policy for the whole of the EEC being conducted from Brussels. We will discuss that question in Chapter 18.

7

WHO WILL PROVIDE THE JOBS?

INTRODUCTION

If there is to be any increase in employment, there must be employers to provide the jobs, taking into account, of course, those who employ themselves. In this chapter we explore some of the possibilities. This is bound to be an uneven and speculative exercise, since the amount of information about various sectors of the economy differs considerably. For instance, we know more about manufacturing than about most other sectors, but nowadays manufacturing provides less than a quarter of total employment. Moreover, trends in manufacturing have been untypical, so that we must be careful about generalisations derived from this sector alone.

There are two issues we want particularly to examine, the one fashionable and the other not. The fashionable one is the idea that small enterprise has a particularly important role to play in the recovery of employment. The unfashionable one is that government might act as a kind of employer of last resort. Public works of course are not a new idea. They were much discussed in the early years of this century as a means of alleviating unemployment, and one suspects that the employment consideration may have been a significant element in more recent demands for expenditure on the infrastructure. But there have also been experiments with various forms of 'workfare' which should be looked at.

LARGE AND SMALL FIRMS

We start with a reminder of changes in total employment, and its industrial composition in the past two decades. We then look at the respective fortunes of firms of different sizes in two large sectors, manufacturing and retail distribution. Although this provides a salutary warning against the over-common practice of generalising from manufacturing, we cannot follow this road further for lack of official statistics. Instead we must have recourse to studies based on samples of firms drawn from all sectors. These studies have been subjected to intricate and critical assessment, which we will try to summarise fairly.

Total employment in Britain in 1988 was about the same as in 1971.

Between these dates it had risen erratically, fallen sharply and at the end risen again. Of twelve industrial groups, five registered a rise in employment over the whole period: Wholesale distribution, hotels and catering; Retail distribution; Banking, insurance and finance; Public administration and defence; and Education, health and other services. The seven whose employment fell were: Agriculture, forestry and fishing; Energy and water supply; Metal manufacturing and chemicals; Metal goods, engineering and vehicles; Other manufacturing; Construction; and Transport and communication. All five of the expanding groups are services and the majority of the declining groups are goods industries. Too much should not be made of this distinction. If a manufacturing firm delivers its output in its own vans, and employs its own drivers, the drivers are employed in manufacturing. But if the firm hired an outside contractor to do the delivery, the driver would be employed in Transport and communication, a service industry. There has been a tendency for some time for firms to stop providing services for themselves, and to hire them from outside specialist agencies. Even so, the shift from goods to services and the relative decline in manufacturing have been widely observed in advanced economies, and in most cases have been going on for a long time. In Britain, the shift could already be seen in the interwar years: but it was reversed after the Second World War, because of the need to improve the net trade balance to make good the loss of income from overseas assets which had been sold during the war. Thus, in 1970, the share of employment in manufacturing was no lower than it had been fifty years earlier. But, since then, the fall has been rapid, being sharply accelerated by the rise in the real exchange rate of 1978–80 and the subsequent recession.

Whether employment in manufacturing was rising or falling, until 1970 the trend in the share of net output produced by the 100 largest firms was upward, rising from 16 per cent in 1909 to over 40 per cent in 1970. In the ten years from 1958 to 1968 the share of employment in the 100 largest enterprises rose from 27 per cent to 37 per cent. The number of establishments with ten employees or less fell from 93,000 in 1930 to 35,000 in 1968, and the change in the number of *firms* of this size cannot have been very different.[1] These trends, of rising concentration in the largest firms, and of decline in the number of very small firms, have since been reversed. The revival of the small firms may have begun in the 1970s, when concentration in the largest firms stopped increasing. As table 7.1 shows, in the 1980s the numbers of small firms were clearly rising. The recession appears to have fallen with especial severity on the largest *plants* in manufacturing (Oulton, 1987), and the table shows also that the share in employment of the largest enterprises has fallen. For instance, the share of employment provided by firms with more than

Table 7.1. *Share of employment by firm size group: United Kingdom manufacturing*

	<100	100–99	200–499	500–4,999	5,000–49,999	50,000+	No. of firms with 500+ employees
1958	15.8	8.0	12.1	29.8	27.0	7.3	1,950
1963	14.0	6.1	9.5	28.0	32.7	9.7	1,774
1968	13.5	5.7	8.5	25.5	31.0	15.8	1,444
1970	15.8	5.6	8.3	24.3	30.6	15.4	1,481
1977	17.1	5.4	7.3	24.6	31.7	13.9	1,428
1979	17.5	5.6	7.3	25.0	31.9	12.7	1,360
1980	18.8	5.5	5.9	25.2	31.2	13.4	1,302
1981	20.3	5.6	6.7	26.3	30.3	10.8	1,177
1982	21.1	5.6	8.1	25.9	30.3	9.0	1,139
1983	22.0	5.8	8.6	25.8	30.0	7.8	1,075
1984	23.4	6.9	9.6	26.5	25.8	7.8	1,082
1985	23.5	6.9	9.8	26.2	26.6	7.0	1,102
1986	24.0	6.5	9.4	25.3	28.9	5.9	1,052

Source: Census of Production, Summary Reports, PA 1002.
Note: There was a change in the sources used to provide estimates for the numbers of small firms between 1983 and 1984.

50,000 employees in 1986 was less than half of what it had been in 1980: the share of small firms with less than 100 employees had gone up by more than a quarter.

We do not have such detailed information about large and small firms outside manufacturing, but in the successive Censuses of Distribution there are figures for single outlet retailers, small multiple retailers and large multiple retailers.[2] Table 7.2 shows the proportion of total persons engaged in retailing in these three classes, which we will call small, medium and large, for a number of years from 1971 to 1986.

The figures for 1980, 1982, 1984 and 1986 are comparable, the first three years having been reworked by the DTI statisticians to put them on the same basis as the new method adopted for the 1986 survey. The figures for 1976 and 1971 have not been reworked, and are not exactly comparable. The 1971 survey, for instance, shows 338,000 single outlet retailers, while in every other year in the table this number lies between 217,000 and 232,000. But, leaving 1971 aside, there is a clear tendency for the large multiples to provide a growing share of employment, and the

Table 7.2. *Total persons engaged and proportion in three size classes in retailing*

	Total persons engaged in retailing (*thousands*)	Proportions in each class		
		Small	Medium (per cent)	Large
1971	2,853	47.0	13.2	39.8
1976	2,503	39.8	15.7	44.8
1980	2,408	38.1	15.5	46.4
1982	2,258	37.6	15.0	47.3
1984	2,317	36.3	14.3	49.5
1986	2,334	35.6	13.9	50.4

Sources: DTI Business Monitor, SDA 25, 1976 and 1986, Retailing.

single outlet retailers a diminishing amount. The impression of increasing concentration is strengthened if we we look at the number of enterprises in each of the three groups, and the average size of enterprise in each group, as represented by persons engaged per enterprise (table 7.3). In 1986, less than 1 per cent of retailers provided 50 per cent of all employment, and 90.5 per cent of retailers, the small shops with one outlet, provided only 35.6 per cent of employment. Put in another way, a declining number of large multiples has been providing a growing proportion of total employment. The medium-sized retailer, that is, the smaller multiples, also gave ground to the larger multiples. The number

Table 7.3. *Number of firms in retailing and average size (employment)*

	Number of firms			Number of persons engaged per enterprise		
	Small	Medium (*thousands*)	Large	Small	Medium	Large
1971	338.2	29.4	1.41	4.0	13.2	819.8
1976	231.1	28.6	1.39	4.3	13.3	791.1
1980	225.9	29.2	1.00	4.1	12.8	1,112.6
1982	220.2	27.7	0.99	3.9	12.2	1,083.1
1984	218.7	27.4	0.83	3.8	12.1	1,377.4
1986	217.2	25.9	0.86	3.8	12.6	1,367.0

Sources: DTI Business Monitor, SDA 25 1976 and 1986: Retailing

of medium firms fell less than the number of large firms between 1980 and 1986, but employment in the medium firms fell by 13 per cent, while it rose in the large firms by 5 per cent.

We do not have employment figures for small and large firms in other service industries, but one has the impression that recent developments in banking, insurance, and building societies have been more like those in retailing than in manufacturing. In any case, retailing is an industry which, in terms of employment, is two fifths the size of manufacturing, and its quite different development must put us on our guard against taking trends in the latter as representative of the economy as a whole.

JOB GENERATION

In 1979, Birch, of MIT, published a report 'The Job Generation Process' claiming that two thirds of the increase in employment in the United States between 1969 and 1976 was provided by firms employing less than twenty workers. This report proved to be immensely influential in the United States, and in many other countries, including Britain, where it was given a warm reception by the incoming Thatcher government. Inevitably, the Birch report has been closely scrutinised by other researchers, and it has not emerged unscathed. A study on similar lines has been undertaken for the United Kingdom by a team of researchers led by Gallagher (1986). The two substantial questions about all this research are whether the statistical results are robust and, to the extent that they are, what is their economic significance. In attempting to give brief answers to these questions we have been very much helped by an excellent review of the whole matter in a book by Storey and Johnson (1987), on which we draw heavily.

The database for the MIT study was the information collected by the Dun and Bradstreet company from 5.6 million establishments in the United States in 1976, covering 82 per cent of all private sector employment, to provide credit ratings. The same database was also used by a team at the Brookings Institution. They estimated that over the period 1978–80 the percentage of new jobs generated by firms with less than 100 employees was 39, whereas, with the MIT approach, the figure would have been 70. Since the same data were used, how could such a difference arise? Storey and Johnson set out the strengths and weaknesses of the database, and they also show that a great deal of manipulation occurs before the final estimates of job generation are reached. Their own conclusion is that the true figure is some way below the MIT figure, but above the Brookings estimate. A number of studies of job generation have also been undertaken for the United Kingdom, but most of them are regional and for manufacturing only. However, two studies by

Gallagher and colleagues use the United Kingdom Dun and Bradstreet source over two periods, 1971–81 and 1982–4, to see how employment in the whole private sector economy changed, according to the size of firm. In neither period was there a *net* increase in employment in Britain, so that one cannot make a straightforward comparison with the Birch results for the United States. In the British case, only the smallest size group (1–19 employees) showed an increase in employment in 1971–81, and the two smallest groups (1–19, and 20–49 employees) in 1982–4. In all other size groups employment fell in both periods. Gallagher and his colleagues tried to overcome the difficulty by constructing a fertility ratio describing the relative contribution to *gross* new jobs (that is, from expansions of firms and new births, but *not* subtracting job losses). Firms with 1–19 employees accounted for 12 per cent of total employment in 1971, but provided 36 per cent of jobs created in the next ten years, while firms employing more than 1,000 workers in 1971 accounted for 42 per cent of employment in that year, but provided only 11 per cent of gross jobs created by 1981.

Hart (1987) has subjected the estimates of Gallagher and Doyle (1986) for the period 1982–4 to a close scrutiny. He points out that comparing univariate size distributions of firms in the two years 1982 and 1984 will underestimate the contribution to employment growth of the small firms, because firms small in 1982, but promoted to a higher size class in 1984, will be excluded from the average of the small firm size class in 1984. Similarly, though for the reverse reason, the contribution of the largest firms will be overstated. What is needed is a bivariate size distribution of firms in 1982 which are still running in 1984. When he constructed such a table, Hart found that the death rate of the largest firms was the same as that of the smallest, which is inconsistent with all previous studies, and puts a question mark against the reliability of the Dun and Bradstreet data. But, even if those small firms of 1982 which survived in 1984 grew a little faster than large firms, what would follow about the contribution of small firms to employment growth? If a small firm of twenty employees increases employment by 5 per cent, that is one employee. If a firm of 10,000 employees decreases employment by 5 per cent, that is 500 jobs. Most employment in most sectors of the economy is in large firms. Arithmetically, the best chance to increase total employment is for large firms to grow.

In the recession between 1979 and 1983, employees in employment fell by over 9 per cent, that is, of the order of two millions. By the early part of 1989, employment had once more reached the 1979 level. Meanwhile, over the whole decade, the number of self-employed was rising throughout, altogether by about one million. It will be some time before details become available to show the increase in employment according to size of firm, but we can get a little distance by noting that the self-employed will include a number of small firms, with a few employees. Between 1979 and 1983, employees in employment fell by 2 million, but self-employment increased by about 320,000, an annual rise of 80,000. From 1983 to 1988, self-employment rose a further 630,000, that is, 120,000 a year, so that we may suppose that in the recovery self-employment was contributing 40,000 a year above trend, of the order of 200,000 in the five years. But in this period employees in employment rose by 1,500,000. Though the employment figures count part-time workers as one, these figures are compatible with, though not a conclusive demonstration of, the hypothesis that most of the rise in total employment was being provided by larger firms taking on additional labour.

Numbers alone cannot tell us what contribution to job generation we may expect in the future from small firms. We need also to know something of the kinds of job they are providing. Storey and Johnson cite three models named after cities in Britain, the United States and Italy. The *Birmingham* model illustrates the case where growth in relative importance of small businesses and the self-employed can be the result of industrial decline rather than the cause of new forms of economic activity and increased employment. Thus, between 1979 and 1984 the West Midlands experienced a net loss of 250,000 manufacturing jobs – a fall of nearly a quarter in five years. Large firms in difficulties will lay off employees, who have no choice in the matter. The proprietors in the smallest firms may, however, keep going however low their revenue falls, and their numbers may be swelled by laid-off workers investing redundancy payments in their own businesses. The increased importance of the small firm may be a reflection of industrial decline. On the face of it, the Birmingham model cannot be the whole of the British story, for self-employment went on rising – in fact rose faster – when civil employment stopped falling and began to recover. However, some of the rise in self-employment could have been the consequence of special policy measures, which we consider below.

The regeneration of employment in Massachusetts is the subject of the *Boston* model. Between 1976 and 1984, there was an increase in total employment of 520,000 or 23 per cent. The contribution of total manufacturing was quite modest, a mere 80,000. But behind that there was a larger rise of 130,000 in high-tech industries, offsetting declines in traditional manufacturing. The majority of new jobs created in small businesses in the Boston model occurred in enterprises outside the high-tech sector, but they would not have come into being without the expansion of that sector, which was developing with the aid of the science and technology of the great concentration of universities in the region.

At first blush the *Bologna* model is a unique example of an area in an

advanced industrial economy experiencing a high growth rate in manufacturing based on traditional low-tech sector consumer goods, such as
clothing, shoes, and leather goods – the very opposite of the high-tech
Boston model. In fact, the Boston and Bologna models have one thing in
common; both their small firm sectors have the capacity to sell abroad as
well as to their own hinterlands. But the Bologna model has a peculiar
feature – it is not an aggregation of small independent firms, but a production system, of considerable antiquity, in which the trade is organised
by large merchants, who place orders with the small manufacturers.

The growth of small firms in Britain in the first years of the 1980s con-
forms to the Birmingham model, that is, it was mainly a response to
recession; it is too early to say whether the continued growth in the later
part of the decade is beginning to show positive features which are
embodied, albeit in different ways, in the Boston and Bologna models.

POLICY TOWARDS SMALL FIRMS

The Thatcher government has stressed the importance of small firms in
the enterprise culture, and, besides lowering rates of direct taxation, has
introduced a number of specific measures intended to assist the self-
employed and small businesses. Under the Enterprise Allowance
Scheme, anyone who has been unemployed for six weeks (previously thir-
teen weeks) and has a viable business idea can claim £40 a week for one
year. In 1988 there were about 90,000 participants at any one time. A
Loan Guarantee Scheme provides a guarantee of 70 per cent of funds lent
by banks to small businesses. There are Small Firm Centres, set up to
give specialised advice to business starters, and the government supports
English Estates, whose purpose is to ensure a supply of premises,
especially in depressed areas.

When there is a large general unemployment, almost any suitably
financed public expenditure may generate employment: Keynes's ironi-
cal example was the filling of old bottles with banknotes, burying them in
disused coal mines, to be dug up again by private enterprise according to
the well-tried principles of *laissez-faire*. Otherwise, general support to
setting up small firms is not, in the British context, a particularly good
way of generating jobs which will last. There is quite a high rate of failure
among such new small businesses: 40 per cent of firms started in any one
year will have ceased trading in three years time. 94 per cent of the smallest firms do not export any of their output. The scheme appears to have
given most support in prosperous areas, and least in areas of the highest
unemployment. The greater part of the job creation is confined to a small
minority of firms which grow fast, the great majority having neither the
aspiration nor the capability to grow.

Considerations such as these led Storey and Johnson to advocate the abandonment of general support for new business, in favour of a selective approach, which would endeavour to pick out the potential winners from the huge field of starters. Specifically, new firms would have to have a track record of three years before becoming eligible for assistance, demonstrating their financial competence and showing above-average employment generation. To attract assistance the firm would also need to demonstrate the capability to sell outside its region, or even abroad. The public agencies set up to foster development would handle only ten or a dozen firms at a time. Hakim (1989) subsequently questioned the feasibility of picking potential winners in this way. She analysed the information provided by the MAS Business Line survey of over a million establishments with less than 50 employees, of which two thirds were independent firms. Only one in ten of such firms was destined to grow fast, but, in her view, it was not possible to *predict* which they would be.

This seems to be a case in which experiment is both feasible and desirable. At present we have a blunderbuss scheme of government aid for every aspiring new business of which only a few will make a significant contribution to generating jobs. Besides the government schemes, there are others, such as those set up by the steel industry and the coal industry to help start up in business steel workers and coal miners who had been made redundant by the policies being pursued by the managements of those industries. That does not appear to be the best qualification to help starters find new areas of productive activity. After all, if those managers knew of productive new areas, why did they not diversify into them themselves? If there is to be assistance to new firms, it should be selective. It should be directed by agencies whose only purpose is to encourage firms likely to make a lasting contribution to job generation. Experiments with different forms could be made, but in the first instance they should be concentrated in the areas of the highest unemployment.

There are signs of small firms on the Boston model beginning in this country. Unfortunately, the high-tech firms and science parks seem to be developing mostly in the South. There may be possibilities of similar enterprises in the North of England, Wales and Scotland. To the extent that there are, they might attract public support, while those in the South develop under their own steam.

JOBS FROM THE PUBLIC SECTOR

Between 1973 and 1979 there was a small increase of 300,000 in the workforce in employment, from 25.1 million to 25.4 million. An increase of 470,000 in the non-market sector (central and local government) was offset by a fall of 180,000 in the market sector (employees in employment in private firms and public corporations[3] *plus* self-employed). In the recession, 1979–83, there was a fall in the workforce in employment of 1¾ million, consisting almost entirely of a fall in the market sector, the non-market sector contributing a fall of a mere 100,000. In the recovery, 1983–8, the workforce in employment rose by 2.1 million. The contribution to this of the non-market sector was tiny – 100,000 – cancelling the fall in the preceding recession. On the face of it, the employment changes in recession and recovery were almost entirely those of the market sector, and changes in non-market employment appear not to have been of any great significance. But the total of the workforce in employment in 1988 included nearly 350,000 people on 'work-related government training programmes': in 1983 these schemes were just beginning and had only recruited 16,000 people. Initially, the training component of these schemes was barely perceptible, their main purpose being to take men and women off the unemployment register. With the passage of time, the training element has increased, albeit the aim of keeping names off the register has remained. If we put this item of work-related training on the non-market side of the line, then, altogether, the non-market sector contributed nearly half a million to the recovery of employment in 1983–8, and this invites us to look a little more closely at the potential role of the non-market sector as a provider of employment.

The *prima facie* case for the government providing jobs for unemployed workers is that they will receive unemployment benefit anyway, so that as long as any contribution they make to GDP exceeds the difference between the wage they earn and benefit, there will be a gain in welfare as well as additional employment.[4] The argument is even stronger if allowance is made for any multiplier effects following from any excess of wage over benefit.

If there is already full employment the argument is quite different, for now government can only succeed in employing an extra worker by reducing by one employment in the market sector. Just how this one-for-one offset is brought about, whether through a movement of wages, or indirectly through crowding out in the market for loans, need not detain us: nor need we dive into the depths of defining full employment. These are matters which are, explicitly or implicitly, decided by governments in practical decisions about financing the extra job. At full employment, with no increase in total employment, the decision is one about the comparative social marginal productivity in the public sector and the market sector. Between the extremes of high general unemployment where the government just adds one to the total of employment and may crowd in a bit more, and full employment where it adds zero, there is a band in which the addition to total employment ranges from plus 1 to zero. Alternatively, there might be open unemployment in some parts of the country and full employment in others. Governments have no great practical difficulty in recognising what kind of situation the economy is in. For instance, when the first work-related training programme was introduced, whose beneficiaries are classed as part of the workforce in employment, no concern was expressed that the expansion of the numbers in the programme from 16,000 in 1983 to 345,000 in 1988 would be at the expense of employment in the market sector. Another example was the Local Employment Act of 1960, in which to become qualified for assistance, a locality had to have at least 4 per cent of its working population persistently unemployed.

One approach to job creation has been to look around for potentially useful work, of no great urgency, which might nevertheless be undertaken when so many people, especially the young, were unable to find normal employment. The Community Programme was of this kind, the jobs being largely organised by public bodies and voluntary institutions: mountain paths in the Lake District were repaired by young people under the auspices of the Manpower Services Commission and the National Trust. So long as such measures could be thought of as temporary, to meet a pressing but transient need, the contradiction between promoting jobs of comparatively low social priority, while at the same time pursuing a policy of curtailing public expenditure of all kinds in the longer term, was not too blatant. But, as Britton (1986b) has pointed out, a permanent distinction between Community Programme work, and normal public sector work is difficult to justify. He suggests scrutinising all public sector spending decisions according to their effects on employment. He foresees that the pressures to contain public expenditure programmes of all kinds is likely to persist, but argues that the employment content of any programme can be influenced according to the price which is put on labour. To a private firm, the cost of labour will be the gross wage plus the employer's contribution to national insurance. But when the public sector takes into employment someone previously unemployed,[5] the shadow price of labour would be the gross wage plus employer's national insurance contribution less the unemployment benefit previously received and less the direct taxes (income tax and employee's contribution to national insurance) which will now be paid by the employed worker.

While the principle of a subsidy to public sector employment to cover the difference between the actual outlays on jobs and their shadow prices is clear, there are practical and political obstacles. We have, for instance, assumed a perfectly elastic supply of unemployed persons, whose employment would not have repercussions on wages in the private sector. This may be the case at some times and in some places, but certainly not always. Such a scheme would appear to give an unfair advantage to the public sector whenever there was competition with private firms. This could happen if nationalised industries were included in the scheme. This objection would disappear if there were a general subsidy to wages (discussed in Chapter 9). Many of the services where additional employment might be given are at present operated by local authorities, and in recent years local authority expenditure has been criticised by Conservatives on the grounds of general extravagance, or because of the alleged link between Labour councils and public sector trade unions, and has been suppressed by extensive capping by central government. Certainly the attitude of those unions to proposals of this kind is of great importance. If the extra employment were to strengthen the hand of the trade unions so as to lead to higher wages, this could put pressure, in a world of cash limits, for the reduction of employment, negating the purpose of the scheme. Finally, the idea of 'shadow prices' may seem to many to run against the current economic ideology – at any rate in its coarser forms – that the 'proper' price for things, including labour, is, or at any rate ought to be, determined by the 'market'. There is a logical correspondence between the shadow price concept and the concept of the externalities of consumption and production. Such externalities are, of course, at the core of environmental economics, and if green policies are to make any headway, politicians will have to familiarise the public with the basic idea. Possibly the idea of shadow prices in the public sector to help in the creation of jobs might be carried along in the wake of the environmental argument. Whether or not the specific suggestion of shadow pricing should prove practicable, the principle remains valid that, according to the degree of unemployment, part, or all, of unemployment benefit can be set against the cost of employing an additional worker in the public sector.

WORKFARE

Before reaching any conclusions about the use of the public sector as a provider of jobs, we should refer to two rather different approaches to this question which have been followed abroad. In recent years a number of American states have adopted workfare programmes, under which people eligible for welfare benefits receive them only if they work off their grants with a sufficient number of hours in unpaid jobs. The imputed wage is typically the state minimum wage and the kind of work to be undertaken is usually menial and of low quality, such as picking up litter or cleaning buildings. Apparently, although compulsion is available, a shortage of places and support facilities means that only a fraction of benefit claimants are in workfare. Supporters of the schemes argue that they discourage the workshy, and make recipients more employable.

Critics argue that the schemes may create a trap of low-paid work rendering the recipients fit for little else. There is no opportunity for them to increase their incomes by working harder and they do not receive any training.

In the Swedish system there is also compulsion, but there the resemblance ends. Counselling from the employment services about training and vacancies in the locality is immediately available for a person about to lose a job. A redundant worker may even go directly into training without entering into unemployment. Where possible, jobs will be provided by the municipality or other public sector organisation. When vacancies are scarce benefits are paid, but they are seen as a last resort. The essence of the approach is to treat an unemployed worker less as a burden on the rest of society than as an opportunity for retraining in order to make a contribution somewhere else. Thus, besides seeking placements in alternative jobs, the employment services will assist those over 20 years of age to start up in business if they so wish. Sweden has followed an active manpower policy for half a century and it has played a major role in keeping the unemployment rate low, even during the recessions of the mid-1970s and the mid-1980s. The system has come under attack for becoming ossified and there no longer exists the assured political consensus for its continuance.

On the face of it there seems little case for inventing 'make-work' schemes in Britain. Many branches of the social services are undermanned and, in some areas, such as the care of the elderly, whether in institutions or in the community, there is a rapidly growing need which, with some financial backing, could be turned into demand. There is also much capital maintenance which has been neglected in the public sector. One of the main problems here is not technical but ideological and political, namely the attitude towards public expenditure as such and the division of public provision between central government and subsidiary bodies, such as regional and local authorities. If a good working relationship between central and local government could be restored there would be much to be said for adopting the Swedish model of linking the public sector as a job creator with a programme for training and retraining workers.

CONCLUSION

The great majority of jobs in the future will be provided in the private sector. The numbers of small firms and self-employed have been growing fast in the past decade, and some have seen the small firm as the main generator of new jobs. Present tendencies in industrial structure are not easy to read. In manufacturing, for instance, until the 1970s it seemed that there was an inexorable tendency for more and more of output to be produced, and employment provided, by fewer and fewer large firms. Yet, in less than a decade, this tendency appears to have been sharply reversed, but it is too early to say how much this was the consequence of exceptionally deep recession, and how much it was a fundamental change of trend. In other fields, in retail distribution, for instance, no reversal of the trend towards higher concentration has taken place. It is true that there have been a number of well-publicised rises of specialised shops: nevertheless a smaller number of large organisations is providing an increasing proportion of employment. These changing structures are the responses of competition to the ever-changing nature of products and processes of production, and the best policy is to let competition continue to take the lead in this regard. Employment considerations alone do not appear to justify undiscriminating assistance to small firms, which is not the most cost-effective way of taking names off the unemployment register. If considerations, other than employment, are taken into account, a case might be made for experimenting with selective assistance, especially in areas of high unemployment, where the object would be to give an impetus to potential winners picked out from among the thousands who appear each year at the start line.

The economic principle that the social cost of taking an additional worker into public sector employment who would otherwise have been unemployed is less than the wage (with various additions and subtractions) retains its validity. So long as the social value of the work done exceeds this social cost, the employment is worthwhile. All the difficulty lies in the measurement of social value, especially for goods and services where no yardsticks are available.

PART 2

THE WAGE QUESTION

8

WAGES AND EMPLOYMENT

INTRODUCTION

Do lower wages cause employment to rise, or does higher employment cause wages to rise? We can set up theoretical models which incorporate the causal link in either direction, or, indeed, in both. But it is economic history and the current real economic situation which tell us which is the direction of causality demanding the most attention at any particular time. In interwar Britain, it was the belief that unemployment was being caused by too high wages which was at the centre of controversy. After the Second World War, the emphasis was all the other way. There was no sign of a return of mass unemployment, and the question now being put was whether low levels of unemployment were causing wages to rise too fast, thereby generating inflation. After the mid-1970s unemployment began to reappear in Britain on a large scale, and the pendulum swung back towards high wages as a cause of unemployment, albeit this time the swing of the pendulum has not wholly extinguished worries about low unemployment causing inflation.

The swings of the pendulum occur mainly in response to changes in economic institutions and in the performance of the economy, but they also owe something to developments in economic theory, as may be seen from a brief examination of the three phases we have just outlined. Let us make it clear at the outset that we are talking about British experience and attitudes. This is not as parochial as it might appear at first sight, since it was in Britain that much of the theoretical debate took place, in the first two of the phases at any rate.

There was not much disagreement about the influence of wages after the restoration of the Gold Standard in 1925. Keynes argued that, in the light of the movement of costs and prices in Britain and the rest of the world during the period of inconvertibility, the decision to restore the prewar parity constituted an overvaluation of sterling of the order of 10 per cent. Downward pressure would have to be exerted on wages, especially in export industries, if international competitiveness was to be maintained. The instrument to provide this pressure was monetary deflation: if there was resistance to cuts in money wages, unemployment might result instead. Keynes's argument was pragmatic. The hassle of trying to get trade unions, one by one, to accept lower wages could have been avoided if the parity of sterling had been put that much lower. This would have entailed less favourable terms of trade, so that *real* wages would have been lower, but the effect would be the same for everybody and, therefore, easier to bring about. In this 1920s debate the direction of causality ran from wages to employment, lower wages improving the competitiveness of British goods in export markets and in competing with imports.

With the departure from the Gold Standard in 1931, the external constraint seemed to have been removed. But world trade had collapsed and there followed a wave of protection, so that it was unlikely that employment recovery could come from improved international competitiveness alone. Nevertheless, wage cuts were still being advocated as a way of restoring employment, which had actually fallen during the Depression. The message which emerged in 1936 from the *General Theory of Employment, Interest and Money*, was still pragmatic. Monetary expansion could achieve the same results as wage cuts, and without the hassle. It was still accepted that for employment to rise, real wages, somehow or other, would have to fall. This was no longer because of international competitiveness. The *General Theory* model had switched to a closed economy. But Keynes made the conventional assumption that if more labour was to be employed with a given stock of capital, its marginal productivity would fall, so that to bring the extra employment about, the real wage would have to fall correspondingly. This assumption was not necessary to the argument in the *General Theory*, and was indeed dropped by Keynes a few years later, in the light of empirical evidence. But keeping the assumption in brings out most clearly the nub of the argument. Even if real wages had to fall, cuts in money wages would not bring it about. In a closed economy, wages are the only direct cost; if money wages are cut, so also will be costs and, in a competitive economy, so also will be prices. Real wages will remain unaltered, as will output and employment. Classical economists might argue that higher employment would still come from second round effects, such as lower interest rates stimulating investment, or increased real cash balances stimulating consumption. The Keynesian riposte was pragmatic: if those are the effects you want, they can be more directly achieved by monetary expansion, thus avoiding the wearying process of grinding money wages down. The context was one in which prices had been steady or falling for many years, and thus different from current experience in which there is always *some* inflation, together with much greater sensitivity to the risk of acceleration. So great is this difference that some might say that no lesson from the past can have any application today, but there is one piece of the analysis which retains its force in the altered circumstances, namely the distinction between money and real wages, and the perception that changes in the one need not necessarily entail corresponding changes in the other.

As to the link the other way, from employment to wages, it is true that some economists were aware of the problem. Joan Robinson (1937, p.15) wrote: 'when labour is scarce not only are trade unions very powerful, but employers themselves throw their weight into the scales of rising wages'. But it was not until after the war that this link moved into the centre of the stage.

In the postwar years, the question: 'what is the effect of an all-round cut in money wages on employment?' continued for a while to appear in examination papers, but interest in the question dwindled as, in Britain, unemployment on any large scale failed to reappear. There were still some variations in the – low – unemployment rates, and it was suggested that there was a connection between these variations and the rate of increase in money wages. In 1958 Phillips propounded a simple relationship in which the level of unemployment determined wage inflation. This led to the idea of a trade-off between inflation and unemployment. Ten years later Friedman argued that if unemployment fell below a critical 'natural' rate, there would be, not only inflation, but indefinitely accelerating inflation. The direction of causality of these and many more elaborate relationships which econometricians claimed to have found, all run from employment, or more specifically, unemployment to money wages. But once the degree of inflation is declared to be an objective of economic policy, the argument can be inverted, and we can work out the level below which unemployment must not go without breaking through the policy-determined inflation ceiling. In Friedman's case, of course, there is an absolute barrier at the natural rate of unemployment, since below this level, sooner or later, the pre-assigned ceiling on wage inflation will be broken through. Thus, through the back door, as it were, wage increases present themselves, once more, as limiting employment possibilities, only this time it is money wages, rather than real wages, which are the prime culprits.

If, in the 1950s and 1960s, there developed the idea of a trade-off between unemployment and inflation, in the later 1970s and in the 1980s we have experienced spells of simultaneously rising inflation and unemployment. With unemployment in Britain staying near to three million for five years, the pendulum swung, and the argument that workers were 'pricing themselves out of jobs' was heard once more. But this time we also continue to hear that wages are causing inflation. When one listens to the exhortations of ministers for wage moderation, it is often unclear which causal link they have in mind. Nevertheless, in looking at some of the evidence we will try to keep the causal distinction. We will start with two examples of the 'real wages cause unemployment' kind – a comparison of the United Kingdom and the United States, and an examination of the share of profits in corporate income. Then we turn to the other link, from unemployment to money wages. The conclusion will be that the British economy does appear to be more prone than its principal competitors to generate wage inflation, and we turn to consider policies which might mitigate this tendency, without requiring persistently high unemployment.

BRITAIN AND THE UNITED STATES

On 20 December 1984, *The Times* published an open letter to Mrs Thatcher, signed by members of both Houses of Parliament, businessmen, and some economists, which included the statement: 'A major reason for our high level of unemployment is simply that real labour costs in Britain have run ahead of productivity. In America 38 million jobs have been created in the past twenty years by holding the rise in real wages to 8 per cent, whereas in Britain real wages have risen by 48 per cent'.[1] Taking a more recent period, we find that between 1979 and 1987 average real weekly earnings in the United States fell by nearly 8 per cent and employment rose by 14 per cent, while in the United Kingdom average real weekly earnings rose by 20 per cent, but employment fell by nearly 6 per cent. If these facts are roughly right then surely it follows that high wages must be a 'major reason' for high unemployment. We shall see in a moment that such a conclusion does not follow at all, but, in the course of disposing of it, a number of questions are raised which are worth pursuing further.

In chart 8.1 we have extended the employment comparison back to 1951. The overall impression is that in the United States employment is always rising (from 1950 to 1987 it rose 2¼ times), while in Britain it was little higher in 1987 than it had been in 1950.[2] Looking more closely, we see that on five occasions employment in the United States fell back, but only for a year before resuming its upward climb. Employment in Britain grew gradually to a peak in 1966; fell back by 4½ per cent to 1972; was back at the earlier peak by 1979; whereupon it fell by 9 per cent in three years, the largest change in either direction since 1950; and finally, after 1983, began to rise again. These figures are for employees, which is the best figure for comparisons with wages. There were under two million self-employed in the 1970s, but this figure increased by more than a million in the 1980s.

Chart 8.2 shows the movement in average real weekly earnings in the two economies since the early 1950s. For the United States, they refer to all production and non-supervisory workers, 88 per cent of all workers in

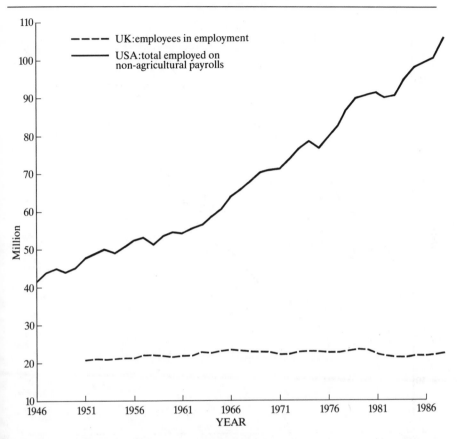

Chart 8.1 *Postwar employment in US and UK*
Sources: UK – *Economic Trends Annual Supplement, 1989*. US – *Economic Report of the President, 1990*, Table C43

1950 and 81 per cent in 1981, and the money earnings were divided by the consumer price index. For Britain, there have been series for weekly money earnings and for retail prices throughout, though the bases of both series have been changed from time to time. The index in the chart was obtained by linking successive series. The comparison falls this time into two parts. From the early 1950s until the early 1970s the general tendency is upward in both countries, with an annual average increase of 2.8 per cent in Britain and of 1.8 per cent in the United States. We know, of course, that insofar as these things can be measured, the *level* of real earnings in the 1950s was a good deal higher in the United States than in the United Kingdom. Both series reached peaks in the 1970s; the United States in 1973 and two years later in the United Kingdom. Thereafter the

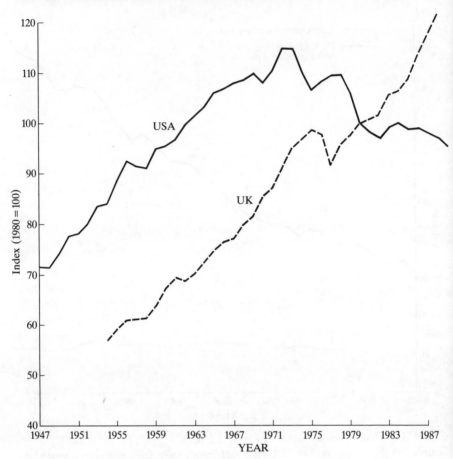

Chart 8.2 *Average weekly real earnings US and UK*
Sources: UK – Average weekly earnings/RPI. *National Institute Economic Review*
and *Economic Trends Annual Supplement, 1989*. US – Average weekly earnings: total
private/CPI. *Economic Report of the President, 1990*, table C44

comparison changes dramatically. In the United States there now
appears to have been a quite marked downward trend, slowed down only
in the later 1980s. In Britain, there was a sharp dip after 1975, but two
years later the upward march was resumed, albeit at a somewhat slower
rate than before, 2.3 per cent per annum on average, compared with 2.8
per cent before.

Looking at the charts together it is apparent that no simple link
between wages and employment holds good all the time. The fluctuations
of the two economies do not coincide, and the subdivisions of the period

Table 8.1. *Average annual percentage change in real weekly earnings and employment in the United States and the United Kingdom, for selected periods*

	United States		United Kingdom	
	Real earnings	Employment	Real earnings	Employment
1957–67	1.5	2.2	2.8	0.3
1967–73	1.2	2.6	3.6	−0.1
1973–79	−1.2	2.6	0.4	0.4
1979–88	−0.9	1.9	2.3	−0.3

Sources: United States: *Economic Report of the President*, 1989. United Kingdom: *National Institute Economic Review* and *Economic Trends* Annual Supplement.

1957–88 used in table 8.1 are a compromise to avoid measuring from troughs to peaks in either case.

In the first period, employment and earnings both go up in both countries; in the second earnings go up in both countries, but employment goes up in the United States and down in the United Kingdom; in the third period employment goes up in both countries, but earnings go down in the United States and up in the United Kingdom; only in the fourth period do we find the desired inverse relation between wages and employment in both countries. But while this extended comparison is sufficient to dispose of any *simpliste* relationship, it leaves behind some awkward questions. During the 'golden age' of the 1950s and 1960s in Britain we became accustomed to regular increases in real wages, and there was talk of a revolution of rising expectations in Britain, and in Europe. Did the revolution not reach the United States? That average real weekly earnings in the United States were *lower* in 1988 than they had been a quarter of a century earlier – with the implication that American workers had become worse off – seems, to a British observer, barely credible. However, if we concentrate on the twenty-year period of 1963–83, during which real weekly earnings fell by over 2 per cent, we find that average real *hourly* earnings rose by 6 per cent, because average hours worked fell from 38.8 to 35 hours a week. To the extent that this fall was voluntary, it means that workers were preferring to take part of their rise in welfare in more leisure than in more income. Then, there were important changes in the industrial composition of the labour force, with the fastest growing employment occurring in the service sectors where earnings are below average. If earnings are weighted with employment, we find that instead of a fall of over 2 per cent in the unweighted average, there is a rise of 3–4 per cent in real weekly earnings, and of 10 per cent in hourly earnings. Finally, there was a large increase in employers' contributions to fringe benefits in this period, and if we count them as a 'social wage', we can see that the real wage behaviour in the United States over this period becomes more credible.

However, the real wage concept used in the open letter, and which we have considered so far, is the 'consumption wage', that is, the real wage as it is seen by the wage-earner. For this purpose, we divide nominal wages by an index of consumer prices. But this is not the concept we need when discussing employment, for, from the employer's point of view, he is interested in the cost of labour relative to the price of the product he sells. For the economy as a whole, an appropriate index would be the implicit GDP deflator. It happens that, after 1978, a significant and widening gap opened up between the consumer price index in the United States and the implicit GDP deflator. The upshot of this, and other factors, which are considered in the Appendix to this chapter on page 244, is that whereas average real weekly (consumption) earnings in the private sector in 1983 were more than 2 per cent below the level of 1963, real compensation per hour of the non-farm business sector (nominal hourly earnings *plus* employers' contributions, divided by the implicit GDP deflator) was 33.7 per cent higher, closely in line with the rise in hourly labour productivity over the same period of 30.9 per cent.[3]

The Appendix, prompted by scepticism about the apparent failure of real wages in the United States to rise in a quarter of a century, is lengthy but not unfruitful. For besides disposing of the open letter as a red herring, it brings us back on to the proper track. What matter for employers are labour costs, of which wage costs are the major component, and we shall proceed to look at this question from two points of view. Firstly, it was argued that in the 1970s in Britain (and in other European countries) profits had been systematically squeezed by the upward pressure of real wages, forcing firms to reduce output, or even into bankruptcy. Accordingly, we examine recent behaviour of the share of profits in the income of industrial and commercial companies. The second approach is to look at the gap between actual wages and the level which would be warranted by the growth of productivity and other factors.

THE SHARE OF COMPANY PROFITS IN THE UNITED KINGDOM

In a paper given to the Bank of England's Panel of Academic Advisers, Hopkin (1984) examined what he called the High Wage Induced Unemployment (HWIU) thesis, which was being expounded by a number of economists and others, which attributed the mass unemploy-

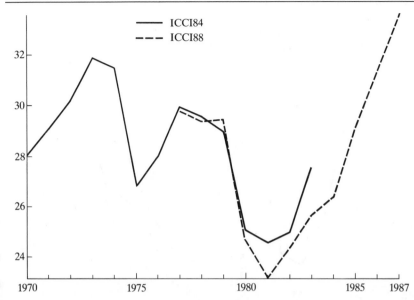

Chart 8.3 *Percentage share of profits in income generated by ICCs (including stock appreciation)*
Sources: 1984, 1988 Blue Book
Note: Pre-1972 North Sea oil not excluded: 1972 and after North Sea oil excluded.

ment of the early 1980s, not so much to lack of demand as to the unwillingness of business managements to supply, because real wages had been set at such a level, in relation to the real product of labour, as to destroy the profit incentive to production. Hopkin did not wish to contest the idea that too high real wages could weaken international competitiveness, and lead to a loss of employment that way. He also pointed out that the argument in question was not the same as that which associates increases in employment with declining marginal productivity, from which it follows at once in classical economic theory that real wages must also fall. In the *General Theory* Keynes had retained the declining marginal productivity piece of the classical model, though he soon abandoned it in the light of empirical evidence. But it is not this employment–real wage link which is involved in HWIU. Nor is it another, and roundabout, link whereby higher *nominal* wages induce higher inflation which the monetary authorities refuse to accommodate, thereby causing demand to fall. This latter is an important link, to which we shall return later, but it is not HWIU. That thesis is concerned with actual real wages, which are to be regarded as exogenous. An example would be if the level of real wages was fixed by trade unions.

For full employment to be achieved, says Hopkin, two conditions must

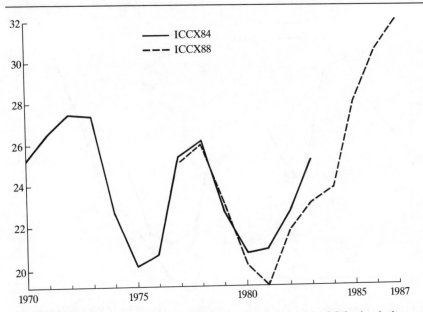

Chart 8.4 *Percentage share of profits in income generated by ICCs (excluding stock appreciation)*
Source and note: As chart 8.3

be satisfied: (1) there is sufficient demand to purchase the output of the fully employed labour force; (2) there is a sufficient level of profit to be made from producing this volume of goods. Failure of the first condition can give rise to Keynesian unemployment, and of the second to classical unemployment. The relevant concept of the real wage for the second condition is, of course, the cost of a unit of labour to the employer. Thus the appropriate deflator for the money value of wages (plus supplementaries) would be the value added per unit of product.

A piece of evidence which might throw light on HWIU would be the share of profits in value added. If there is pressure to raise real wages which becomes excessive, presumably the share of profits in value added will be reduced. Unfortunately, there are other influences which can have a similar effect, notably a worsening of international competitiveness, and a change in the pressure of demand in the economy. The tendency of profits to fluctuate more widely than income from employment in the ups and downs of the business cycle is well known. At the time he was writing Hopkin had available time series of profit shares from 1972 to 1983, a dozen observations in all, which ruled out econometric analysis, and he adopted the method of a careful historian with a good knowledge of the period, a method which we shall attempt to follow. The National Income

Blue Book carries tables of GDP by sector and type of income: in particular, there are figures for income from employment and gross trading profits for industrial and commercial companies, and also for half a dozen industry groups. The two series used by Hopkin were for industrial and commercial companies, excluding North Sea oil companies, and for manufacturing. He gave arguments for preferring the concept of profits, inclusive of stock appreciation, as an indicator of the incentive to production rather than profits on the basis of replacement cost, that is, excluding stock appreciation. In charts 8.3 and 8.4 we show the share of profits on both bases for industrial and commercial companies, excluding North Sea oil companies. The heavy black line uses the data contained in the 1984 Blue Book, which was used by Hopkin, and the hatched line comes from the 1988 Blue Book. The two lines illustrate a phenomenon familiar to users of these statistics, namely that profit estimates are the subject of frequent revision for three or four years after they are first published. In the charts we have also included figures for 1970 and 1971: these are taken from earlier Blue Books, and they include North Sea oil companies' profits, which would however have been a small positive or negative amount. The inclusion of these two years further emphasises the strong cyclical element in the movement of the profit share. United Kingdom international competitiveness, as measured by such indicators as relative export prices or the IMF normalised index of labour costs, was improving between 1972 and 1976/7, deteriorating sharply until 1981, improving again until 1986, after which there was renewed worsening. Notwithstanding the very large and obvious cyclical variations, the visual impression from chart 8.3 of the share of profits, including stock appreciation, is one of some downward *trend* between 1972 and 1981. The influence of competitiveness would presumably have been to make profits higher than otherwise between 1972 and 1976/7 and lower than otherwise until 1981. Taking out this influence would leave a flatter trend. The HWIU thesis, of course, requires a downward trend in the 1970s with, possibly, a reversal after 1980 as the power of trade unions is reduced by the stream of industrial relations legislation, as well as by the great increase in unemployment. After 1981, the factors of cyclical recovery, of output, if not yet of employment, and of improving competitiveness are both favourable to profits. But so also would be the HWIU factor, working through the curbing of trade unions. Thus all three influences on profit share are working in the same direction, and there is, indeed, a sharp improvement in the profit share. The figures after 1985 are exaggerated by the arrival in ICCs of newly privatised companies such as British Telecom.

Looking at manufacturing only (chart 8.5), the impression of a downward trend in profit share between 1972 and 1981 is, perhaps, a trifle

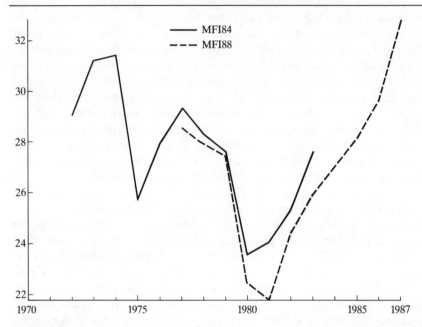

Chart 8.5 *Percentage share of profits in income generated by manufacturing ICCs including stock appreciation)*
Source and note: As chart 8.3

greater. This is what one might expect since manufacturing is proportionately more exposed to international competition than ICCs as a whole. A reasonable conclusion is that it is perfectly possible to tell the story of the profit share in terms of demand fluctuations and international competitiveness alone. There may be room to add in an influence of HWIU, pulling the share down in the 1970s, and allowing it to rise again in the 1980s. But over the whole period, at the end of which the profit share recovers to the peak of the early 1970s and then surpasses it, the influence of HWIU can only be of minor significance.

THE PRODUCTIVITY GAP

Following OPEC 1 the unemployment rate in Western Europe rose, from 2.7 per cent in 1973 to 4.6 per cent in 1979, and after OPEC 2 it had nearly doubled again by 1986. Unemployment in the United States also rose in the mid-1970s, and it rose still further in the recession of the early 1980s, but then it dropped right back. The persistently high unemployment in Western Europe was attributed by many economists to real wages being 'rigid' and remaining 'too high', whereas in the United

Table 8.2. *Real wage gaps in manufacturing industry, 1970–86 (percentage deviations from 1973)*

	1970	1975	1980	1981	1982	1985	1986
Belgium	−16.3	13.5	21.5	27.3	19.1	15.9	..
Denmark	−3.3	4.1	2.2	2.6	−1.8	−6.6	−11.4
Finland	−5.0	−3.0	−4.8	−2.3	−2.8	−4.3	−1.0
France	−2.0	3.3	5.6	8.1	12.2	3.4	−2.6
Germany, FDR	−1.8	2.5	7.3	8.3	4.8	2.5	−1.5
Italy	−3.7	4.4	−3.2	1.7	0.8	−2.7	−6.9
Netherlands	−4.3	9.0	16.3	16.6	10.7	6.6	..
Norway	−3.6	3.2	8.4	7.3	7.5	3.7	−3.5
Sweden	3.7	−1.2	5.1	4.7	−0.3	−6.8	−10.0
UK	−4.5	8.0	6.2	8.2	5.4	1.8	−2.5
US	−6.2	−5.8	0.3	−2.3	−2.6	2.3	−3.5
Canada	3.2	−3.3	−4.7	−1.4	5.9	3.1	..
Japan	−6.2	13.2	12.1	11.6	11.2	11.5	..

Source: ECE Secretariat.

States, real wages were said to be more flexible, enabling unemployment to fall back from the peak of the recession. One approach to this question has been to postulate that there is a level of real wages which is warranted by the level of productivity achieved and by full employment, and then to measure the gap between the actual real wage and this warranted amount. This was the line adopted by Bruno and Sachs (1985), and was followed up by the UN Economic Commission for Europe (1988).

The Commission's procedure starts from the share of compensation (earnings *plus* supplementaries) in value added. For a given product wage, the movement of this share would reflect cyclical fluctuations in productivity, so that a cyclically adjusted share could be obtained by replacing the actual share with a trend value. It was assumed that actual and trend coincided in 1960, 1973, 1979 and 1985, productivity trend rising at constant exponential rates in the intervals. 1973 was taken as the benchmark year in which there was full employment. Wage gaps were then defined as the percentage deviation of the normalised labour share from the share in the benchmark year. The exercise was confined to manufacturing industry. The ECE Secretariat acknowledged that this limitation is controversial, but argued in justification that much of the Western European unemployment problem seems to have arisen from the weak performance of this sector.

Table 8.2 shows the wage gaps calculated for a number of countries for selected years from 1970 to 1986. In most Western European countries the wage gap rose after OPEC 1 and in the subsequent recession, and the pattern was repeated after OPEC 2 in 1979. Thereafter, the general tendency was for gaps to fall, and by 1986 they were all negative. The behaviour of the United States wage gap was different. To begin with, it was small throughout and, in contrast to the Western European countries, it fell after both oil price rises. To draw general conclusions from this evidence is not easy. So far as trends go – the tendency of wage gaps in Western Europe between 1970 and 1981 was upwards, as was that of unemployment. After 1981, the trend of wage gaps was downwards, most becoming negative by 1986, but unemployment continued to rise strongly. In the United States there was a slight upward trend in the wage gap from 1970 to 1979, and after that a slight fall: the trend in unemployment was slightly upward throughout the period from 1970 to 1986. As to inflexibility of real wages, the fact that the wage gap declined in recession in the United States, and rose in Western Europe, has been cited as evidence of greater flexibility in the former. Thus, if we confine our attention to the 1970s the evidence gives some support to the view that too high real wages kept unemployment up, and rigidity prevented it from falling. But, if we confine ourselves to the 1980s, the evidence supports neither view.

Other writers, notably Gordon,[4] have made estimates of wage gaps for manufacturing and for the whole economy, for many countries. One of the most striking results is that, since 1971, Japan had a much more severe real wage problem than France, Germany or the United Kingdom, yet it was the European countries which were to experience the highest unemployment in the 1980s. The logic of the wage gap approach is to relate actual real wages to the levels which would be warranted at full employment. But these levels, it is argued, are not unique, depending on other factors such as the stock of capital, which in turn could have been influenced by demand management policies pursued in preceding years. On these grounds, the results cannot be claimed as definitive.

THE CLASSICAL UNEMPLOYMENT HYPOTHESIS

Pencavel (1987) has adopted an alternative approach to the attribution of slow employment growth in OECD Europe, as contrasted with North America, to the downward rigidity of real wages in the former, and the greater flexibility elsewhere. He begins with a model of an economy in which wages are determined by market clearing between a demand function and a supply function for labour, and compares this with one where the labour market is unionised or government regulated. The presumption is that in response to an exogenous shock, employment will change more in the unionised economy than in the market clearing case, where wage changes will contribute more to the adjustment. We should therefore expect that wages are less volatile and employment more volatile in the unionised case, than in the market clearing case. Is this so?

Pencavel selects seven variables related to the labour market for study: hourly compensation; consumer prices and the GDP deflator; employment and weekly working hours; GDP and unemployment. He calculates three measures of volatility for the period 1960–84 for each of the variables: their standard deviation; their standard deviation after removal of trend (split at 1973); and a measure derived from the coefficients of an ordinary least squares linear regression of the variables (again split at 1973). The three measures are calculated for eight countries: the United States, Canada and Japan; and five European countries including the United Kingdom. The first finding is that the volatility of manhours and employment across countries tends to be negatively correlated with the volatility of both real and money wages. However, those economies whose employment has grown most do not appear to be those showing greater flexibility: on the contrary, there appears to be a negative association between growth of employment and wage volatility. Canada and the United States, with the largest employment growth, have the lowest values for the standard deviation of real product wages.[5]

According to the classical unemployment hypothesis, movements in exogenous variables determining the supply of labour should have zero coefficients in equations accounting for variations in employment. Pencavel considers the case of the replacement ratio (of unemployment benefit to wages). A cut in this ratio should shift the supply curve of labour to the right. However, if wages are always kept above market clearing levels, this should have no effect on employment. When applied to Britain, the conclusion of this test is not wholly satisfactory. On the one hand, it rejects the notion that employment was affected by the replacement ratio: on the other hand, Pencavel found himself unable to come up with a satisfactory labour demand function.

As so often happens, the results of this very well-conducted empirical study do not all point unambiguously in the same direction. The author's own phrase is that 'they lean in the direction of rejecting' the classical unemployment hypothesis. Nor, taken together, do the two empirical studies we have summarised decisively reject the classical real wage hypothesis for the different groups of countries examined, over slightly different time periods. But they do not offer it much support either. The special test did seem to exclude it for Britain, but it did leave a loose end. This is not a wholly satisfactory position, but we shall not try to pursue the real wage hypothesis any further. For there still remains the obstacle that whatever statistical association can be found between real wages and employment or unemployment, the variable involved in wage settlements is the nominal, or money, wage. The desire to achieve some target real wage may well figure among the factors influencing trade unions in deciding how much to ask for. In some cases a settlement may include an indexed component, though it usually has a nominal element as well. But the majority of settlements are still made in nominal terms, and it then depends on how prices rise during the contract period whether or not any real wage target is achieved. We should, therefore, shift our attention to the determinants of nominal wage increases.

NOMINAL WAGES AND EMPLOYMENT

In considering the wage–employment nexus, the direction of causality usually runs from the real wage to employment. But for nominal wages, it is the other way round, at any rate if we are considering unemployment rather than employment. If unemployment is high, there will be downward pressure on money wages, but if it is low, and labour becomes scarce, employers may compete for labour and money wages will rise. This idea was familiar to the first generation of Keynesians (Robinson, 1937), and to economists studying the prospects for full employment after the Second World War,[6] although the relationship was not conceived in any precise quantitative way. The publication in 1958 of Phillips's paper put a different complexion on things, for it appeared that he was propounding a simple econometric law. He plotted the annual change in money wage rates against unemployment for the period 1861–1913. He fitted a hyperbolic curve to these points and went on to assert that, given the levels of unemployment which actually occurred, the wage history of the interwar years 'could have been predicted fairly accurately from a study of the prewar data'. He also claimed that keeping unemployment at 2½ per cent would ensure a stable level of product prices.[7] As regards the influence of prices on money wages, Phillips argued that the cost of living would have little separate effect, except in cases where retail prices had been forced up by sharp rises in import prices, such as occurred in wartime. Throughout the postwar period before 1958, unemployment had been less than 2 per cent, but there had been an average price inflation of around 3 per cent a year. The idea that persistent inflation, leading to intermittent balance of payments crises, might be ended at the cost of a comparatively small rise in unemployment had its obvious attractions, but the more important message of the Phillips curve was the idea of a trade-off between unemployment and inflation. The Phillips curve entered the vocabulary of economics with extraordinary rapidity, despite warnings against the dangers of over-simplification. But, in little more than a decade, the simple trade-off between the change in money wage rates and unemployment was in retreat. This was partly the consequence of the increasing availability of the computer, allowing the generation of more and more wage equations. On the one hand alternative dependent variables, such as earnings, or earnings net of direct tax, could be tried, and on the other side the range of explanatory variables could be extended to include the change in unemployment as well as the level, and also prices. One interesting idea to emerge from the empirical studies in this country was the idea of a target real wage: specifically, trade unions, having formed expectations about how much prices could be expected to rise in the coming period, would set a nominal target which would cover this amount *plus* a premium which would yield the real increase. However, equations estimated from past time periods respond only slowly to changes occurring in the real world. What was disconcerting was that from the end of the 1960s, more and more countries began to experience simultaneous increases in inflation and unemployment. This phenomenon does not require that one should immediately jettison the Phillips model: one can take it on board by incorporating shifts in the whole curve. That does mean, though, that one must find an explanation for the shift.

NAIRU

For some economic theorists the erosion of the Phillips curve acted as a stimulus to make a superior model, and in 1968 Friedman provided one of the first of these, in a powerful exposition of the natural rate hypothesis.[8] The key feature of this and subsequent similar models is that when unemployment is below the natural rate, there would not be just more inflation, as with Phillips, but accelerating inflation. If unemployment were above the natural rate, wage and price increases would slow down, and then go into reverse, with prices falling indefinitely, although this aspect of the model received very little subsequent attention. According to some versions of the theory, there might still be a trade-off between money wages and unemployment in the short run, but, in the long run, the Phillips curve would become vertical.

The natural rate, or NAIRU (non-accelerating inflation rate of unemployment), was absorbed into the vocabulary of economists as quickly as its Phillips predecessor, and was incorporated into models developed by the rational expectations school of theorists. But there remains some obscurity about its status. Flemming has remarked that the view that 'the natural rate of unemployment is a known constant has never been tenable and has probably never been entertained'.[9] This may be true of the maintenance, but hardly of the entertainment: certainly, many economists have acted as though there was a number out there, waiting to be found. The first estimate for Britain was probably that of Laidler in 1975, when he put the natural rate below 2 per cent.[10] Nickell and Layard[11] have given estimates, using the male unemployment rate in Britain, of 2 per cent in 1955–66, 4 per cent in 1967–74, 8 per cent in 1975–9 and 10 per cent in 1980–3. Estimates have been made for other countries which show similar large variations in the natural rate from one sub-period to another.[12] The most remarkable set of estimates is that provided by Minford. These are of particular interest since he is one of the leading exponents in Britain of the rational expectations idea. In the first edition of *Unemployment: Cause and Cure*, published in 1983, Minford put the natural rate in Britain at 7.25 per cent, or about 1.75 million, and added: '... since then it has probably risen to the range of 2 to 2.5 million'. In the second edition, published in 1985, the natural rate in 1980 was of the order of 13.5 per cent, that is, 3.25 million. Minford's first estimate was derived from a system of equations, using annual data, estimated over the period 1955–79, using 'over 1,100 observations' of British economic behaviour. Less detail is given about estimation in the second edition, but reference is made to 'over 1,300 observations', suggesting an estimation period of 1955–83, or 1955–84. Not only did this extension of the period increase the natural rate dramatically, by 1.5 million between 1979 and 1980, but it also had remarkable effects on the estimate of the natural rate for the *same* year in the past. Thus the chart on page 27 of the first edition suggests a natural rate for 1971 of just over one million, but the chart on page 28 of the second edition puts the rate for 1971 at 2.4 million. Later on, in a paper presented to a conference organised by the National Institute of Economic and Social Research on policymaking with macroeconomic models, held in December 1987, the natural rate 'today' had been brought down to 'around one million' (Minford, 1989).

Whatever may be the merits of the natural rate of unemployment as a tool of economic theory, its empirical base is hardly strong enough to be of practical use in policymaking. In some cases there is little or no attempt to provide reasons why the NAIRU should have changed between one period and another. Layard and Nickell are an honourable exception. For example, of an increase of 7.1 per cent in the measure of the male NAIRU for Britain between 1956–66 and 1980–3, 20 per cent is attributed to employers' labour taxes and 60 per cent to increased trade union pressure. They remind us, however, that all their numbers are based on estimated equations, where many of the coefficients are not determined with any degree of precision.

In a more recent paper Nickell (1988) expressed some dissatisfaction with the natural rate story. After 1982, wage inflation in Britain did not fall for four or more years, yet unemployment remained a 'staggering' 10 percentage points higher than in 1979. 'Must we conclude that the natural rate of unemployment has risen by an equally staggering amount?' In order to explore various possible explanations he used as a framework a three equation model which he had earlier developed in conjunction with Layard. He reached the tentative conclusion that changes in duration composition of the unemployed are of crucial importance. An increase in the proportion of people who have been out of work for long periods attenuates the downward pressure of unemployment on wages. This is an interesting conclusion, with implications for policy which will be considered elsewhere (see Chapter 9, page 107). But it is also, though Nickell does not say so in as many words, a nail in the coffin of the natural rate concept.[13] When Friedman spoke of the level of unemployment which would be 'ground out by the Walrasian system of general equilibrium equations', he was retaining the familiar distinction between the structure of the economic system, embodied in the parameters of those equations, and the variables. He did not claim that the parameters never changed: on the contrary he gave a list of the structural characteristics of labour and commodity markets, changes in which could well alter the natural rate. But he did *not* include in that list the past values of any of the variables. To do so would be to change the goal posts, and to alter the perception which we have hitherto had of the status of the natural rate. Taken with the bewildering variety of estimates of NAIRU, it would seem that the coffin had best be buried. Regrettably, there is no procedure for the official interment of misleading terminology: the best we can do is to do without it whenever we can.

THE INFLUENCE OF PRICES

Phillips had explained money wages in terms of unemployment. The natural rate and NAIRU originated as a critique of the Phillips framework, but ended by virtually obliterating the explanation. If unemployment differed from NAIRU, money wages would be either rising faster and faster, or slowing down and then falling faster and faster. If unemployment was at NAIRU there would be steady wage inflation, but any rate would do, the particular rate being an accident of history. This is fine, if you believe the story, but if you do not the problem still remains.

The modern reader may be surprised that Phillips gave hardly any role to prices in the determination of money wages, except in rare circumstances. But, over the period 1861 to 1913, there was little discernible trend. The slow decline in consumer prices until the end of the century was followed by a gentle upward move to 1913. And after the rise and fall of the First World War and its aftermath the pattern was repeated in the interwar period. In the Second World War, though prices rose, they were kept under better control and it took some time after the war before the public began to appreciate that we had entered a new world in which prices would rise somewhat every year, and hardly ever fall. In wage settlements, the price element was retrospective, adjusting for increases that had already occurred, rather than those which were expected to occur. This was even more evident for salaries, which were adjusted in steps at infrequent intervals, and decades had to elapse before they joined the annual round.

The notion that nominal wage increases *ought* to compensate at least for price rises since the last settlement became part of the conventional wisdom, at any rate on the trade union side, in the 1960s. Blackaby observed that during the period 1962–9, during which there was some form of incomes policy in place, the government always stressed that price increases were 'no longer' to be considered a justification for wage increases (Blackaby *et al.*, 1978, page 383). Stage III of the Heath government's incomes policy which came into operation in November 1973 made provision for a 40p pay increase for every 1 percentage point the retail price index exceeded by 7 per cent the level of October 1973.[14] Up to this time, there was no hint of wage claims to cover *anticipated* price rises. However, claims on this basis were soon to appear. When the Labour government came into office in March 1974, while continuing to honour Stage III of its predecessor's incomes policy, as well as retaining elements of statutory price control, it abandoned statutory control of wages, relying instead on a 'social contract' with the TUC, which embraced the principle of voluntary wage control. But it quickly became apparent by the autumn, that settlements of the order of 20 per cent were being reached *in anticipation* of further price rises in the coming twelve months. Although rates of both wage and price inflation have been brought down to single figures since then, we may reasonably suppose that workers and their representatives, when bargaining, may still keep one eye on future price rises as well as on those which have already occurred. But how important are such anticipations or expectations in actual wage settlements, as compared with making good past increases in prices?

Brown (1985, chapter 8) provided an interesting treatment of the question whether price expectations had become influential in wage settlements. He started from the original Phillips curve, relating the rate of change of money wages to unemployment, drew charts for six major countries since 1951, and considered whether the fit of the curves could be improved by varying the lag between unemployment and wage changes, and whether shifts in the curves could be identified. One possible explanation of the Phillips curve was that, when there was a regular business cycle, trade unions held back in recession years and struck, in both senses of the word, in boom years. This effect could be removed by averaging over the cycle, which in most countries tended to be about four years. When this was done, traces of the Phillips relationship remained in some cases, though not in all. Brown concluded that some influence on inflation, other than unemployment, had become progressively more important during the period. 'This was so to a small extent for Japan and Germany, overwhelmingly for the United Kingdom and Italy, with the United States in between'. It seems that there was never a discernible influence of unemployment on wage inflation in France. The simplest Phillips relation can be written: $\dot{w} = k\,(\bar{U}-U)$, where U is unemployment and $\bar{U}$ the equilibrium rate where the curve crosses the x-axis, and $\dot{w}$ is the rate of change of money wages. One should add v_t, a random variable of zero mean, but we exclude it for convenience. To introduce price expectations, we write: $\dot{w} = k\,(\bar{U}-U) + \dot{p}^e$, where $\dot{p}^e$, is the expected price change. How are expectations formed? For a long time economists used forms of adaptive expectations, but the snag is that in periods of rising inflation, expected inflation would always lag behind actual inflation. If, however, expectations were formed rationally or consistently, the best guess for $\dot{p}^e$ would be the $\dot{p}$ which the model would deliver, that is, we would write: $\dot{w} = k\,(\bar{U}-U) + \dot{p}$, or $\dot{w} - \dot{p} = k\,(\bar{U}-U)$. Since $\dot{w}-\dot{p}$ is the rate of change of *real* wages, we now have an equation for real wages in the same form as the original Phillips equation for money wages. The procedure now is to compare the charts for each country of nominal wages and of real wages against unemployment. This comparison shows up the influence of correct price expectations on nominal wages. Brown's conclusion is that continuation of current rates of inflation was never fully built into wage settlements except in Italy, where, of course, there was indexation, a conclusion which is in line with other evidence for OECD countries.

AN HISTORICAL PERSPECTIVE

Where does all this leave us? Common sense tells us that unemployment and price changes must have an influence on nominal wages, but the econometric evidence has not yielded any stable relation which would be of much use in the conduct of policy. Let us try a different tack, and run our eye over the whole postwar period in the United Kingdom. There exists only one continuous series for nominal wages, and that is for the basic weekly wage rates of manual workers, which runs from 1948 to 1983, when it was discontinued. This index was never highly regarded as a measure of labour market conditions, but it is good enough to indicate orders of magnitude. Table 8.3 shows averages of annual changes in the index over the previous year for five year periods, together with equiv-

Table 8.3. *Averages of annual percentage changes in United Kingdom basic weekly wage rates of manual workers, and of the retail price index*

	Wage rates	Retail price index
1950–4	5.5	5.2
1955–9	5.2	3.4
1960–4	3.8	2.8
1965–9	4.9	4.3
1970–4	14.1	9.6
1975–9	16.9	15.7
1980–4	10.2[a]	10.3
1985–8[b]	–	4.6

Source: *Economic Trends* Annual Supplement.
Notes: [a] 1980–3. [b] Four years only.

alent figures for the retail price index. By subsequent standards the four quinquennia of the 1950s and the 1960s stand out for their comparative tranquillity. Throughout these two decades, the economy was near to full employment. Any Phillips curve variations were of the order of a few hundred thousand at most. There was no obvious acceleration, and it is not surprising that Laidler found a NAIRU less than 2 per cent. Nevertheless the danger of wage inflation under full employment was recognised from the outset by many economists, including those members of the Economic Section of the Cabinet Office who were advising the government. There was a spell of wage restraint after the 1949 devaluation, which the TUC supported but, during the 1950s, the government limited itself to exhortation towards wage moderation. The competitive edge gained by devaluation was gradually eroded, as British export prices rose a little faster than those of principal competitors, and in the 1960s there started what was to prove a sequence of varied incomes policy measures, including an outright freeze on wages and prices in 1966, intended to put a brake on inflation. Nevertheless, a devaluation of sterling proved necessary by the end of 1967, to restore international competitiveness.

OPEC 1 came just at the end of a boom in all the advanced industrial countries, all of whom experienced higher inflation in the 1970s. But, notwithstanding the very different circumstances, Britain's rate was still at the top, matched only by Italy. After OPEC 2 all major countries experienced recession. Britain's was earlier and deeper than the others, and unemployment was proportionately higher than elsewhere. Inflation came down, as it did throughout the world but, once again, Britain's

Table 8.4. *Unemployment, and percentage changes in average nominal earnings and retail prices in Great Britain, per cent*

	Unemployment[a]	Increase in earnings[b]	Increase in retail prices
1976	4.1	–	–
1977	4.4	9.0	11.6
1978	4.3	13.0	8.3
1979	3.9	15.5	13.4
1980	5.0	20.8	18.0
1981	8.0	12.9	11.9
1982	9.4	9.4	8.6
1983	10.4	8.4	4.6
1984	10.6	6.1	4.9
1985	10.8	8.5	6.1
1986	10.9	7.9	3.4
1987	9.8	7.8	4.2
1988	7.8	8.7	4.9

Source: *Employment Gazette*, April 1989.
[a]The unemployment percentages have been revised many times in recent years, almost always downwards. Thus the figure of 10.4 for the year 1983 compares with the figure reported at the time of 12.2 per cent.
[b]The earnings series changed in 1980, but the old and new series overlapped.

inflation remained higher than the other majors. It is worth looking more closely at the course of wage inflation in the most recent period (table 8.4). This time for wages we use a more representative figure, namely, average earnings for the whole economy (Great Britain), against which we put retail prices and unemployment. Against the year 1981, say, the table shows the percentage change since 1980 in the wage and price indexes, and the level of unemployment, in percentage of the total labour force, for the year 1981.

Following the breakdown of the Labour government's incomes policy in the winter of 1978–9, both wage and price inflation rose and peaked in 1980, after which they fell back sharply, but there was no further deceleration after 1982: the annual growth of nominal earnings, in particular, settled at a steady figure of just under 8 per cent. Meanwhile, unemployment, which had been slightly falling in 1979, began to rise strongly, surpassing 10 per cent in 1983, far higher than anything previously experienced since the end of the war, and comparable with the unemployment in the Great Depression fifty years earlier. Moreover, in contrast with the 1930s, this time unemployment went on gradually climbing for three more years. The inflation rate, though much lower than in the 1970s, settled around 4¾ per cent per annum, still, unfortunately, rather higher than our principal competitors.

But, does the fact that Britain tends to have a nominal wage inflation which delivers a somewhat higher price inflation than its major competitors matter? The view taken in the 1950s was that it did not.[15] The system of free collective bargaining meant that different groups of workers sought, in an annual wage round, to keep up with, or even to get one ahead of the others. No doubt, at the time the settlement was made, each group believed it was achieving a real wage increase as well, though it would find, as prices continued to rise, that any such increase was being eroded until the time came round for a new increase. No doubt, also, that the aggregate of claims, in real terms, exceeded the capacity of a fully employed economy to produce. But the consequent increase in nominal labour costs could be defended as acting as a safety valve dissipating the excess of claims over resources, thereby averting direct confrontation between the various groups. Particular groups, such as pensioners, who did not participate in the annual merry-go-round, might suffer, but they could be helped directly, for example, by indexation. If the rate of price inflation was moderate (as it was at between 3 and 5 per cent), it might even be regarded as a useful social invention.

For all the success in maintaining employment and rising output in the 1950s, there were still balance of payments crises which, though quickly corrected, led to growing concern about the competitiveness of British industry, and brought two ideas forward onto the political agenda in the 1960s. The first idea was to try to do something directly about inflation, and it took the form of incomes policy or prices and incomes policy, varieties of which were to cross the political stage in the next twenty years. The second idea was to accept the inflation rate, and to offset the damage to competitiveness by lowering the parity of sterling in the International Monetary Fund: advocacy of devaluation grew during the 1960s, and eventually devaluation arrived in 1967. At the time, this was hailed as a success: the Brookings team of distinguished American economists who had set out to diagnose the 'British disease' reckoned that the 1967 devaluation should enable Britain to 'find itself in a strong balance of payments position, when the effect of these measures takes hold' (Caves *et al*, 1968). When, in 1972, the Heath government embarked on a programme of expansion, the Chancellor of the Exchequer indicated that he would not let a fixed exchange rate stand in his way. When the pound was allowed to float, in June, it was introduced as a temporary measure, but in the event inaugurated a new period of floating, and in the circumstances, it probably intensified wage inflation. Incomes policy came to be seen, not as an alternative to devaluation, but as complementary. If successful, it might avert it; if not, it was needed to damp down its inflationary consequences.

In all the varieties of incomes policy tried out in the 1960s and 1970s, the maintenance of full employment remained a primary objective of government policy. The Labour government of 1974–9 was unable to achieve it, and full employment, as a target of demand management, was formally abandoned by its successor.

CONCLUSION

Britain is an open economy, with exports and imports constituting nearly a quarter of final expenditure. Labour costs play a large role in international competitiveness and, if the latter is judged inadequate, then in that sense real wages may be considered too high. If the inadequacy was expressed in a trade deficit, its correction need not entail unemployment. But, in order to achieve the necessary switch of resources from the domestic economy to the trade balance, real wages would have to fall. The alternative correction would be to deflate aggregate demand, reducing imports, but also reducing domestic output and employment. In this case we could say that unemployment was being caused by too high real wages.

As regards the domestic economy, we thought that the fall and rise of the profit share could be accounted for by demand movements and changes in competitiveness, but because the timing coincided there was a little bit of room for a story about rising pressure on profit margins by trade unions in the 1970s, followed by relaxation of pressure in the 1980s, as unemployment and the new labour legislation got to work. But the more serious problem appears to have been the persistent tendency, over virtually the whole of the postwar period, for nominal wage inflation to be on the high side, that is, generating an inflation of costs and prices higher than that of our major competitors. This was not a threat to employment, so long as the British public was prepared to tolerate the moderate inflation, and the monetary authorities to accommodate it, and so long as the exchange rate could be adjusted, or allowed to adjust, to preserve competitiveness. These conditions ceased to apply in the 1970s, and the level of employment has become the residuary legatee of an anti-inflation policy. This raises two questions. Why is British nominal wage inflation too high? And can it be slowed down directly, by means other than the contraction of demand and employment? These questions are addressed from different angles in the following chapters.

9

WAGE SUBSIDIES

From time to time, and in different ways, the existing system of wage and price determination has been seen as an obstacle to full employment. Among remedies, wage or employment subsidies have been proposed. They were advanced in the interwar years, and interest in them has revived with the return of high unemployment in more recent years. The proposals have ranged from a general subsidy to all employment, to marginal subsidies to extra workers employed.

There has been comparatively little practical experience in this field in postwar Britain. The most interesting case, probably, was the Regional Employment Premium, which was introduced in the late 1960s, and although it may have had some effects (see Chapter 6, p. 59) it was phased out in the early 1970s. We shall not, however, attempt any comprehensive survey of practical measures applied in Britain, or elsewhere, nor of the many schemes of this kind which have been proposed. We will simply pick out some of the main proposals with a view to exposing their varying theoretical underpinnings, and pointing to some of the practical problems they raise.

The chapter on wage subsidies incorporated in the third edition of Pigou's *Economics of Welfare* in 1928,[1] may be said to be the classic exposition of the classical view on the subject. It starts with a closed economy, with a homogeneous labour force of $x + h$ workers, of whom x are employed at a wage w. For all $x + h$ to be employed, it would be necessary for the wage to be at a lower level, w_1. This reduction in real wages would be the simplest solution to the unemployment problem; however, trade union power is sufficient to insist on wage w. Given that insistence, the additional h workers could still be brought into employment if a subsidy, s, equal to $w - w_1$, were to be paid to employers for every worker employed. The effect of this is to reduce the cost per worker of each employee from w to w_1 – and hence the extra h workers will be taken into employment. The extra output will lie between hw and hw_1 – this is because of declining marginal productivity.[2] To complete the picture, we suppose that previously unemployed workers had received amount r in unemployment benefit, which had been paid for by income tax falling only on employers. It is also supposed that the subsidy is paid for in the same way. Pigou calculates the net outcome of the subsidy by considering first the x workers already employed. They themselves continue to receive wage w: the employers receive a subsidy s, but they pay for it out of income tax. The additional h workers also receive wage w, so that wage earners as a whole are better off. With respect to them, employers receive subsidy hs, which is paid for by income tax. Thus altogether employers pay $(x + h)s$ in income tax. But they save hr, the unemployment benefit previously paid. Moreover, there is the additional output hc – where c is in the range between w and w_1 – so that the net change in employers' income is $h(r + c - s)$, which is positive so long as $(r + c)$ exceeds s.

It will be noted that employers receive a subsidy towards the wages of the x workers who would be employed anyway, as well as, of course, paying the income tax for it. This 'deadweight' effect is of much concern to more recent writers, but Pigou had no qualms. He does not, in fact, mention any possible adverse effects upon activity of the income tax, such as reduced investment. Pigou also maintained that if subsidies were applied in export industries, the balance of gain and loss would work out less satisfactorily, because foreigners, instead of domestic users, would get the benefit of the price reduction due to the subsidy. However no mention of any price reduction was made in the exposition of the closed economy case. Pigou states that: 'workers already in work will receive no more than before' – implying unchanged prices, and hence real wages for the worker, while the employer pockets the subsidy, for which he has to pay the income tax.

If prices *did* fall, then real wages per worker would rise and not remain at the original level. To sort out this problem requires the separate specification of nominal wages and prices. This was done by Kaldor (1936) in the mid-1930s when he argued that the general subsidy to wages would have far greater effects on employment than an equivalent general reduction in money wages. The postwar Kaldor was generally regarded as a leading Keynesian, but when he came to print his original 1936 paper in his collected *Essays in Economic Policy*, Kaldor (1964) acknowledged that the approach was 'pre-Keynesian'. He still thought that the conclusions were sound, but that the argument was not. He also mentioned that he had received a letter from Keynes himself in 1935[3] arguing that a general subsidy to wages would have no effect at all on employment. This was, of course, in line with the more familiar Keynesian argument that an all-round cut in money wages would simply lead to a corresponding cut in prices, and no change in real wages or employment. But, as Joan Robinson (1937, pp. 77 *et seq.*) pointed out, with the general subsidy *nominal* wages remained unchanged, while prices fell, so that real wages rose. At the same time, nominal profits would initially fall, with real profits the same. Real profits would rise to the extent that output rose, but they would be reduced by the income tax to pay for the subsidy. Since, in the early Keynesian canon, the rich were supposed to save more than workers, the transfer of real income from the former to the latter would raise the propensity to consume, inducing an increase in consumption and a temporary rise in investment. Along this route, there could be a rise in employment and output.

That was the position of the debate as it stood before the Second World War. It is not surprising that no more was heard of the subject for many years after the war, since there was already full employment. The issue of a job subsidy was raised again in the later 1970s, in Britain, though the approach now differed from that of Pigou in a number of important respects. Firstly, the proposals considered are of a subsidy to *marginal* output or employment: the deadweight aspects of any general subsidy are now seen to be a serious disadvantage, especially in the effect on the budget – albeit on both sides of the account. Secondly, while in the Pigovian original the best results were achieved in a closed economy, in the revived version one of the merits claimed was to bring about an improvement in the balance of payments, equivalent to that which might be achieved by a devaluation, but without the adverse effect on the price level which, by instigating a wage–price spiral, would lose the ground initially gained. The underlying reason is that whereas in most classical theorising, foreign trade is always brought back into balance, in the modern approach a change in the trade balance is one of the many ways to influence output and employment, when there is initial unemployment.

Layard and Nickell (1980) made the case for subsidising extra jobs in the *Economic Journal*. Specifically, they proposed a subsidy to all new jobs created, whether due to the subsidy or not. After introduction, the scheme would last for two years, after which the subsidy would fall progressively to zero over, say, four years. The subsidy would apply at the level of the firm and not the establishment, to preclude the creation of spurious new jobs by switching workers from one establishment to another, and back. They set up a Keynesian model of the economy within which to make estimates of the quantitative effects of such a scheme. They estimated, for instance, that a marginal subsidy of one third of average earnings would have a medium-term employment effect equivalent to a devaluation of 1½ per cent. In comparison with government expenditure, the budget deficit per additional job may be less (though it may be more) and the balance of payments effects are always more favourable. The strongest case for the marginal employment subsidy appears to be as a disguised form of devaluation, improving the balance of payments, and creating employment, but without adverse effects on the price level.

Some years later, Jackman and Layard (1986) put up an apparently different objective for a combination of a tax on wages and a subsidy to employment. They postulated a natural rate of unemployment below which inflation would accelerate, and act as a bar on conventional Keynesian expansion. Their objective was to shift the natural rate itself. They considered two possibilities: in the one it is firms which set wages, and in the other trade unions. In the former case they believe that there will be a downward shift in the wage-setting relationship, that is, firms will be prepared to pay the going wage at a higher level of employment. If wages are set by unions, they will be less inclined to push for higher wages at any given level of employment. In both cases, the natural rate is reduced.

Yet another proposal is for a subsidy to employing the long-term unemployed, those who have been out of work for more than a year, say. One argument for this is because it seems that the longer a person remains unemployed, the harder it becomes to get employment once more. Another is that it appears that, unlike short-term unemployment, long-term unemployment has no effect on wage inflation. Yet another objective for subsidies is to give preference to the employment of persons in some regions or districts and not others. Several of these proposals appeared in a programme for reducing unemployment put forward by Layard (1986). Layard makes the important point that for the layman subsidy may be a dirty word. By the same token, 'reducing employers' national insurance contributions' arouses little passion. From the point of view of presentation, the 'restructuring of the tax on jobs' may get off to a better start than 'a subsidy to employment'. On the face of it, employment or wage subsidies have been proposed with a number of different objectives in view and each scheme needs to be judged with these primary purposes in mind and compared with other possible means of achieving the same ends. A comprehensive survey of such proposals might be useful, but is not intended here. Rather, we would draw attention to a feature which they all have in common, namely the desire to get round some intractable obstacle. In Pigou's case (1928) there was no question as to what was his preferred solution. If there was unemployment, real wages ought to come down to the requisite level. Unfortunately, the obstinacy of trade unions stood in the way. His wage-subsidy plan was a device to circumvent this obstinacy. Interestingly, Pigou did not consider the possibility that lower unemployment might make trade unions even more obstinate, insisting on an even higher level of real wages, thus frustrating the subsidy solution. Layard and Nickell (1980) clearly approve devaluation, were it not that the real wage resistance of trade unions might lead them to push up money wages, in an effort to restore real wages, causing inflation until the gains of the devaluation had been cancelled. The marginal employment subsidy is designed to get round this obstacle. But might not foreigners rumble the plan, and retaliate? There is, perhaps, less of subterfuge in a scheme to shift the natural rate, or to pick out those unemployed believed not to exert an influence on wage bargaining.

The element of subterfuge does not, of itself, invalidate all subsidy schemes. The art of the possible is an essential ingredient of most policies in democratic countries, and the various schemes should still be considered on their merits. However, since at the root of most schemes is the notion that the existing arrangements for the determination of wages and prices are not compatible with full employment, one ought to consider proposals which claim to go to the root of the matter. One such is profit sharing.

10

PROFIT SHARING

INTRODUCTION

The remuneration of workers by a share in the crop, as in agriculture, or in the proceeds from the sale of the product, as in sliding-scale agreements linking wages to product prices, which have been used at one time or another in the coal and steel industries, goes a long way back in the history of capitalism, but the practice was becoming less common in advanced countries in the past half century. However, interest has been revived by the claims made by Weitzman (1984) that profit or revenue sharing would provide a powerful antidote to stagflation, having strongly favourable effects on employment, as well as tending to reduce inflationary pressures. Weitzman's arguments received an initially favourable reception from a number of distinguished economists, but have since failed to find support in historical and empirical studies. We will first set out the essentials of the argument and draw attention to the key assumptions about firms' behaviour which are necessary for the conclusion about stagflation to be realised. Then we consider the results of some recent historical and empirical studies of profit sharing.

THE WAGE SYSTEM AND SHARING

Weitzman contrasts the behaviour of a profit-maximising firm under a wage system, in which workers receive a fixed wage, specified in advance and not tied in any way to the revenue or profit performance of the firm, with a sharing system in which part, at least, of the remuneration is proportional to the revenue or profit of the firm. There are many such possibilities, but the essence of the argument can be exposed by taking the case where the worker's remuneration consists of two parts, one part specified in advance, and the other part proportional to the profits of the firm.

Consider a typical firm operating under conditions of monopolistic competition. This means that, in order to sell more of its product, the firm would have to reduce its price – as against perfect competition, where a firm could sell any amount at a given price. The firm's costs of production may initially fall when its output is very low, will reach a minimum at some optimal scale of production, and then start to rise as output is expanded further. To hit upon the profit maximising output, the firm will equate marginal revenue (MR) with marginal cost (MC). Since the demand curve is downward sloping, MR, the addition to revenue of selling one more unit of the product, will be less than the price, and marginal cost less than average cost. In the long run, average revenue must cover average cost by an element of 'normal' profit:[1] if not, either new firms will enter or existing firms start to leave the industry. This is just the textbook case of firms in monopolistic competition with one another. Now simplify further, and suppose that the only costs which vary with output are labour costs. The problem is now to compare the behaviour of two firms, which are similar in all respects except that in firm A workers are paid a fixed wage w, while in firm B they are rewarded by a fixed amount x (smaller than w), the rest of their remuneration being in the form of a share of the profits P, so that the wage of an individual worker would be $x + \alpha(P/L)$, where L is the total number of workers currently employed, so that P/L is the profit *per worker*, and α is a fixed coefficient. In this example, L and P are the employment and profits which profit maximising firm A would settle on with the given demand curve, and with the wage set at w. x (lower than w) is now set as the fixed wage element for firm B, and initially α is derived so as to ensure that $x + \alpha(P/L) = w$. Thereafter, α remains constant in the comparison of the behaviour of firms A and B.

To have reached the postulated point of profit maximising, firm A will have been taking on additional workers so long as the extra (marginal) revenue exceeded marginal cost, which in this case is w per additional worker taken on. Thus at the profit-maximising point MR per worker equals w. Now turn to firm B. At this same output, its marginal cost (per worker) is only x, the fixed element of the workers' remuneration, which, by definition, has been chosen less than w. So, in a situation which is one of equilibrium for firm A, in that it has no incentive to take on any more workers, firm B still has an incentive to expand. Whether it *can* expand is a different matter. If there is a fringe of unemployment around the industry, then it will expand beyond the point at which A stopped. But, if there is already full employment in the industry, it will still wish to take on more workers, but will not be able to because they are not available. B could only secure more workers by bidding up the wage element x, in competition with other firms. The argument so far seems almost too good to be true, but it will be quickly seen that there is a joker in the pack. When firm A takes on an additional worker, paid w, it does not affect the remuneration of workers already employed, who continue to receive w. But in the case of B, while the element x remains unaffected, total profit *per worker* will fall: workers already employed will be *pro tanto* worse off.

The kernel of the argument may, perhaps, be most easily grasped by considering an extreme case of monopoly, where, in addition, the elasticity of demand for the monopolised good is one, that is, price is inversely proportional to output sold, so that total proceeds are constant. If remuneration of workers were on a fixed wage basis, the optimal output would be zero![2] For every additional worker taken on adds to costs, without being accompanied by any additional revenue. If, however, all remuneration were on a profit-sharing basis, then the smaller the share per worker the larger the number of workers who can be profitably employed. More generally, in the situation Weitzman envisages, in which firms are typically confronted with falling demand curves, but with a sizeable elasticity (he makes frequent use of a numerical example in which the elasticity is 3, that is, a 1 per cent fall in price would elicit a 3 per cent increase in the volume of output sold, and a 2 per cent increase in total revenue) the smaller is the pure wage element and the larger the profit-sharing element in workers' remuneration, the larger will be the profit-maximising level of output for the firm, and hence the employment it will give.

Suppose that firm A is in a profit-maximising position, and that B is producing the same output, but is unable to expand because there is full employment. If a general recession in demand occurs, A will respond to the fall in profits by reducing output and laying off workers. For B, however, the situation is quite different. In the initial position, the firm had an excess demand for labour, which it had been unable to satisfy. Now, some labour has become available, released from the A-type firms. Thus firm B will first of all maintain output by lowering its price a little, but it might go further and take the opportunity to increase total profits by *expanding* output, and taking on more labour. Profit sharing makes B-type firms at full employment like vacuum cleaners sucking in additional workers if they become available, and thus acting as a stabiliser. The amount of employment a firm can offer is, of course, affected by many factors besides short-term changes in demand for its present products, notably innovation and investment in new processes and products. But Weitzman wishes to concentrate on the problem of Keynesian unemployment. His case does not rest exclusively on the profit-maximising algebra of monopolistic competition: he argues that it is no accident that in Japan, which has tended to have exceptionally low unemployment, profit sharing is widespread.

ASSUMPTIONS

The crucial assumption from which the argument starts emerges if we scrutinise carefully the equation $x + \alpha(P/L) = w$. In a wage system, if firm

A was confronted with a wage w payable to all workers, it would, in the given demand situation, set employment at L and reap profits P. We then looked at firm B, in the identical demand situation, and similar in all other respects, except that it paid its workers a (lower) uniform rate x *plus* a 'profit share' $\alpha(P/L)$, where α was the number which would equate w and $x + \alpha(P/L)$ at the initial level of employment L. At that particular level of employment, the total remuneration of a worker, under either system, was the same. But, at every other level of employment, the remuneration would be different. In situations where employment was less than L, A workers would receive less than workers in B firms: but if employment were greater than L, A workers would receive more than B workers, it being supposed that profit *per worker* is a declining function of employment, in the postulated conditions of supply and demand. From the workers' point of view, the two systems present different risks. In the wage system, there is a rate for the job, and the worker knows what he will earn, over any contract period, irrespective of the profit success or failure of the firm. The income variability risk is all taken by the employer. Under the sharing system, the unemployment risk for some workers will, by the Weitzman argument, be reduced. But, there will now be the risk of loss of income for all workers already employed, when employment expands beyond L. If workers were sharply divided between insiders, who are always employed, even when employment is below L, and the rest, there is a clear difference of interest between the two groups. In real life, there is some overlap between the two groups, so that even insiders may bear some small unemployment risk. But, there is no reason, in principle, why the balance of risk preferences should be such that L workers can be found who would accept either a wage system, with wage w, or a sharing system, with the remuneration $x + \alpha(P/L)$, with this equal to w when employment is at L. Either x or α might have to be bigger to find as many as L workers to agree on a change from a wage to a sharing system.

The sharing which Weitzman proposes is confined to income, and does not extend to any other aspect of the business. The maximand is profits. It is true that, with any given α, maximum profits P_{max} will entail maximum profits $(1 - \alpha) P_{max}$ for the managers and shareholders. But the decision whether to expand or contract employment rests exclusively with the owners: the workers have no say at all. Yet profit sharing might be just one manifestation of the desire of the workforce for a larger share in the conduct of the business generally. But, if workers go for codetermination, to borrow the German expression, might not those already employed (the insiders) vote against expansion since, even though total profits might rise, the profit element in their own remuneration would fall?

Nuti (1987) has queried whether the vacuum-cleaner effect of excess demand at full employment can persist. Would firms be content to regard only the fixed wage component of pay as 'marginal cost', and not include in that concept the cost consequences of bidding up wages in competition with other firms similarly placed? In the same vein, the spotlight should be turned on the assumption that the normal market situation of firms is one of monopolistic competition. What this implies is that a firm can always expect to sell more if it lowers the price of its own product: indeed it is suggested that it can always achieve a significant increase in revenue this way (in technical terms the elasticity of demand is taken to be substantially greater than unity). This may well be a situation in which some firms find themselves. But there are other situations of only a few firms in competition with one another, and where one firm might increase its total revenue by a price cut, provided that the others did not respond with a similar cut, whereas, if they did, its total revenue would fall. It is the fear of this response which might inhibit price cutting so that, in the event of a general fall in demand, the B-type firms would respond in the same way as the A-type firms, namely, keeping price the same and reducing output and shedding labour.

So far, we have concentrated on the output and employment responses of sharing firms. Weitzman also claimed that sharing would reduce inflationary pressures. Our own view is that the wage–price spiral has been an important and persistent element in British inflation. In particular, it seems that when demand falls, it is output and employment which respond, while wages and prices remain sticky: when demand recovers there is the possibility of nominal wage increases, and price rises. Fluctuations in demand may, therefore, have a ratchet effect on the price level. To the extent that, under sharing, there is a larger price response to falls in demand, the ratchet effect is diminished and average price increases over the cycle will be less. But this does depend on firms following price and output policies in the manner Weitzman prescribes.

In bringing out key assumptions, we have concentrated on the claim of profit sharing as a cure for stagflation. This happens to be a novel claim. Historically, the claim for profit sharing rested on other grounds, that it improved workers' motivation, reduced industrial conflict or raised productivity. We mention these traditional claims because the historical and empirical evidence we are about to describe deals with them as well as the specific stagflation question.

HISTORICAL AND EMPIRICAL EVIDENCE

Matthews (1989) has lately written an historical survey of profit-sharing in Britain in the past hundred years. Britain has had more experience of profit sharing than other countries which, as Matthews drily remarks, might be predicted 'since she suffered most from labour troubles'. There is very good documentation of profit sharing inasmuch as the Labour Department made annual reports from 1891 to 1938, which are published in the *Labour Gazette*. There is no similar systematic source since the Second World War, and reliance has to be placed on the occasional studies available: 'we know more about the extent of profit-sharing in 1880 than in 1980'. The definition of profit sharing adopted is that a scheme had to give a large proportion of employees (not just supervisory staff or managers) a bonus in addition to wages, related to profits in a predetermined manner. Matthews suggests three groups of motives for setting up schemes: business, political and philanthropic. Profit sharing is consistent with firms' profit-maximising behaviour and firms might hope to achieve higher productivity, or lower costs, or else to reduce industrial conflict, which would help the other two. A related motive was to strengthen managerial control of the workforce: the socialist Webbs opposed profit sharing precisely because it might weaken collective bargaining. The political motive is that such schemes could provide an education for the workers in the virtues of capitalism, stressing the common interest of employers and workers in maximising revenue, rather than their difference in dividing it between them. Among motives for giving tax relief in the 1987 Budget to workers taking a proportion of their pay as a share of profits of their company was surely support for the enterprise culture. From time to time it is suggested that it is inherently right to give workers a share of the profits they helped to generate: the John Lewis Partnership and the Scott Bader Commonwealth are names which come to mind. Nevertheless, the evidence points to the philanthropic motive being the exception, the dominant motives being business and political.

The number of schemes rose steadily between 1910 and 1930, from 120 schemes covering 50,000 employees to 320 schemes and 230,000 employees. They fell back in the 1930s. Contrary to popular belief it seems likely that the numbers of schemes and of the employees they covered increased in the 1950s and 1960s, although the fastest rate of growth was to come in the 1970s and 1980s. It was estimated that in 1987, there were 700 schemes covering two million employees. Although the statistical correlation between schemes and industrial disputes is not significant, the peaks and troughs of schemes and disputes roughly coincide and, in an interesting historical narrative, Matthews discloses his own belief that industrial militancy makes for the formation of profit-sharing schemes, and that employers lose interest when labour relations are peaceful: certainly, the only time when scheme formation fell was the 1930s. It is true that schemes grew very fast in the 1980s, when industrial disputes fell to very low levels, but a possible influence were the 1978 tax concessions for share schemes.

Although the share element of pay is related to profits, the mean bonus payment has been a fairly constant proportion of wages, between 5 and 6 per cent. Since the general tendency of the share of profits in value added during this century has been downwards, this implies that the mean bonus payment, as a ratio of profits, must have been rising although any such tendency will have been reversed in the second half of the 1980s when the profit share rose very sharply. Matthews concludes that the historical evidence suggests that profit sharing was usually a strategy of labour discipline by profit maximising companies. The bonus payments were, in effect, additional wages. There was little evidence that profit-sharing firms performed better than others in terms of productivity, or profits, though these schemes may have contributed to better industrial relations.

In the historical survey, no trace seemed to emerge of the Weitzman idea that, if workers were to take part of pay as a share of profits, employment prospects would be improved. The approach adopted in the first of the empirical studies which we consider (Wadhwani and Wall, 1990) is more direct. The economists begin by setting up a model, in the form of equations, which when estimated from data of firms' performance, should enable them to test whether or not the Weitzman hypotheses about profit sharing and employment are validated. The models are designed to show also the effects of profit sharing on wages and productivity.

The original data are the published accounts of 219 manufacturing companies over the period 1972–82. In order to be doubly sure that the crucial information concerning a company's payments in the form of a profit-sharing bonus was correct, this data set was compared with another, and eventually estimation was made from a sample of 101 firms, of which 21 had operated a scheme at one time or another during the ten year period. From the coefficients estimated from a number of different equations, the authors reached the following conclusions. Firstly, that under a profit-sharing scheme, firms view the total remuneration, and not just the basic wage, as the marginal cost of labour. This conflicts with a key assumption of the Weitzman argument. Secondly, the evidence is consistent with the view that the bonus payments are largely an extra, in addition to the normal wage. If this is so, profit sharing may increase, rather than decrease, inflationary pressure. Thirdly, the evidence from some, though not all, of the equations, was consistent with the view that profit sharing boosts productivity, but the effect upon employment was as likely to be negative as positive. These results, the authors rightly stress, are derived from a small sample of firms, confined to the manufacturing sector: moreover, some of the crucial coefficients are not statistically significant.

Blanchflower and Oswald (1988) analysed the answers given on income sharing in the 1984 Workplace Industrial Relations Survey of a sample of 2,000 establishments in the United Kingdom. They found that there were three forms of income sharing already in use: share ownership, profit sharing and value-added bonus. The survey included questions on the comparative financial performance of the establishments, and the information was analysed statistically to test whether profit-related pay, in the broadest sense, had the kind of beneficial consequence claimed by Weitzman. Besides noting that in Britain some form of sharing is already more common than is generally realised, they concluded that, at conventional confidence levels, there was no evidence that sharing establishments had superior financial performance, and they found that sharing and non-sharing establishments appear to have had similar employment growth.

In *The Share Economy*, Weitzman buttresses his theoretical argument with the evidence of the success of the Japanese economy since the Second World War, pointing out that 'most regular industrial workers are paid a significant part of their pay in the form of a twice-yearly profit-sharing bonus'. One should not be distracted by enthusiasm for Japan's spectacular growth performance from the issue at stake, which is employment. There are difficulties in comparing unemployment rates between countries, but we accept here the standardisations which have been attempted by the United States and OECD statisticians. Japan has certainly had a much lower unemployment rate than the United States throughout the postwar period, but there have been other countries with rates as low. In the 1960s, for instance, other major economies had similar rates to compare with Japan's 1.3 per cent: Germany, 1 per cent; France, 1.5 per cent; the United Kingdom, 1.9 per cent. In the 1970s and 1980s Norway and Sweden have continued to turn in rates as low as Japan, and Switzerland persistently lower. Even if one confines the comparison to the United States and Japan, there are problems, for labour-market institutions differ in more respects than the profit bonus. There are also the Japanese 'lifetime employment' and 'seniority wages', for instance. It seems that both lifetime employment and profit sharing occur mostly in the larger companies, and they must surely be related. Annual turnover of labour in United States firms is quite high, so that only a certain proportion of the workforce at the end of a year was there at the beginning. The working of bonus schemes is clearly easier when labour turnover is low than when it is high. But, if bonus systems, lifetime employment and so on, are all part of a specifically Japanese labour relations package, can one single out one element of the package as the key to better employment performance?

Our own concern is with British employment prospects, and we do not think that Weitzman's Japanese example outweighs the negative impression which was left by our brief study of the British experience. We do not see in profit sharing, as such, the key to full employment without inflation, and there is no evidence that schemes have been introduced with employment creation in mind. But the evidence on productivity and reducing industrial conflict does not exclude the possibility that there were cases where profit sharing improved performance. Be that as it may, the idea of profit-related pay (PRP) has caught the fancy of the British government, and there are now tax incentives to encourage PRP. If this leads to more schemes being formed, at least the sample of cases to be studied will increase.

11

INCOMES POLICY

INTRODUCTION

Wage subsidies and profit sharing have a common origin in the perception that the existing arrangements for wage and price determination stand in the way of full employment. Incomes policy, an expression which entered the vocabulary of economics after the Second World War, refers to measures intended to influence directly the level, or the rate of change, of money incomes, especially wages and salaries. It is normally taken to exclude monetary and fiscal policy, whose influence on wages and other incomes is indirect. Historically, wages policy and incomes policy were first discussed as means to contain the cost inflation which accompanied the full employment which came to be taken for granted in the years following the war. Analytically, the incomes policy concept fitted comfortably into the Keynesian paradigm, and can be illustrated by reference to the Phillips curve in its original form, which postulated a simple inverse relationship between the level of unemployment and the rate of change of money wages, sometimes called wage inflation. If, in a closed economy, changes in productivity were taken to be exogenous, and if, in addition, prices were determined by costs, the Phillips relation between unemployment and wage inflation could be transformed into one between unemployment and price inflation – or inflation *tout court*. If such a relationship were found to rest on strong empirical foundations, it follows that there would be a trade-off between unemployment and inflation. Demand management, that is, fiscal and monetary policy, could choose between different combinations of higher inflation and lower unemployment, or lower inflation and higher unemployment. Changes in aggregate demand, whether spontaneous, or the consequence of deliberate policy, would be represented by movements to and fro along the Phillips curve. In this mode, incomes policy denotes measures which shift the curve bodily downwards to the left, so that for any given level of unemployment, there would be less inflation. The analytical distinction between the direct, incomes-policy effect on wage levels, and the indirect impact of fiscal and monetary policy, can be retained, even if the original Phillips curve relationship turned out not to be empirically well founded, which proved to be the case.

The forms of incomes policy could vary widely. One could imagine, for instance, a highly centralised system in which all money wages were fixed by a single authority. At the other end of the spectrum, the policy might consist of no more than jawboning, resorted to, at one time or another, by virtually every postwar Chancellor of the Exchequer, urging all concerned to exercise restraint in claims for higher wages or salaries.[1] Incomes policies can be embodied in voluntary agreements between workers and employers, or between workers' and employers' organisations and the government, or they can be imposed by law. They can be permanent features of the economic landscape, or they can be introduced temporarily in response to some economic crisis.

A closed economy was chosen simply for the purpose of exposition. In an open economy, labour ceases to be the only direct cost, and inflation ceases to be a purely domestic affair. In an open economy, in a regime of fixed exchange rates, a rise in the world prices of imported materials or intermediate products will raise domestic production costs in the same way as would a rise in wages, and feed through into the prices of domestic output. In a regime of floating rates, a fall in the exchange rate can have similar effects. Although domestic wage inflation ceases to be the only factor influencing price inflation, this does not so much reduce the importance of incomes policies as extend their scope, for they can now be used to reduce wage inflation as an offset to imported inflation. The occasion of introducing incomes policies in Britain has often been an external balance-of-payments crisis.

While the incomes policy concept fits comfortably in the Keynesian model, it might seem to have no place in the monetarist world. In that model the Phillips curve becomes vertical at the natural rate of unemployment. With unemployment below the natural rate, inflation is accelerating. Monetarists, however, do not exclude the possibility of lowering the natural rate, by microeconomic measures to improve the labour market, weaken the power of trade unions, and so on. But this amounts to shifting the vertical Phillips curve to the left, so that, in a manner of speaking, incomes policy is smuggled back into the picture.

Monetarists, whether old- or new-fashioned, would probably say that in practice incomes policies are not necessary, and in any case create distortions. But some might concede that if, for instance, an incomes policy norm was accepted by major employers and trade unions, it could lower inflationary expectations and thus reduce the unemployment cost of getting inflation down.

OTHER INCOMES

While contemporary economists have no difficulty in treating wages and salaries as costs, they are less comfortable with rent, interest and profits. Rents are rarely mentioned at all. Profits are sometimes treated as a residual: at other times, such as in the treatment of profit margins, they appear as costs. In deep recessions, not only will total profits fall, but firms may be forced to reduce margins as well. In recovery, profits will rise, and firms may take the opportunity to restore, or even increase, their normal margins. Higher margins, in the context of strong demand, might well be regarded as a form of 'profit push', insofar as they induce increased pressure for higher wages. Interest is awkward. A rise in interest rates is seen as deflationary, likely to reduce aggregate demand, and hence inflation; but it is also seen as raising cost inflation, as, for instance, with higher mortgage interest in the retail price index. While many economists would assert that what really matters in incomes policy are wages and salaries, politics is likely to insist that other incomes cannot be left to look after themselves. Dividend limitation has frequently appeared in incomes policies, as also has price control – extending the policy to prices and incomes.

MONEY AND REAL INCOMES

Any spontaneous change in money wages is likely to have *some* effect on real wages, not to mention other variables such as exports or employment. But it was the essence of the theory propounded by Keynes in the *General Theory* that this effect would be small. The context was one of general unemployment in which, according to classical theory, real wages should fall, bringing the economy back to full employment. The point on which Keynes insisted was that what workers, or their union representatives, could offer was not a cut in real wages but only one in money wages. The latter, however, might achieve little more than a corresponding fall in prices, leaving real wages, as well as the level of employment, unchanged;[2] all this, of course, in the context of a closed economy. To the extent that the economy is open to foreign trade, it brings scope for the classical link to operate.

Some confusion has come about in Britain about the objectives of incomes policies, because they have often been introduced at a time when a fall (or restriction in the rate of rise) in real wages was in any case desirable, not to say inevitable. Take the case of an open economy in a regime of fixed, but alterable, exchange rates. The economy is initially at full employment, and in external trade balance. A trade deficit emerges, because of, say, a rise in the world price of materials, which is expected to last. The immediate effect will be a rise in the import bill and a worsening of the trade balance. If the latter is to be restored, then extra resources must somehow be diverted into the balance, whether by reduced imports or increased exports. The mechanisms for bringing this about will differ according to whether an alteration of the exchange rate is, or is not, allowed. But, whatever the mechanism, and even if full employment is maintained, the amount of resources available for domestic absorption must be reduced. Most plausible scenarios for the adjustment would call for a reduction in real wages. If workers, and their unions, passively accept the economic facts of life, well and good. But, as like as not, they may try to recover their real wage, by claiming and securing, higher money wages. But, if the trade balance is to be restored, the recovery of real wages *cannot* be allowed. The higher money wages *must* go to waste in higher prices. It is precisely to prevent such a jump in inflation that an incomes policy might be introduced. But its purpose would not be to cause a reduction in real wages, but to prevent a rise in money wages, aimed at restoring a cut in real wages, which was called for by the need to restore external balance.

OTHER OBJECTIVES

Were it not for the chronic, and eventually accelerating, inflation in the postwar period, incomes policies might never have been heard of. Certainly, there is no trace of them before 1939.[3] They are undoubtedly the product of full employment with some inflation.[4] But while inflation may have been the reason for putting them on the agenda, once there it was open to anyone to suggest further objectives for such policies. They might be used to influence the distribution of income: in particular, if a cut in real income was necessary, the policy could be directed to ensure that the burden fell more heavily on some shoulders than others. Some policies made productivity gains a precondition for wage increases. In varying ways, policies for personal and corporate incomes have been linked with other policies of government towards productivity, investment and employment. In countries with highly centralised systems of wage determination, such linkages formed a regular feature of the policymaking process. Faxen[5] cites the Scandinavian example where the 'main course' for the economy is agreed by the economists of the workers' and employers' organisations and of the government, and a 'corridor' is also drawn within which there is scope for collective bargaining, all parties agreeing in advance that there is no point in either side pushing beyond these limits. An attempt was made by the British Chancellor of the Exchequer to achieve a similar result in a less formal way. His primary objective in 1977 and again in 1978 was to get a lower norm for wage settlements. Well in advance of the Budget, he offered two alternative tax scenarios. If the unions would agree to his norm, scenario A would come into operation: if not, there would be a more severe tax scenario B. Rather surprisingly, the TUC did not respond favourably to this injection of an element of bargaining.

EXPERIENCE OF INCOMES POLICIES: TESTING

Some writers have maintained that to the extent that incomes policies have achieved their primary objectives, they have only done so at the cost of disadvantageous side effects. One such, frequently alleged, is the squeezing of differentials. Faxen claims that there is not much evidence of this. There was some narrowing in France after 1968: in Germany there appears to have been stability. In the United Kingdom, where some compression might have been expected, he found little evidence,[6] whereas in Italy, despite the absence of incomes policies, differentials *were* compressed. Trends among the smaller countries, with highly centralised systems, were equally diverse. In Britain, incomes policies were not a permanent feature of the economic landscape, but were introduced intermittently by various governments, usually in response to some crisis, for example, in overseas payments.

The earliest example was the wage restraint inaugurated in 1948: it was largely voluntary, but for two years it had the full backing of the TUC. The Conservative government elected in 1951 started off with non-intervention in wage determination, but in 1957 it set up a Council on Prices, Productivity and Incomes, whose task was to ascertain the facts and present them to the public. From then on there was a succession of incomes-policy measures and institutions: in 1962 the National Incomes Commission; in 1965 the National Board for Prices and Incomes; in 1972 the Price Commission and Pay Board; in 1974 the Social Contract, followed by a new incomes policy in 1975. In the 1960s and 1970s there were alternations between Conservative and Labour governments. Each incoming administration began by scrapping most, or all, of the incomes-policy machinery of its predecessor, only to set up, after a year or two, a new apparatus of its own, almost always in response to a crisis, of inflation or the balance of payments.

Many attempts have been made to test whether any of these incomes policies worked. They include a number of econometric tests, which typically introduce into a wage equation dummy variables to denote periods of 'policy on' and 'policy off', and some have included 'catch-up' dummies, in an attempt to capture the effect of an apparent rush to secure larger settlements once the incomes policy has ended.[7] Sometimes 'catch-up' is claimed to restore the original rate of inflation. Other studies find no significant influence of incomes policies on the rate of inflation. There are some difficulties about these procedures. In the first place, they appear somewhat mechanical. Policy is either 'on' or 'off', usually with uniform intensity, though some studies try to introduce an element of gradual tightening. One suspects, however, that there may be cases where informal understandings between the social partners may exercise a greater influence than some statutory policies imposed on unwilling social partners. Secondly, these methods cannot establish whether the policies have altered the climate of inflationary expectations. Finally, there is always the possibility that important variables, for example, world prices, are not included. Such objections can, of course, be raised against almost any econometric procedure: nevertheless the generality of application does not exclude the particular case.

A FUTURE INCOMES POLICY

The Thatcher administration started off with Monetarism Mark 1. It was going to have no truck with incomes policy, inflation being a purely monetary phenomenon. Nigel Lawson, then a junior Treasury minister, argued that trade unions could not generate inflation. If they insisted on higher wages, they could, at worst, cause unemployment. Nevertheless, the government introduced a series of bills whose effects were intended to reduce the bargaining power of trade unions. The scale of settlements in the mid-1980s was, indeed, very much reduced, although some experts have argued that this owed as much to three million unemployed as to the new legislation. Though never acknowledged explicitly, it is also plain that the government has a kind of incomes policy for the public sector. As a major employer, it could hardly not have. In the case of schoolteachers, for instance, their normal bargaining procedure was abrogated in 1987 and their pay settlement imposed: and, it was apparent in 1989 that the government was anxious to impose an upper limit of 7 per cent increases in the public sector.

For a while, in 1983, price inflation dropped below 5 per cent per annum, helped, it should be added, by falling world commodity prices, but despite the continued rise in unemployment, wage inflation got stuck between 7 and 8 per cent. After 1986, demand rose rapidly and unemployment fell, to well below two million at the end of 1989. Wage inflation started to rise again, beyond 9 per cent, and prices began to rise faster also. The government relies mainly on interest rates to restrain demand, though there is increasingly open recognition that fiscal policy also matters in this context. The question at issue is whether demand can be restrained to the required extent without engendering a sharp recession.

We should ask what is wrong with 5 per cent inflation. A quarter of a century ago, it was possible to argue cogently, as Reddaway (1966) did, that the kind of inflation experienced since the war may have done more good than harm by acting as a safety valve for the relief of pressures from different sectors of society for ultimately irreconcilable claims on real income. But twice since then we have experienced explosions in which price inflation has been carried beyond, or just short of 20 per cent. Even the comparatively small increase in the rate of inflation in 1988 and 1989 has revived fears of acceleration, and called for restraint of demand. The danger of violent lurches, one way or the other, might be lessened if monetary policy was reinforced by fiscal policy. Even so, unemployment remains the residuary legatee of anti-inflation policy. With a run of unbroken good luck employment might be allowed to continue to rise. But, if there is a shock, such as occurred in the 1970s, the expansion has to be stopped.

Incomes policies are certainly out of favour with the present government, but then the subject was unmentionable in official circles in the first two years of the Heath administration in 1970 and 1971. Possibly the pendulum may never swing again. But one of the clearest lessons to be learned from British experience since the National Incomes Commission was launched in 1962, is that nearly all the policies were introduced in a hurry, usually in response to a crisis, so that, even if they achieved some initial success, they soon began to show strains of one sort or another. If it is prudent to consider the shape of a future policy, and we think it is, the first requirement is that the arrangements should be planned to stand the test of time.

When one reviews the experience of other countries, it is apparent that the corporatist version of incomes policy has had the most lasting success – the cases of Germany, Austria and Sweden spring to mind. The first requirement is that the social partners, the government, and the bodies representing trade unions and employers should be in agreement on macroeconomic objectives for the economy, such as high employment and productivity growth, but also including the need to keep wage inflation within bounds. Not all three parties need be equally involved. In Sweden since the 1950s collective bargaining was conducted by the Swedish Employers' Federation and the Swedish Confederation of Trade Unions. The aim was to reach settlements which were in accordance with the government's macroeconomic policy, which would not call for government intervention. In fact, such intervention became more frequent in the 1970s.

Support for some kind of corporatist policy in Britain appeared to be growing in the late 1970s. In 1977 and 1979, the CBI proposed a national economic forum, with links to Parliament. The idea of a forum was mooted in a Conservative Party document in October, 1977, and a similar idea appeared in a joint statement by the TUC and the government in February, 1979. There was no lack of candidates to be put on the agenda of any corporatist forum. Perhaps the first item was the norm; whether such a figure should be set below the desired increase in *average* earnings, thus leaving room for settlements above the norm in special cases, such as low pay, labour shortage, or for increases in productivity. Should the policy be voluntary, or receive statutory backing? Then the forum might discuss reforms in the system of pay bargaining: one suggestion was that major bargains should be synchronised within a short span of a few weeks or months, so that bargainers would be made more immediately aware that one person's pay rise is another person's price rise.

But, while these issues were being written about and talked about, events were taking place in the real world which diminished the feasibility of any corporatist approach in Britain for many years to come. Although both Conservative and Labour governments have introduced incomes policies, it was long thought that Labour would find it easier to reach agreement with trade unions whenever the macroeconomic situation called for wage restraint. The incomes policy brought in in 1975 was, in fact, agreed by the TUC and the government, without any official involvement of employers. But though that policy succeeded in its earlier years in bringing down wage inflation, it crumbled in the Winter of Discontent in 1978–9. If it is true that trade unions, and especially the miners, brought down the Conservative government in 1974, it is equally plain that the trade unions contributed to the defeat of Labour in the 1979 General Election. The Thatcher administration conspicuously ignored the trade unions in matters of economic policy, and began the sequence of Acts of Parliament designed to limit their powers in industrial disputes. The whole thrust of government policy has been against nationwide bargaining, as was expounded in the document *Employment for the 1990s*, presented to parliament by the Secretary of State for Employment in December, 1988: 'National agreements which affect the pay of half the workforce all too often give scant regard to differences in individual circumstances or preferences ... Job growth in the 1990s will depend on replacing these outmoded concepts with pay arrangements which reflect a greater responsiveness to local labour market conditions, changes in product markets and technology, differences in performance, merit and skill, the continuing profitability of the enterprise, and international competitiveness'.

The government has not intervened in the private sector, but in the public sector it has attempted, with varying success, to move towards local flexibility, in the steel industry and the Post Office, for example. The White Paper, just quoted, said that the proportion of workers covered by multi-employer national agreements declined from 60 per cent in 1978 to 54 per cent in 1985. This is not a dramatic fall, but further efforts have been made since 1985, culminating in the abolition of the National Dock Labour Scheme in 1989. The present government has no intention of introducing an incomes policy and, on the evidence of its recently published policy review, nor would any future Labour government. By the time any future government did decide to re-embark on the incomes policy course, and we accept that this is only a possibility, the dissolution of multi-employer national agreements, and public sector national agreements, might have gone too far to make any corporatist policy feasible. Any future policy would have to be directed to individual settlements, whether in the private or the public sector.

The first need is for a *referee* to declare whether or not a proposed settlement is in accordance with national policy. But how is that defined? There would still, it seems to me, have to be a norm, with, possibly, a list of exceptions: the longer the list the further below the desired *average* rise in earnings would the norm have to be set. There is room for debate whether the norm should be set by the government, or by the referee. The objective of the policy is to restrain inflation. The referee should not therefore be directly concerned with relativities, but he should be aware of possible knock-on effects of particular settlements. If a settlement is negotiated below the norm, there is no call for the referee to intervene. If the dispute is about a figure above the norm, then the dispute has to be passed to the referee for arbitration. The special Review Boards which currently exist should be extinguished, their functions being taken over by the referee.

The next question refers to the sanctions to be imposed to ensure the observation of the arbitrated settlement. One suggestion, widely canvassed, is that any excess above the approved settlement should be subject to a tax, which could fall on the employer, the workers, or both. Tax-based incomes policies (TIPs) are attractive, insofar as they leave an element of choice, albeit at a cost, to the bargaining parties, but there are serious practical difficulties in estimating the tax due, and there might also be difficulties of collection. If taxes are not used, there have to be other penalties on employers, employees, or both, who reject the terms of the arbitrated award.

These proposals resemble the procedures of the National Board for Prices and Incomes, which operated from 1965 to 1970, except that they exclude any attempt at price control. In the real world of actual competition, there will always remain pockets of monopoly, but these are likely to be already subject to regulation by bodies such as Oftel, or Ofgas.

Though not conceived as representing the social partners, the referee clearly has to earn and maintain the confidence of employers, workers and the government. There needs to be a board of men and women respected for their experience and independence. It should probably include some economists, but should in any case have at its disposal a strong secretariat of economists, statisticians, and others with expertise in industrial relations. The first task of the board is to establish the norm, if it has not already been given it by the government. In either case, it needs to explain to the public the considerations taken into account in reaching it. Next it has to explain what kinds of exception it is prepared to consider, whether for low pay, productivity or whatever. The norm and the exceptions from it are at the heart of any incomes policy, and they are not at all easy to decide. Take, for instance, the question of productivity. Subject to some qualifications about import prices, the idea that nominal wages for the whole economy should not run ahead of productivity if prices are to be stable seems reasonable enough. But it does not follow that the same wage–productivity formula should apply to each individual settlement – a trap into which successive generations of politicians fall whenever they start worrying about wage inflation. Productivity (output per person employed) is apparently easy to measure in some industries, for example, tonnes of steel or coal, and hard, if not impossible, to measure in others, for example, banking or teaching. Even in the apparently easy cases, there is the question of quality. And when we are satisfied that productivity is correctly measured, it does not follow that every increase justifies a corresponding wage increase. Many productivity increases originate in new equipment, whose operation requires less skill and less effort than the equipment it replaces. Why raise wages? Should not prices come down? If every productivity rise is absorbed by the workers directly involved wages would rise and rise in those sectors where measured productivity rises can be easily achieved, and stay put in those sectors where they cannot. There is no reason to think that the pattern of wages which would emerge would correspond to the relative demands and supplies for labour in different sectors of the economy. Alternatively, if wages keep pace with productivity in sectors where it grows fast, and then have to be raised in other sectors in order to secure the supply of labour required, prices in these sectors will rise, and we shall find ourselves with 'productivity-generated' inflation.

The rules of an incomes policy have first to be worked out, according to whether it is confined to containing inflation, or has wider objectives affecting the distribution of income. Once settled, the final interpretation of the rules remains to be decided by the board, and explained, in each individual case. The point of having only one referee is that over time the board will build up a series of judgements and precedents, similar to the case law created by judges.

We have written so far about wages and salaries as though they were the only incomes which mattered. In any one year, this may be pragmatically justified: if the major settlements in public and private sectors are within the norm, it may be supposed that other settlements will follow suit. In the longer run, however, its writ has to run over all

employment incomes, including company chairmen and managing direc-
tors. If the norm is 4 per cent, and top management sets things off by
awarding themselves 20 per cent, they must expect more trouble than if
they themselves had begun at 4 per cent. An economist might take a
similar pragmatic view about profits and self-employment incomes: if you
have a good hold on the major wage settlements, competition will keep
other incomes in line. But politics may require some *quid pro quo* to secure
the willing acceptance of trade unions. In past incomes policies, there
have been dividend limitations and, when its obvious weaknesses became
clear to all, price control. Whether, in any future incomes policy, a *quid pro
quo* would be needed depends upon the circumstances in which the new
policy is brought in.

CONCLUSION

When the Thatcher government came into office, it turned its back on all
forms of incomes policy. It was able to dwell upon the distortions and
failures of the policies of all previous administrations, whether Labour or
Conservative, confident in the knowledge that its own monetarist policy
would scotch inflation for good and all. Now, ten years on, with inflation
once more rising, and with individual settlements in double figures
beginning to appear, it looks a little different. Incomes policies may have
failed, but the alternative, which involved five years of unemployment
near the three million mark, if it has not yet failed, has not succeeded
either. The Heath government, it will be remembered, began in 1970 by
rejecting incomes policy, only to come back to it little more than two years
later. Perhaps just one more recession will deliver the *coup de grâce* to
inflationary expectations. But, perhaps not. It is not impossible that
incomes policy will come back on to the agenda.[8] We would not ourselves
regard the employment of government economists on the thorough
examination of all feasible alternatives as a misuse of public funds. For
there is one very clear lesson of past experience. If you are thinking of
bringing in incomes policy, it will not last very long unless you have
worked it out thoroughly in advance.

PART 3

MACROECONOMIC POLICY

12

THE THEORETICAL BACKGROUND

INTRODUCTION

In this part of the book we consider whether the prospects for employ-ment can be improved by macroeconomic policy. We mean by that expression: fiscal policy; monetary policy; and incomes policy. The term is a clumsy one, and since we have already considered incomes policy in Part 2, as an aspect of the Wage Question, it was tempting to use the expression demand management. However, this term normally excludes incomes policy, which we wish to consider as an adjunct to the other two.

Whether there is scope for macroeconomic policy to influence the level of employment depends on one's view about how a predominantly private enterprise economy would behave if left to itself. There are many views about this, but among them one can pick out two dominant strands – classical and Keynesian. According to the former, if the economy has been subjected to a shock, which has caused unemployment, there are forces within the economy which will bring it back automatically towards full employment. According to the latter view, these forces may not always work in the prescribed manner, leaving the economy stuck with persistent unemployment.

The classical position has the longer pedigree. In Britain until the 1930s it was the dominant view, an application of mainstream economic theory. Then, during the Second World War, and for a quarter of a century after, it was no longer to be seen. But it began to re-emerge in the 1970s, at first under the banner of monetarism, adding later on the more exotic flag of the New Classical Economics. Whereas, until the 1930s, important contributions to classical economics were being made in Britain, the centre of gravity of the classical revival had moved to the other side of the Atlantic. The Keynesian thesis that capitalist economies can get stuck with persistent unemployment was articulated in the *General Theory of Employment, Interest and Money* in 1936 and, by the time the Second World War ended, Keynesian ideas were well on the way to becoming the mainstream of economics, and they were to remain so until the revival of classical ideas in the 1970s.

A classical economist, whether of the older or more recent variety, believing that the economy is self-adjusting, will not be on the lookout for policies to boost employment even when unemployment is high. Rather he will be anxious to avoid policies which might hamper the working of market forces in the process of readjustment. On the other hand, a Keynesian economist, believing that the economy can become bogged down with unemployment, and believing also that the readjustment mechanisms will not always work or will only work slowly, will search for policies to increase demand and employment.

This distinguishing of two broad strands of economic thinking, the classical and the Keynesian, is very simplified, and some might say too much so.[1] What about the Marxists, for instance? After all, they have been saying for more than a century that capitalism generates periodic crises and needs a 'reserve army of labour'. In challenging the self-righting properties of a market economy, they were making the same point that was made by the Keynesians in the 1930s. The difference lies in the fact that the Keynesian analysis quickly convinced a whole generation of economists and statesmen that it led to a feasible reform programme, which would tackle unemployment directly, while the implication of the Marxist analysis seemed to be that nothing short of a revolution, scrapping the capitalist system and creating an entirely new one, would do. It may be that a Keynesian programme is not so feasible after all: that indeed, is the subject of our enquiry. But in the Western world, the Keynesian categories have entered the language of economics in universities, in governments and international organisations, in a way which makes this strand of thinking more significant than the Marxist strand.

Though we have confined ourselves to only two strands of thought, they are sufficient to generate *prima facie* contradictions. Thus, most Keynesians would argue that an increase in public expenditure, not matched by tax increases, would generate additional imports, and lead to a loss of reserves if the exchange rate were fixed, or to a fall in the exchange rate. But economists in the classical tradition would argue that a budget deficit causes the exchange rate to rise. The explanation lies, I suspect, in differences in important, but unstated assumptions. Classicals normally assume a fixed money supply, and possibly also full employment. Keynesians normally assume either an elastic money supply of private banks, or monetary accommodation by the central bank, and they do not always assume full employment. In the former case the rate of interest does not rise, in the latter it does, attracting funds from abroad, thus putting up the exchange rate. Members of each group have a tendency to suppose that everyone shares their own implicit assumptions, which need not be the case. Another example is a change in public expenditure matched by a change in tax revenue. A standard piece of Keynesian economics is the balanced budget multiplier theorem, in which a (revenue) matched increase in public expenditure increases employment. But in the Treasury macroeconometric model, which incorporates some classical assumptions, a decrease in public expenditure increases employment.

If contradictions can be traced to alternative assumptions or differences about facts, one might have supposed that an alliance of logical rigour with econometrics would have ironed out most of the important differences by now. But this has not happened. Anyone who has worked for any length of time in economic modelling and forecasting is aware of the rise and fall of particular equations purporting to explain the behaviour of earnings, personal savings, or the exchange rate. Sometimes, once-successful equations cease to perform well for some years and then come back into favour as they appear to be doing well once more. For econometrics to have a sharp cutting edge in distinguishing between alternative hypotheses, it would seem that we need very long time series observed under stationary conditions, but to suppose that economic history provides us with series of this kind is not believable (see Solow, 1985). This does not mean that econometrics can tell us nothing. It can often pretty convincingly exclude whole ranges of hypotheses as being untrue or in need of modification. But its results are best treated as circumstantial evidence of varying weight. The best that any economist can do is to argue with rigour, and in the handling of evidence to be as honest as he can.

When we encounter contradictions, as like as not will lie behind them differences of assumption and inconclusiveness of evidence. But it would be tedious to disinter them on every occasion. It is, however, possible to indicate some of the principal differences separating the Keynesian and classical strands which occur over and over again, and this, in a moment, we shall attempt to do.

There is a quite different source of possible misunderstanding in the fact that the economy which is subject to policy is not necessarily coextensive with the political authority exercising power. Though there exist fora such as the IMF, OECD, GATT or the European Commission in which policies affecting all member countries can be discussed and agreed, by far the greatest weight of policy decisions is still to be found in national governments. Their decisions tend to be taken mainly in the light of their anticipated impact on their own nationals. But they also have effects on foreigners, which may be given little weight when policies are being judged. For instance, if unemployment is high a national government might attempt to raise employment by cutting taxes or, alternatively, by engineering a fall in the exchange rate. In the former case, imports are likely to rise, giving employment to foreigners who supply them: in the latter case, exports may rise, but imports may fall, reducing the employment of foreigners. In both cases, British employment rises but the impact on the employment of foreigners is quite different and in the latter case may provoke retaliation. There are thus two sorts of difficulty. In the first place, in much discussion of macroeconomic policy the problem does not get mentioned at all: the theorist, by implication, has assumed a closed economy. Secondly, questions of substance arise because some policies, for example, fiscal expansion, which might prove very effective if concerted by a number of trading partners, might fail if undertaken by one country on its own.

With these preliminaries over, we follow a conventional route, considering both theory and practice first in a closed economy, and then extending the discussion to the international dimension.

CLASSICAL AND KEYNESIAN MODELS

The name, indeed the very idea of macroeconomics is a product of the Keynesian revolution. A contemporary student of economics is confronted with sections of the library labelled microeconomics and macroeconomics. No such distinction was made before the Second World War. The Keynesian model deals throughout with aggregates, such as consumption, savings, investment, employment and unemployment. It is not concerned with investment in the chalk industry as compared with the cheese industry, nor is it concerned with the relative prices of those commodities. By contrast, the classical model, at any rate in the British tradition, never had much to say about aggregate income or employment as such. It was concerned, in the first instance, with the relative prices of chalk and cheese, and the relative prices of the factors of production, especially labour and capital, which were used in their production. These prices were the outcome of the interaction between supply and demand, the former being determined by conditions of production and the latter by the subjective valuation of users and consumers. The results for particular markets were then extended to the whole economy. If the total supply of labour exceeded the total demand for it, so that there was some unemployment, then, just as in any particular market, the price of labour would fall, increasing the demand for it and reducing the supply, until they were brought into balance without any unemployment. The price of labour, that is, the wage, was conceived in real terms. To get more workers to come on to the market, or to induce workers already in jobs to work longer hours, the inducement has to be not just extra money, but more of the things that money can buy. The supply price of labour would be influenced by the presence or absence of an alternative source of income, in particular social security benefits. Such payments are not normally available unconditionally, being dependent on the willingness to take work if it is available. But if the conditionality is not too strictly applied, the inducement to work is no longer the total wage, but the difference between the wage and social security. The higher the latter, the higher must be the wage to induce a given supply of labour. In the classical model, so long as obstacles are not put in the way, wage flexibility will always assure full employment of those willing to work.

The Keynesian model starts off in a totally different way. In a closed economy, all incomes, specifically wages and profits, are generated in producing output either for current consumption or for investment in plant, equipment and inventories needed to produce new output. So income, Y, equals consumption, C, *plus* investment, I. But income is either spent on consumption or it is saved. At low levels of income, most will go on consumption and little will be saved. As incomes rise, saving will rise, and so too will consumption, but not by as much as income. The simplest possible consumption function would be $C = \alpha + \beta Y$, where $\beta < 1$, and is called the marginal propensity to consume. Our model now consists of two equations:

$$Y = C + I \tag{1}$$

and

$$C = \alpha + \beta Y \tag{2}$$

From these two equations it follows that:

$$Y = (\alpha + I)/(1 - \beta) \tag{3}$$

This means that the level of income is determined by the level of investment and the two coefficients which define the consumption function. National accounting tells us that total output = total income = total expenditure.[2] So total output also depends on investment and the two coefficients. We now bring employment into the picture, and make it depend on the level of output. If the level of investment was just right, it would call forth a total output just sufficient to employ all the labour available. Call this amount I_F. Then, if investment were greater than I_F, the system would be trying to employ more labour than it has got. We should have to amplify the model to deal with such a case. But if investment were less than I_F, no such amplification would be needed. The model would tell us that there will be output, but not enough to employ everyone: some would be left unemployed. Not only that. If investment did not change but, somehow or other, employment got above the indicated amount, it would have to fall back, and similarly, if employment fell below the indicated amount, it would have to rise. In this simplest of models, the value of Y indicated by the model in equation (3) is stable.

One way of conveying the essence of the Keynesian theory is to say that the behavioural parameters, α and β, describing the consumption function, may be such that the model will deliver too little output to secure full employment and, if so, there is no reason, *within the model*, for unemployment to go away. This is a result from an extremely simplified model, but the Keynesian argument can be very easily extended to models with many more variables, and correspondingly more behavioural parameters. The latter may be such as to allow the model to deliver full employment. But they may not, so that the model delivers persistent unemployment.

Up to this point the classical and Keynesian strands seem to have been moving on quite different planes. But Keynes was able to provide a link by re-examining the classical adjustment process in the case of unemployment. In the classical model, for employment to rise, real wages would have to fall, because of declining marginal productivity, and Keynes accepted that *if* employment were to rise, there would have to be an accompanying fall in real wages. However, he pointed out that workers are not paid real wages, but sums of money, per day or per week. What they, or their trade union representatives, might offer, therefore, would be to work for less money. But if they did, two things would happen. Total monetary expenditure of workers would fall; and labour costs, expressed in money, would fall at the same time. It is quite likely that competition among employers would bring prices down in line with any cut in wages, with the result that *real* wages would remain unchanged. In the conditions assumed by both classical economists and Keynes himself, this would mean that output and employment would also remain unchanged. The classical model's treatment of the supply and demand for labour as wholly independent functions of the real wage is, therefore, illegitimate: the supply and demand schedules are interdependent.

But this was not a knock-out blow to the classical idea of automatic adjustment. Even if a fall in money wages were matched by a fall in prices, and real output was initially unchanged, there would be a fall in nominal income and this would bring about a fall in the rate of interest, thereby stimulating investment, consumption, or both. Keynes countered with the observation that the consumption effect might be weak or non-existent while there was a lower limit below which interest rates could not fall, and this could happen before enough extra investment had been stimulated.

The classicals had another shot in their locker. If lower interest rates did not do the trick, presumably wages and prices would still be falling, so that the real value of money itself would be rising. Anyone holding any money would feel himself to be wealthier and wealthier. This wealth effect would cause any such person to save less out of any given income, and increasing consumption expenditure would put the economy back on the road to full employment. A possible Keynesian counter to this argument, which played a prominent role in the earlier days, is that money wages are 'sticky', downwards at any rate.[3]

The efficacy of the classical escape routes to full employment is something on which empirical light can be shed. It is not excluded that they are routes which might work well at some times and badly at others. It is not the intention to dig any deeper into theoretical foundations, but one addendum needs to be made. We noted that in the *General Theory* itself, Keynes accepted the classical view that for employment to rise real wages would have to fall, in line with declining marginal productivity. In the light of evidence produced a few years later, he withdrew from this position. If there were both considerable unemployment and also excess plant capacity, there could be cases in which rising output is accompanied by constant, or falling, rather than rising, costs. If so, a fall in real wages might not be necessary to secure higher employment. Once more, these are empirical questions.

It is possible to tell the wage-adjustment part of the classical story without any very obvious intervention of money. In the schedules of the demand and supply of labour the independent variable is the real wage. On the supply side, the workers measure up the advantages of the real wage (or its excess above social security) against the loss of leisure, or alternative pursuits. The demand for labour is provided by firms which aim to produce output at minimum cost, by combining appropriate amounts of labour and capital. If, in the short run, the latter is taken as given, then workers will be employed so long as the wage is no greater than the marginal product of labour, which is supposed to fall as employment rises so long as capital is fixed. In the longer run, when capital may also be varied, there is a similar equating of the rate of interest with the marginal productivity of capital. It is, perhaps, easier to tell this story with the aid of money, but it is not necessary.

One way – paradoxically in view of the so-called 'monetarist' counter-revolution – in which Keynes parts company with the classical approach is in his persistent emphasis on the distinction between the monetary and the real. The classical wage adjustment fails precisely because wages are contracted and paid in money. The real value of those wages emerges only when we know what prices have been during the period of a wage contract and that, as we have seen, depends on the money wage contract itself.

In the classical model, the amount of capital formation is determined by the intersection of the demand and supply of savings, both being taken to be simple functions of the (real) rate of interest. Once more Keynes made the objection that the two schedules are not independent of one another. If people wished to save more, they would spend less of any given income on consumption. This cut in consumption would reduce other peoples' incomes. The equality of savings and investment would be brought about by a fall in income and output. Indeed, with income falling, investment might be adversely, rather than favourably, affected. Classical economists could reply that, even so, the rate of interest would also fall. Once again we have an empirical question: is the negative effect on investment of reduced income wholly, or partially offset by the positive effect of the interest rate fall?

MONEY, OUTPUT AND PRICES

The relation of the different views of the economy within the two broad strands we have distinguished, can be illustrated by making use of the famous Fisher equation for the Quantity of Money, namely: $MV = PT$. In this equation, M stands for the quantity of money, and V is its velocity of circulation – the average number of times the money stock is turned over in a given period, a year say. In every transaction, money is exchanged for a good or service, so that MV is a measure of the money value of all transactions taking place within the year. T is the average number of such transactions[4] and P the average price of that which is transacted. PT also, then, is the money value of all transactions taking place within the year. Hence $MV \equiv PT$. By adding the third line to the equality symbol, we indicate that more than equality is involved, but identity – an identity ensured by the way V was defined. So far, nothing operational has been said about the economy. We try now to introduce causality.

Both classical economists and Keynes himself postulated that M, the quantity of money, was fixed by the monetary authorities (for example, a central bank) and for the moment we accept this. V, it might be argued, is essentially determined by institutional matters, such as the frequency of income receipts, whether weekly or monthly, the time lags between receipt and payment of bills, and such like. On the face of it, there is no reason why V should be altered if all prices and incomes were increased, or decreased, by the same factor. That would be the position of some economists in the classical strand. But some, following Keynes, would accept that, because of the need to cover unforeseen contingencies, and because of speculation about future changes in prices, people might wish to hold an average stock of money larger than the bare minimum to cover regular payments, and that this amount would vary with the rate of interest. High interest rates would induce people to keep their cash holdings low; with low interest rates, they sacrifice less by holding money.[5] V then, in this view, is a function of the rate of interest.

On the other side of the equation, there may also be differences. For the classical economists, T, the volume of transactions, which we will suppose here is tied to the level of activity, is determined by real things such as the size of the labour force and the state of technology. An increase in monetary expenditure will not increase the volume of transactions, but only the average price of each transaction. The Keynesian, however, sees the possibility of the economy running well below its full potential with unutilised plant capacity and unemployed labour, so that a change in money expenditure may cause firms to increase output – and employment – rather than to raise prices. Once full employment is achieved, however, the Keynesians rejoin the classical strand. In the *General Theory*, there is a vivid passage describing the modification of the Quantity Theory of Money: 'So long as there is unemployment, *employment* will change in the same proportion as the quantity of money; and when there is full employment, *prices* will change in the same proportion as the quantity of money'. We can summarise the argument so far in a little table, setting out what happens when there is an increase in M:

Classical	*Keynesian*
Since V is fixed, rise in MV	Rise in M may cause V to fall. *Either* no change in MV *or* a rise in MV
Since T is fixed, rise in P	If rise in MV, then rise in T or P or both, depending on supply curve. If already at full employment, then rise in P

Whether or not V responds to changes in the rate of interest, and whether or not supply curves are elastic,[6] and over how big a range, are clearly empirical questions. But one notices that models made in the classical mode tend to assume, sometimes explicitly but quite often not, a framework of full employment, whereas Keynesians tend to focus on the possibility of underemployment. Most classicals and many Keynesians regard M as being autonomously fixed by the authorities. Nevertheless the $MV \equiv PT$ identity allows for quite another direction of causality. Suppose M were determined by the demand for it alone, any demand being supplied by private banks or an 'accommodating' central bank at a given rate of interest. In that case a spontaneous change in T or P could cause a rise in M. Spontaneous changes in T are more likely to be falls, brought about, for example, by a natural disaster or a general strike. Spontaneous rises might come from an improvement in confidence inside the economy, or from outside as a result of a rise in world trade; we will take up the latter case when we leave the closed economy for an open one.

It is the spontaneous change in P which is the more immediately interesting. This could happen to the extent that product prices are taken from costs, so that an autonomous rise in wages is passed through into P, If M had been fixed, a rise emanating from the right hand side of the equation, PT, requires that V must rise in sympathy. Otherwise T would have to fall. But, if M is accommodating, there is no problem.

It follows that there are two types of price rise, which, if sustained, we would call inflation. In the one case, the motor is a change in M – this is the demand inflation which monetarists and some Keynesians put in the forefront. But if the autonomous impulse comes from P, on the other side, we have cost-push and, if there is monetary accommodation by private or central banks, cost-inflation. The once popular argument that 'trade unions cannot cause inflation' rests on the (often unstated) premises that M is fixed and V will not give, so that any rise in P has to be taken out in a fall in T, and hence in employment. This brief excursion into the Quantity Equation of Money shows how quite different ways of thinking about the economy can be contained within the same formal mathematical expression. The point is so obvious that it is frequently forgotten altogether.

The extension of the argument to the open economy case does not bring in much that is new. It opens up, as we saw a moment ago, the possibility of spontaneous changes in T originating outside the economy. There is also, now, another source of a spontaneous rise in P, brought about by a rise in the prices of imported materials and goods. Otherwise, opening up the economy is likely to bring the classical and Keynesian strands nearer to one another. A Keynesian might argue that in a closed economy money wage changes would have little effect on output, but in the open case wage changes could alter the competitiveness of British producers *vis-à-vis* foreigners, for instance, making exports more expensive and imports relatively cheaper. The effect on employment would be just the same for a Keynesian as for a classical economist.

POLICY IMPLICATIONS

Because the classical view postulates that the economy will always find its way back to full employment, neither fiscal nor monetary policy is needed to help it on its way. Monetary policy, therefore, can be exclusively addressed to controlling the price level. On the face of it there seems to be no role for fiscal policy, and some monetarists, such as Friedman, appear to have taken that position. Others, notably the British Treasury, in the original version of the Medium Term Financial Strategy (1980), have seen fiscal policy as a necessary adjunct of monetary policy. Budget deficits, moreover, will crowd out productive investment, so that there is no room for – and, in the limit, no possibility of – demand management. Any influence of fiscal policy on real output is seen by classical and monetarist economists to come from the supply side. 'High taxes destroy incentives' is a common cry. High, and easily obtainable, social security benefits push up wages and/or reduce employment.

The Keynesian policy prescription is, precisely, demand management. Left to itself, the economy may deliver either persistent demand deficiency, with accompanying unemployment, or persistent excess demand as in a war or in the years following.[7] Both monetary and fiscal policy can be used to supplement, or curtail, aggregate demand. However, Keynesian policy has to deal with three problems. Firstly, if the economy is generating persistent demand deficiency, which was the context in which the *General Theory* was developed, and the gap is made good with the aid of a budget deficit, will there not, in consequence, be a perpetually rising national debt? Excess demand could, of course, generate surpluses, but can we rely on periods of surplus balancing periods of deficit?

Secondly, if the economy requires demand deficiency to be made good by low interest rates and budget deficits, what will happen to the general price level? What if money wage settlements are made in excess of any rise in labour productivity. Costs and prices will rise. Real wages also may rise, in line with productivity, but the increase will be less than the money wage increase originally obtained. Since monetary policy is assumed to be accommodating, what is to stop the trade unions trying again next time round, starting off an indefinite spiral of wages and prices? We have already examined this most important question in Part 2, where we also looked at the possibility of incomes policy, which would aim by statute, or by intrusion into the bargaining process between employers and trade unions, to put a ceiling on total money wage increases, *irrespective of the level of unemployment.*

The third potential constraint on macroeconomic policy is to be found in relations with the rest of the world. Fiscal policy will affect the balance of payments on current account; monetary policy may do so as well, but, in addition, it will affect the capital account. Both will have effects on the reserves, or on the rate of exchange itself, according to whether the regime is one of fixed or floating exchange rates. For classical economics, bringing foreign trade and payments into the picture does not introduce anything essentially new. The self-adjusting properties of markets will continue to function in this wider context. It is no surprise, therefore, that the most intensive discussion of the external constraints has been by economists in the Keynesian strand, who believe that macroeconomic policies can have effects on the real economy. Keynes himself and many followers have at various times advocated forms of protection. Most international trade theory rests on the assumption that all the trading partners are at full employment. The arguments for protection look different when unemployment is taken to be a serious possibility. It is then easy to show that protectionist policies can be devised to benefit a single country: the question is whether they must necessarily harm other countries, and whether other countries will retaliate. The further question arises as to whether international cooperation in macroeconomic policies is feasible, or desirable.

FLUCTUATIONS AND STABILISATION

Neither classical nor Keynesian theory requires the economy to move smoothly from one equilibrium to another. Both allow for fluctuations. In the classical case these are, as a rule, the result of unforeseen shocks, followed by adjustment to a new equilibrium. If the adjustment is slow enough, a succession of random shocks could then generate cycle-like movements.

Keynesian theory can be extended quite easily to account for a regular cycle generated by the interaction of a consumption function with an investment function, with time lags. A number of such theoretical models were developed in the first decades of Keynesian analysis, and modern macroeconometric models will generate cycles, usually damped. For Keynesians, therefore, the idea of policies of counter-cyclical stabilisation emerges naturally from the theory. Some monetarists, Friedman for example, accept that such policies are conceivable, but argue that they are undesirable, because too little is known, particularly of the lag structure of the economy, so that demand management could as well accentuate oscillations as damp them down.

WHAT EVIDENCE DO WE NEED?

To measure the effects of a particular macroeconomic policy, we need to know how the economy would develop in its absence. In logic, therefore, evidence about how the economy works is prior to evidence about policy. Accordingly, in the next chapter we report on some recent findings concerning the theoretical relationships we have been looking at. We then turn, in the following chapter, to experience with macroeconomic policies in a number of countries, attempting to judge their effectiveness. This separation of economy and policy acting on it is not easy to make. For instance, between 1979 and 1981, there was a decline in output and a steep rise in unemployment in Britain. Was this because the economy had begun to behave in ways not previously experienced, or was it because the objectives of policy had changed, giving much higher priority to reducing inflation and much lower priority to keeping unemployment down, with a corresponding alteration in the setting of the instruments of economic policy? A formal approach to this question is to construct a mathematical model of the economy, consisting of a set of equations which represent the observed behaviour of economic variables such as output, employment and prices, in terms of other variables thought to determine them, and then to simulate the effects of an increase in interest rates, or a reduction in income tax. We shall report on studies which adopt this approach. In practice, this approach is limited. Models have not been constructed at all for some countries. Where, as in the United States and Britain, several models have been constructed, they do not always agree on important relationships.

In recent years, some economists[8] have raised more fundamental objections to the separation of the economy and policy just described. In the first place, in countries where the authorities have been pursuing active policies for some time, for example, raising and lowering interest rates, or cutting taxes and public expenditure, the values of economic variables which we observe, and are the raw data for estimating the coefficients in the equations of our model, are the outcome, not only of other parts of the economy, but also of all the earlier policy changes. To use these equations as representing the pure economic mechanism would thus be a mistake. Even supposing that this difficulty could be overcome, there is a second obstacle in the way. We have told only one side of the story, that of the government finding out how industrialists, consumers and other economic agents behave. But these agents are not automata, changing behaviour only in response to impulses from government policy. They are sentient beings, and just as governments try to find out what they are up to, they are trying to find out what government is up to. Once they have found out the policy rules which government follows, they may bring into consideration expected policy reactions to future changes and modify their own present decisions. Some economists have argued that the ability of economic agents to predict the policy reactions of governments is high, and they adjust their own behaviour accordingly, in such a manner as to render macroeconomic policy ineffective. We do not believe this ourselves. If we did, we could spare the reader the chapter on the evidence of economic policy. But we felt it our duty to warn the reader that first, the economic modelbuilders have not agreed among themselves in all respects how the economy works, although there is less disagreement on some things than on others. Nor is it obvious that governments do in fact pursue systematic policy rules which are transparent to the outside observer. Nevertheless, the point which is being made may at times be important.

13

EVIDENCE RELATING TO THE ECONOMY

Evidence about how the economy works can be usefully considered under headings suggested by the discussion of $MV = PT$, and we begin with the question which was at the centre of the original monetarist view of the world, namely whether or not the demand for money was stable. Suppose, to take the simplest case, we could show that the demand for money, that is, the amount of money people wished to hold, depended on their level of income, and upon nothing else, we should be home and dry. For, if the authorities chose to increase the *supply* of money, of which, let us assume, they have the monopoly, then the level of money income would have to rise accordingly.

Brown (1985) has recently examined the statistical evidence of the relations between variables in the quantity of money equation for a number of countries, including all the main industrial countries, over the period 1950–79. To start with, he looks at the closeness of association between pairs of the variables. He uses a particular form of the Fisher equation, $MV = PQ$, where Q stands for real income, rather than the T used earlier, which stood for all transactions. This choice is quite legitimate, since the definition of V, the velocity of circulation, is complementary to Q. Q is an index number, and there is also a complementary index number of prices such that $PQ = Y$ the nominal national income. If we write $m = \log M$, and similarly for the other variables, we obtain the logarithmic form of the money equation: $m + v = p + q = y$, and this is the form used for examining the data, which are drawn from fifteen countries.

There is, it turns out, some similarity between the price changes in the different countries, as measured by the correlation between pairs of them, over the period 1953–79, and it was reassuring to find that the closest association was that between the United States and Canada. When the period was split into two, 1953–67 and 1967–79, the former corresponding roughly to a regime of fixed exchange rates and the latter to one of floating, it was found that the links between price changes in different countries were more clearly seen in the latter period of floating, as well as much bigger price movements than in the former period. The similarity between output changes was much smaller than between price changes.

Brown also looks at the international similarities in changes in nominal income, in money stock and in velocity, but for us the more interesting results concern the relations between the variables within each country. There are, it should be emphasised, two versions of the Quantity Theory of Money, the first asserting that money and nominal income move together, and the other, older, version asserting that money and prices move together.

When changes in money income are correlated with money stock, using both narrow and broad definitions of the IMF, it is found that there is a correlation at the 1 per cent level of significance for six countries, which include the United States and the United Kingdom, but in three countries, including France and Germany, the level of significance is well below 5 per cent. Splitting up the period indicates that the relationships are highly unstable.[1] Many versions of the Quantity Theory allow for time lags between changes in money stock and changes in money income. A simple test is to correlate m and y simultaneously, and with a one year lag in each direction. Counting up correlations at the 5 per cent level of significance, and making use of both measures of money, it was found that there were $15\frac{1}{2}$ cases where money led income, $14\frac{1}{2}$ cases of simultaneity, and 5 where income led money (the halves refer to a dead heat).

The more common version of the Quantity Theory is the one which relates money to prices. This time there were $11\frac{1}{2}$ cases where money led prices, 5 of simultaneity and $9\frac{1}{2}$ where prices led money. These figures suggest that money is somewhat more closely associated with money income than with prices, and this is in accordance with a number of other studies for the recent period. The country where money most closely leads the other variables is the United States, but the strongest probability of the opposite is Japan in the case of money income, and the United Kingdom in the case of prices.

Brown's data show that changes in the velocity of circulation from year to year are not so much less variable than the changes in money growth that velocity can be reasonably treated as a constant. Yet the constancy of velocity lies at the heart of the argument in the massive study of *Monetary Trends in the United States and the United Kingdom* (1982). Since Friedman clearly influenced the views of Mrs Thatcher on monetary questions, it is worth stepping aside to consider *Monetary Trends*. The study covered the period 1867–1975 in the United States and the United Kingdom and assembles time series for money stock, nominal national income, price deflators, interest rates, the sterling-dollar exchange rate, and other variables, which are the subject of analysis. The data are 'decycled' by means of an unusual device of 'triplets' of neighbouring cycle phases (two ups and a down, or two downs and an up). *Monetary Trends* formed the agenda of a meeting of the Bank of England's Panel of Academic Consultants in October 1983 (Bank of England, 1983). Besides the Friedman and Schwartz book (hereafter F&S), a number of journal reviews were tabled, and in addition two specially prepared papers by Hendry and Ericsson and by Brown. The former concluded simply that a number of the F&S assertions about their money demand equation 'were found to be without empirical support' and their failure to produce evidence pertinent to their main assertions 'leaves these devoid of credibility'. This is strong language. It can, however, regrettably be applied to a good deal of contemporary economic analysis, and I shall, once again, draw heavily on the paper by Brown. He summarised his critique by posing a number of questions which bear on the position which F&S took. The first concerned the claim that the variation of output growth in the United Kingdom was insignificant. Brown pointed out that the F&S 'smoothing' process starts off by eliminating the chief variations, which occur *within* cycles. Even so, there was a good deal of variation left, in the Great Depression, or in the slowdown after 1973, which would have been more apparent if the study had not ended in 1975. Moreover, if the two war and immediate postwar periods are excluded, variation in growth rates of output within cycles had a wider amplitude than those of inflation. Brown concurs that in the long run, and with some qualifications, the growth of money income is related to money. But in the short run, it is not. It is velocity, not money, which carries much of the variation of money income growth within cycles. Between the wars, it carried most of it.

Next comes the question of how an expansion of money income is partitioned between changes in output and in price. Generalisations about the long run are difficult, because during the wars and again since the late 1960s, there was evident inflation, whereas from the 1870s to the 1890s, and again from 1920 to 1932, the trend of prices was downward, while that of output was upward. The pattern within cycles is clearer. In the absence of internal wage explosions or external inflation, extra demand has gone mostly into output when there was spare capacity and into inflation when full employment was approached. Finally, when Brown asks the question whether F&S make their case that United Kingdom experience supports a simple quantity theory, with money controlling prices, and output controlled by other factors entirely, he says; 'In a word, no'.

THE MEDIUM TERM FINANCIAL STRATEGY (MTFS)

That is where an academic economist might be content to leave it. However, the macroeconomic policy of the first Thatcher government rested heavily on Friedman's ideas about money, and could well be regarded as a large-scale laboratory test of monetarism. The first full statement of the medium term financial strategy (MTFS) appeared in March, 1980, in the *Financial Statement and Budget Report, 1980–1981*. There it was stated that: 'Control of the money supply will over a period of years reduce the rate of inflation'. To this end, targets were set of the upper and lower limits within which the growth of money supply should fall for several years ahead, starting from a range of 7–11 per cent in 1980–1, and gradually falling to a range of 4–8 per cent in 1983–4. While not setting targets for the PSBR, the government stated that fiscal policy should be conducted so as to be consistent with achieving the planned reduction in the growth of the money supply over the medium term with lower interest rates. The chosen measure of the money stock was £M3. This measure of broad money, besides including the note circulation and non-interest bearing bank deposits, also includes interest bearing deposits. Over the ten-year period 1978–88, £M3 increased 4¼ times, almost exactly twice the rise in prices over the same period. In his speech at the Mansion House in October, 1989, the Chancellor of the Exchequer, Mr Nigel Lawson, who, as Financial Secretary to the Treasury, had launched the medium term financial strategy in March 1980, acknowledged that: ' ... the plain fact is that for the past ten years now, broad money has proved to be an unreliable guide'. The unreliability of broad money was, indeed, apparent from the very beginning, exceeding the upper limit of the target range at a time when inflation was slowing down. In subsequent years new monetary aggregates were paraded, and varying statements made about their significance: the aggregate in favour at the end of the 1980s was M0, which is in the main the total of notes and coin in the hands of the public. Over the ten-year period, M0 increased by just over three quarters, which was one fifth less than the rise in prices, and *a fortiori* less than the rise in money GDP, which increased one and three quarters times – hardly surprising, in view of the growing replacement in current transactions of cash by credit cards and other new instruments. M0, explained the Chancellor, is a 'coincident indicator' of money GDP, the first quarterly estimates of which do not appear until three months after the end of the quarter, whereas M0 is immediately available. However, the change from £M3 to M0 involves more than just a change in measure. In the original MTFS, £M3 was the main *instrument* of anti-inflation policy, the subsidiary instrument being control of the PSBR. Setting £M3 would determine inflation in the medium term, after the elapse of several quarters. The link was causal. The reference to 'coincident indicator', which is a term of art, means that all idea of causality has disappeared. It is not suggested that the way to reduce inflation is to cut the number of bank notes in circulation! M0 is put forward as an *indicator* of a magnitude which already exists, but whose amount will not be known until the statisticians have had time to collect all the bits and pieces of information used in estimating it. Thus the move from £M3 to Mo involves *two* shifts, of the concept and of the number used to measure it. We may note that there have been two further shifts within the framework of the MTFS. It appears from the more recent *Financial Statements* that the specific objective of macroeconomic policy is no longer the price level, but money GDP. The fourth is that policy appeared to be directed towards holding the exchange rate at a certain level, or within a certain range. Since the Chancellor claimed to have only one instrument at his disposal, namely the rate of interest, he clearly could not have *independent* objectives for money GDP and the exchange rate, and it was a matter of continuing speculation which was the one to which he was attaching the greatest importance at any particular time, with the added complication that the Prime Minister might not always agree with his priorities.

We will consider the relevance for employment of the policies actually followed in the United Kingdom after 1979 later in this chapter. Our concern with MTFS at this point was as a test of monetarism. The doctrine that inflation was determined by the money supply came to grief on the question – Which money supply? But there was another aspect of monetarism on test, namely the idea of the 'simple rule' which should be adopted to replace discretionary fine-tuning. The MTFS began in the spirit of the simple rule, but within very few years fine tuning, in the form of discretionary downward and upward adjustment of interest rates, was back. Not only that. It was asserted that discretionary fiscal policy was out, and for a brief spell in 1988 we heard about the idea of balancing the budget. But that idea was abandoned within twelve months, when a large surplus in the budget which had appeared was maintained. If it is said that the early return to discretionary fine-tuning does not prove that a monetary rule would not have worked better, one can only ask, in the light of the huge disparity in the movement of different measures of money actually observed: 'To which measure should the rule have been pinned?'[2]

TYPES OF INFLATION

What Brown's evidence suggests is that there may be some times in some countries when money is driving money income or prices, and other times when the right-hand side of the equation is driving money. The former cases carry the implication that the authorities choose M, which then determines PT, with possible slippage through V. Any rise in prices brought about in this way is characterised as demand-pull inflation, or demand inflation *tout court*. Not all of the changes in M will reach P; some will be absorbed by Q, and of particular interest to us is how changes in demand are split between prices, P, and output, Q, the latter having direct influence on employment. In the nineteenth century, and into the interwar years, it was almost universally assumed that M was in the driving seat and that its changes would affect P. The main issue for stabilisation policy was whether to stabilise the domestic price level or the exchange rate.[3]

A subsidiary question was whether a gently rising price level would be more favourable to enterprise than complete stability. In the interwar years, and especially in the Depression of the 1930s, unemployment emerged on an unprecedented scale, and there were clearly many instances of underutilisation of capacity as well as of labour, so that the supply of output might be quite elastic. The question now arose how a rise in MV would be split between rises in prices and rises in output, an issue which has come to the fore again with the renewed unemployment of recent years.

There was an argument widely used in the 1980s to demonstrate that the notion of trying to stimulate output by increasing demand was no longer realistic. It went something along these lines. In the 1960s the growth of 8 per cent a year in the nominal income of OECD countries was split between output of 5 per cent and price increases of 3 per cent; that is, only 37 per cent of money income increase was 'lost' in inflation. However, this proportion of 'loss' rose steadily, and by 1980–2 it had reached 94 per cent of a faster growth of nominal income. In some individual countries, including the United Kingdom, the proportion lost was over 100 per cent on several occasions! However, the proportion lost in prices has since fallen back below 60 per cent. But these simple percentage losses may not be what we want. In the first place, if the inflation originates spontaneously on the right-hand side, that is, we have a cost inflation proceeding, then the share of output in any rise in nominal income is going to be smaller, the larger the cost inflation: but what we want to know is how *additional* demand will be split between price and output.

Demand pull, whether or not starting from an increase in M, can clearly lead to extra inflation in some cases. But there is another possibility, namely that inflation originates in a spontaneous rise in P. Trade union militancy could accelerate the increase of nominal wages, or a rise in world prices, whether of materials or final products, not offset by a corresponding rise in the exchange rate, could cause non-wage costs to rise. Monetarists might argue that, even so, by hanging on to the monetary target, the pressure on P could be deflected into a fall in output. But there is the possibility that V is more responsive to rising monetary demand than is commonly thought. Monetarists are apt to exclude the very possibility of cost inflation, by the assumption that money is exogenous. But such an assumption is not justified. Institutions vary from country to country, and from period to period: and policy can vary within any given institutional framework.

Clinging to the exogeneity of money may seem to give assurance that the genie of inflation can always be kept in the bottle. But once the stopper of exogeneity is taken out, who can tell to what heights the inflation could soar? This is, indeed, a question which has to be faced by any economist who does not believe that inflation is determined by money and money alone. A great many Keynesians would find themselves in this category.

Two types of answer can be given. The first passes the buck to the 'rest of the world'. Firms in a country which trades with the rest of the world in any substantial degree must keep their prices in line with the competition in export markets, and in home markets accessible to imports. By way of example, consider a small country in a world of fixed exchange rates. The prices of its exports cannot deviate far from the prices of its competitors, subject to detailed qualifications concerning tariffs, transport costs and the like, and similarly for home industries open to foreign competition. Price levels in the tradeables sector will, therefore, be set by rest of the world prices, where that expression is shorthand for the lists of particular export markets and import competitors. According to the growth of productivity in the tradeables sector, wages will correspondingly be determined, it being understood by all that if wages are driven up beyond the warranted level markets would be lost, so that it would be at the expense of employment. The market for labour is supposed to be sufficiently competitive for changes in the wage level in the tradeables sector to bring about similar changes in the non-tradeables sector. If productivity growth in the latter industries is less than in tradeables, then costs will rise faster (or fall more slowly) in these sectors than in tradeables. There will thus be a premium on price increases in the non-tradeables sector over the rises in the tradeables sector. The overall national price level is a weighted average of the two sectors, and it will rise faster than world inflation by an amount depending on the weight of the two sectors and the differential in productivity growth between them.

This brief outline of the Scandinavian model of inflation was given as an illustration of the kind of mechanism which might link domestic inflation to that in the rest of the world (Maynard and Van Ryckeghem, 1976). It happens that the evidence in favour of this particular model is not all that strong. Nevertheless, it has been found that in smaller countries the influence of world prices on domestic inflation is greater in relation to unit labour costs than in large countries.[4]

But what if the exchange rate is free to float? In theory a change in the exchange rate could offset precisely any difference between domestic and rest of the world prices of tradeables. In practice, as with the Scandinavian model, the evidence that offsetting is always achieved is not strong. However, if the real world did work according to the rules of pure theory, 'clean' floating would shift the burden of responsibility for the inflation rate onto the shoulders of the domestic economy.

What looked at one time to be the most promising anchor for the rate of inflation in a closed economy was the Phillips curve, which appeared to pin the rate of change of money wages firmly to the level of unemployment. However, as we saw in the chapter on Wages and Employment, the simple relationship did not survive the intensive econometric scrutiny to which it was subjected in subsequent years, for different periods and different countries. It is not that it was incontestably demonstrated that unemployment exerted no influence whatever on wage inflation, but that no influence was found which could be relied upon to remain firm enough to act as precise guide to policy. As for the models which purported to supersede the Phillips curve, even had the empirical evidence given strong support to the existence of a natural rate for instance, it would have done no more than to say that inflation would be either accelerating, or decelerating, according to whether unemployment was below or above the natural rate. Moreover, the fact that estimates of the natural rate in Britain jumped by more than ten percentage points in less than ten years, was hardly encouraging.

Does the fact that the econometric evidence does not seem to throw up clear, unambiguous and stable relationships mean that rational macroeconomic policy is not possible? Not necessarily. It may be that the methods employed are not well adapted to take account of historical change. To give but one instance: after two decades in which inflation rates in Britain have been over 10 per cent per annum on more occasions than they have been below, quite a lot of people would regard 5 per cent a year as a reasonable rate, provided that it could be guaranteed. But in the 1930s, or again in the 1950s and 1960s, a target of 5 per cent a year would have been regarded as unacceptably high. Instead, therefore, of setting out with the idea of finding constants, which would be the same for all economies at all times, we might try a different approach and examine the success or failure of particular macroeconomic policies as they were applied in different countries at different times.

14

EVIDENCE RELATING TO POLICY

In studying the behaviour of the economy, we were looking for statistical generalisations, though the results were not always conclusive. With macroeconomic policies, there may be some questions, for example, stabilisation, where it is, in principle, sensible to look for generalisation, but, as a rule, the particular circumstances of economies at particular times make it unlikely that the general approach will be very fruitful. Much of this chapter will, accordingly, be historical and discursive.

In retrospect, the postwar development of the advanced economies seems to have had two phases. In the first phase, priority was given (in varying degrees) to the maintenance of employment and, in most cases, not only was this achieved but output grew at higher rates than ever previously experienced.[1] In Britain, GDP grew between 1951 and 1973 at an annual average rate of 2.8 per cent, which implies a doubling in every 25 years. This was low by comparison with European countries and Japan, but was faster than in any period of comparable length since at least the middle of the last century. More striking still, productivity, that is, output per man year, was already rising at 2 per cent a year in the 1950s, and was to rise faster still in the 1960s. But Matthews and his colleagues (Matthews, *et al.* 1982) have also shown that ' ... the postwar period is unique in British history (since the time of James I) in having a sustained and substantial rise in prices'. In this first phase, inflation in Britain was, if anything, slightly falling. Elsewhere, experience varied, but there was no obvious acceleration of inflation. In the earlier postwar years there still existed many government controls within the domestic economy, such as consumer rationing, the allocation of materials and building licensing, and there were also stringent controls of foreign trade and payments. Over time, both internal and external controls were relaxed and dismantled. Tariffs were reduced in successive rounds of GATT negotiations. The Bretton Woods system of fixed, but occasionally adjustable, exchange rates was in operation throughout.

The Golden Age ended in the early 1970s, since when the advanced capitalist countries have generally experienced slower growth of output and productivity, higher inflation and higher unemployment. In the mid-1980s, in Britain, growth rates of output and productivity have once more reached the levels of the 1960s, though unemployment remains very high, and inflation has still to fall below that of the 1960s. The United

States stagnated in the late 1970s, and output per person employed stopped rising altogether for several years, but after 1982 there was a good recovery, with rising output, rising employment and falling unemployment, with productivity moving up positively, if slowly, once more. In most other advanced economies, however, the slower growth rates persisted through 1987. These slower rates can be seen as a falling away from the achievements of the Golden Age, but they can also be seen as a return to the longer-term historical average. In this latter perspective, it was the rates of the 1950s and 1960s which were abnormal. Nevertheless, current unemployment rates in many countries are still well above any long-term average. Different countries entered the second phase at somewhat different dates, but there were some elements common to all. Among them was the first of the OPEC oil price rises in 1973–4, which contracted demand, but at the same time boosted costs across the world. All countries were affected by the crumbling of the fixed exchange rate system, and its replacement by floating rates. As inflation worsened the commitment to full employment became weaker and weaker, and was increasingly replaced by a commitment to reducing the rate of increase in prices. In the view of some economists the poorer performance of the second phase is evidence of the failure of policies which were being attempted in the first period. In the eyes of others, changes in economic behaviour – particularly with respect to costs and pricing – were the prime movers, so that the earlier policies were no longer appropriate. Let us, therefore, begin by examining the effectiveness of policy in the first phase.

THE 'GOLDEN AGE'

The Second World War had been immediately preceded by the Great Depression, which many believed had contributed to making war more likely. It was natural that governments should wish to avoid mass unemployment in the future. The commitment to maintaining employment was expressed in a number of cases in Full Employment Acts, and the objective of full employment appeared in United Nations documents, such as the Final Act of Bretton Woods setting up the International Monetary Fund (IMF). The degree of commitment varied. Among the most committed were Britain, Norway, Austria and Sweden; and among the least were Germany and Switzerland. While the United States had a Full Employment Act, and a Council of Economic Advisers was established, its employment policies were initially somewhat passive, and it was not until the 1960s that they entered an activist phase.

The context of the *General Theory* was the interwar unemployment, and particularly the Great Depression, and the diagnosis was one of deficiency of demand. The two principal remedies to emerge from this analysis were low interest rates to stimulate private investment and deficit spending by central government.[2] The use of monetary policy, of course, went back a long way. The novelty was the idea of deliberately unbalancing the budget, associated with the belief that fiscal policy would be more powerful and more certain in its effects than monetary policy. In the first postwar phase the economy was on average near to full employment, and the pressure of demand was clearly higher than in the interwar period. Matthews and his colleagues have estimated that between 1952 and 1973 in Britain, the average ratio of actual GDP to full employment GDP was 10 per cent higher than in the period 1925–37, and they estimated the contribution to this increase from the three variables, investment, exports and income from abroad, and the two propensities to save and to import (Matthews *et al*, 1982).

Much the largest contribution came from investment, with a smaller, but still substantial contribution from exports. There was a rise in the overall savings propensity, within which public sector saving of central and local government, which was near to zero before the war, rose substantially. On the face of it, therefore, deficit finance made no contribution to postwar full employment. However, if one examines the changes which were occurring during the period, a little more can be said. A strong rise in personal and corporate saving took place between 1948 and 1953, and this was matched by a fall in public sector saving. Had it not been, demand deficiency might well have reappeared. What Keynesian policy requires is not any particular balance of the budget, whether it be deficit or surplus, but that the budget balance should be the regulator which supplements or offsets private sector saving, according to the requirement that saving should equal investment at full employment.

When the *General Theory* was written, the problem was, as we have noted, one of substantial demand deficiency. The challenge to policymakers after the war was to keep excessive demand under control, and later on, to damp down the fluctuations which still occurred, albeit at a much higher average level of activity than before the war. Were they successful in this objective? Bispham and Boltho (1982) have pointed out that a selective reading of the literature would actually suggest that in Britain demand management was at best ineffectual and at worst destabilising. But such a conclusion is open to question. What one needs to know is how the economy would have behaved if budgetary policy had been neutral or passive, leaving the economy to look after itself. Unfortunately there do not exist agreed macroeconometric models of United Kingdom and other countries which could be used for such an exercise.

Output in advanced countries grew at a much faster average rate after the war than before. There continued to be fluctuations, not so much the alternation of absolute rises and falls, but phases of faster and slower growth, around a rising trend. The amplitude of these fluctuations and their period was in most cases smaller or shorter than before the war. Taking the root mean square deviation from trend as a percentage of the corresponding trend value as the measure, it appears that in Britain fluctuations of GDP between 1958 and 1973 were smaller than in any other industrial country of any size, and that those in industrial production were as low as all but two of the ten countries listed (NEDO, 1976).

WAS POLICY STABILISING?

This evidence still, of course, leaves open the question whether policy made fluctuations better or worse. One of the best known international studies of fiscal policy was undertaken by Hansen (1969) for the OECD. Starting from a Keynesian model of national income determination, he attempts to isolate a 'pure cycle' which would have occurred in the absence of both automatic and discretionary fiscal policy changes.[3] It is then possible to compare the trends of the actual cycles and the pure cycles over the period under consideration, which was 1955–65 for most of the seven major economies investigated. It appears that general government was on average an expansionary element, with the exception of the United Kingdom, where the contribution was zero. Short-term stabilisation was measured by comparing the deviation from their respective trends of the actual cycles and the pure cycles. The particular formula chosen to measure stabilisation had a value of 100 if stabilisation was perfect, zero if there was none at all, and negative if the effect of fiscal policy was perverse. According to this index, the best performer was the United States, with a score of 56, a little surprising in view of the belief that American fiscal policy only became active in the 1960s.[4] Other countries had smaller, but positive results. In Germany, *not* surprisingly, the index was zero, and in the United Kingdom it was small, but negative. Boltho (1981) has questioned the inclusion of public enterprise investment in fiscal policy, which Hansen had done, on the grounds that there were differences in the degree of real control over public enterprise investment exercised by governments, and in the extent that such control was exclusively used for counter-cyclical purposes. Accordingly, he excludes public enterprise investment, and recalculates the stabilisation index. Most indexes improve, including that for the United Kingdom, which becomes positive though still small. Only the index for France deteriorates, and that is a case where it is known that the planners intended to use public enterprise investment counter-cyclically.

Boltho went on to modify the formula, measuring stabilisation against potential output rather than against the two trends, and he made estimates for the period 1966–71 as well. The change of formula raises the stabilisation success of all countries but one, the exception being the United States. The United Kingdom is, however, still the least successful. The performance of most countries deteriorates in the period 1966–71: once again Britain is the exception, the net result being that it joins the pack. However, not too much weight should be placed on general measures of this kind. First of all, they appear to imply that fiscal policy is the only important stabilisation instrument.[5] One ought, in principle, to take into account monetary policy, and other instruments, such as the direct control of consumer credit. Secondly, one may question whether stabilisation was always the primary objective of policy. This does not, of course, affect the index so much as the interpretation one places upon it. But it may be that in concentrating on year-to-year changes, one is missing altogether the point that what really mattered in this first phase was that businessmen came to believe that governments were (a) committed to the avoidance of serious slumps, and (b) knew what to do if they discerned any signs of one appearing.

The objection that Hansen's study did not take account of monetary policy, though formally valid, may not be so serious in practice. In the early postwar years, monetary policy in most countries was accommodating. In both Britain and the United States, the wartime policy of keeping interest rates very low was continued. That such policies were pursued at a time of very high pressure of demand may come as a surprise to some modern readers, but the view was taken that the economy was being adequately steered, and demand constrained, by fiscal policy, buttressed with direct controls. In particular, there existed in most cases stringent controls over imports and international payments. What need, then, to invoke changes in interest rates, which were thought to be weaker and less certain in their operation?

THE REVIVAL OF MONETARY POLICY

More active monetary policies began to be developed in the 1950s. Had the purpose of monetary policy been exclusively to support fiscal policy in maintaining high employment, the degree of stabilisation success attributed above to fiscal policy alone, would have to be ascribed to the combination of fiscal and monetary policy. However, matters were more complicated than this. In the course of the 1950s, quantitative restrictions on imports were steadily reduced and controls over payments relaxed. By 1958 something approaching convertibility, at any rate for current transactions, was achieved between the major currencies. In some countries there emerged surpluses in the balance of payments on current account, and in others deficits. In many cases the revival of active monetary policy was directed towards this conflict between domestic and external balance.[6] This was particularly so in the British case. The characteristic response to balance-of-payments crises was a package of measures, including tighter monetary policy. The latter was not so much higher interest rates, although they figured increasingly in successive crises, but restrictions on bank advances and stiffer terms of hire purchase (consumer credit). If the Goes of Stop-Go were mainly encouraged by relaxing the stance of fiscal policy, the Stops were mostly engineered by monetary policy, in its wider interpretation.

The freeing of trade and payments offered no immediate threat to the domestic policies of those countries whose balances moved into surplus, but for countries with intermittent deficits the conflict between domestic and external objectives became from time to time acute. The rules of the International Monetary Fund permitted adjustment of parities and, from the end of the 1950s, there was increasing resort to devaluations, to correct current account deficits and, in the cases of Germany and Switzerland, to revaluations upwards, to avert excessive pressure of demand and inflation. The pressures on deficit countries to devalue were on the whole stronger than the pressures on surplus countries to revalue, and this lack of symmetry was one of the factors leading to the crumbling of the fixed exchange rate system of the IMF which occurred at the end of the 1960s and in the early 1970s.

Although governments expressed concern about inflation throughout the Golden Age, the concern did not, as a rule, lead to very strong action. The great inflation of the Second World War had largely subsided by 1953, after a final fling during the Korean War. In the next fifteen years consumer prices in the industrial countries were to rise at rates between 2 and 5 per cent a year on average. In many cases such figures were high by historical standards, but they did not show any tendency to acceleration. Prices of internationally traded manufactures rose very slowly.

Tobin (1985) has argued that postwar recessions in the United States can be attributed to deliberate policies to restrict aggregate demand to bring the inflation rate down. This was the case, for instance, in 1957–8 and 1960, where recessions took unemployment up from around 4 per cent to 6 or 7 per cent, but reduced inflation from 4 or 5 per cent to less than 2 per cent. In Britain, restrictive demand management was usually occasioned by the desire to correct deficits in the balance of payments, rather than to curb inflation, although the latter was invoked in 1957 at the time when bank rate was raised to a then astronomical 7 per cent. A year earlier Tinbergen had enunciated the principle that, if the government had distinguishable objectives, such as full employment, stable prices, external balance and so on, it would need as many policy instruments as objectives. In establishing the Council on Prices, Productivity and Incomes in 1957, the British government was implicitly endorsing the Tinbergen principle. The Council had no statutory powers to control collective bargaining or price fixing, being limited to finding the facts about prices and incomes, and making them public. Successor bodies remained restricted to exhortation and the encouragement of voluntary restraint in wage settlements, and when statutory powers were introduced in the wage and price freeze of 1966, the objective was as much the balance of payments as of stable prices. But, from then on, incomes policies were to become a semi-permanent feature of the British scene until the end of the 1970s.

Until the mid-1960s it was possible to maintain that the creeping inflation experienced in Britain and elsewhere, if indeed it was the consequence of maintaining high levels of employment, was nevertheless an acceptable price to pay. Up to this time, therefore, it was also possible to argue that fiscal and monetary policy were sufficient to secure full employment, reasonable price stability and, taken with occasional alterations of exchange rate parities which were permitted by the IMF rules, a reasonable external balance as well. As we have already noted, however, the foreign exchange rate regime of Bretton Woods was crumbling. And, on the inflation front, the outlook changed significantly between the mid-1960s and the mid-1970s. Under the Bretton Woods regime, the dollar had been effectively the base of the world's currencies. In the United States the annual increase in consumer prices in the early 1960s was of the order of 1½ per cent, or less, but after 1965 there began a gradual acceleration in the annual rate, which exceeded 5 per cent by the end of the decade, and which is commonly attributed to the expenditure on the Vietnam war and President Johnson's Great Society programmes, not matched by sufficient taxation: that is, it was a demand inflation. Elsewhere the impetus seems to have come as much from costs. Clustered around the year 1969 there occurred in many countries a distinct jump in the rate of increase of money wages, which Phelps Brown (1983, page 159) has christened the 'Hinge', and which he regarded as 'the outcome of a continuous drift in the attitude of wage earners'. Older workers remembered the Great Depression of the 1930s, and tended to rate job security above militancy, but younger workers, who had experienced only high employment and rising living standards, had higher expectations and believed that they knew how to fulfil them. Year by year the balance tilted away from the older workers towards the younger, until the attitudes of the latter predominated. The second cost impulse was OPEC 1, at the end of 1973. By itself, the rise in the price of oil, even if followed by other fossil fuels, would have added only 2 per cent directly to the industrial world's price level, but if allowance is made for knock-on consequences, the total rise attributable to OPEC could have been several times as large.[7] The average rate of inflation in the leading industrial countries over the period 1950–73 had been 4.1 per cent a year: in 1973–9 it more than doubled, to 9.5 per cent a year. At the lower end of the scale, Switzerland had an increase from 3 to 4 per cent: at the upper end, Britain's rate rose from under 5 to over 15 per cent. These increases were sufficient to lead many governments to give the highest priority to the containment of inflation, even at the expense of abandoning the maintenance of employment.[8]

THE SECOND PHASE: 1973 TO DATE

We have seen that towards the end of the Golden Age, doubts were growing as to the sufficiency of demand management – that is, fiscal and monetary policy – to secure the objectives of full employment and stable prices. Governments might differ in the degree of commitment to the objectives, and in the degree of belief in the effectiveness of the instruments at their disposal; nevertheless, the orthodox view was still that demand management had a positive role to play. One has only to look at any report published by OECD at the time to see this. Yet, by the mid-1980s a new orthodoxy had emerged, to the effect that macroeconomic policies were impotent in securing lasting effects upon the real economy: specifically, they could not raise employment or reduce unemployment in the long run. Macroeconomic policies should be directed towards controlling inflation, or, in some versions, towards controlling the money value of national output. Reductions in unemployment could only be achieved by microeconomic measures, which term embraces breaking up, or reducing the power of, cartels, and trade unions, and other measures to make markets work more freely. The new orthodoxy has been adopted by the British government[9] and, if one may judge by some recent documents, by the Secretariat of the OECD. The question which most concerns us is how this transformation has come about, and how far it can be supported by evidence of the ineffectiveness of demand management of the previously orthodox kind.

THE RISE OF MONETARISM

Academic economists can claim some of the credit for the shift in orthodoxy. The 1970s were the decade of the monetarist ascendancy: first, the Friedman version that inflation followed changes in the supply of money, with 'long and variable lags', and then the speeded-up versions, incorporating the 'rational expectations hypothesis'. The implication of all these versions was that there was little or no scope for monetary or fiscal policy to exercise lasting effects upon output or employment. Most of these theoretical ideas originated in the United

States, but they were beginning to find their way into the reports of governments and international organisations by the end of the decade. But governments are also influenced by experience, and that is our primary concern here. What they found in 1974 and 1975 were unemployment rates and inflation rates, each more than double those to which they had become accustomed, and occurring simultaneously. OECD used to publish a 'discomfort index', which was the simple sum of the unemployment rate and the annual increase in consumer prices. Such an index for seven Major Countries (OECD, 1977, page 42) was around 5½ percentage points through the 1960s decade; an average unemployment rate just below 3 per cent combining with average inflation above 2½ per cent. In most years, moreover, the two separate indexes moved in opposite directions, so that the discomfort index was fairly steady. It began to rise at the end of the decade, and by 1974 and 1975 it was 17 per cent. This was an entirely new experience, and governments reacted differently. The rise in the oil price had given a strong impulse to costs in oil importing countries. Britain was one such, the first North Sea oil platform only coming on stream in 1975. At one extreme, some countries, notably Germany and Switzerland, followed a relatively non-accommodatory monetary policy. At the other end of the spectrum, in an attempt to offset the contractionary effects of the oil price rises, Britain and Italy relaxed the stance of demand management, so that the rise in oil costs was allowed to pass through into the wider economy. Other countries adopted intermediate positions. The result was that the inflation rate reached much higher peaks in Britain and Italy than elsewhere.[10] The diversity in initial response to the OPEC price rise reflected very much the priority given in different countries to curbing inflation as against avoiding unemployment.

Output in OECD as a whole *fell* in 1975 for the first time since the Second World War, albeit by only a tiny amount, and then gradually resumed its upward path, but at a rate nearly everywhere about half of what it had been before 1973.[11] Inflation generally subsided, though it seemed to reach a floor at an annual rate more than three times that of the 1960s, and unemployment remained stubbornly high at rates nearly twice as high. Policy in this new era of 'stagflation' was hesitant. Many countries experienced larger budget deficits, larger balance-of-payments deficits, or both. For those with inelastic demands for imported oil these were only to be expected. Higher oil prices raised import bills, and worsened the trade balance *pro tanto*, since it was to take some time before the oil-producing countries were to increase their own imports of manufactures. The oil price rise also reduced real demand in the importing country, and this would have reduced output and employment if it had not been offset by a fall in either the private or the public propensity to save, the manifestation of the latter being an increase in the budget deficit. In the context, the latter did not denote an increase in demand, but merely restored the *status quo ante* in that regard. However, this reasoning was not everywhere understood, or accepted.[12] Instead, some feared that the deficit denoted increased inflationary pressure, while others interpreted the fact that the deficit had increased without any corresponding *increase* in output and employment as evidence that conventional fiscal policy no longer worked.

Even though the increase in current account deficits might be attributed to OPEC 1, this did not prevent governments being inhibited from expansionary demand management. Such inhibitions did not apply to countries, notably Germany and Japan, which remained in persistent surplus, and it was agreed at the summit meeting in Bonn in mid-1978 that it would be sensible if these countries, by domestic expansion which would increase imports as a consequence, would act as a locomotive to pull the rest of the industrial world out of recession. Germany undertook to take measures aimed at adding 1½ per cent to GDP by 1980, the spill-over being estimated to add ½ per cent to the GDP of Germany's closest trading partners. This was hardly a sensational programme, but it did signify an attempt at a consistent international policy. The immediate effect was that Germany's output rose by 4 per cent in 1979, and its current balance moved into deficit. These developments were in the right direction. However, unemployment remained stuck and then, just at the wrong moment, OPEC 2 injected another boost to cost inflation. The German authorities responded by trying to reduce the budget deficit, and by raising interest rates. The locomotive was brought to a halt.

If the stubbornness of unemployment caused concern, so too did that of inflation. Perhaps the greatest success of the monetarist campaign was to convince politicians that inflation was primarily a monetary matter – that it would be possible to bring inflation down, sooner or later, by controlling the supply of money, without either large, or prolonged, detriment to output and employment. During the 1970s, central banks and governments became increasingly persuaded of the merits of adopting, and announcing, monetary targets. The announcement of such targets, and the determination of the authorities to stick to them, would, it was argued, lead to desirable modifications in the behaviour of the private sector.[13] In particular, trade unions would cease to press for excessive wage demands, appreciating that, in the new monetary regime, such claims, if granted, could only bring about unemployment among their members. Germany was an early practitioner of targetry and it was argued that the announcement of targets was followed by success: certainly the reduction in inflation which followed was remarkable (Thygesen, 1982). But Germany was a special case, inasmuch as there had always been an exceptional public antipathy towards inflation and for many years it had practised 'concerted action' between the 'social partners' and the government: it did not follow that the announcement would be equally effective in countries lacking such arrangements. Switzerland was held for many years to be a good example of monetarist virtue, because of the determination of the authorities to adhere to targets, and the near zero rates of inflation which were the apparent consequence. However, in 1978, the dollar weakened and the Swiss franc rose, creating a dilemma for the Swiss: either to allow the franc to appreciate, with adverse effects upon competitiveness, or to allow the inflow of funds to drive up the supply of money well above the target. They chose the latter course: the money supply did rise way above target, but the inflation which did follow was mainly accounted for by OPEC 2. Whether or not such an influx of capital will have inflationary consequences depends on the intentions of the owners. If they intend merely to hold the funds and not spend them, there need be no effect upon the domestic price level.[14] But, although doubts were expressed by many economists about the monetarist doctrines, the tide was running strongly in favour of action against inflation, and after OPEC 2 all major countries had adopted monetary targets and agreed to give priority to curbing inflation. This time there was to be no attempt to accommodate the cost impulse of OPEC 2.

THE RECESSION OF THE EARLY 1980s

The recession which followed was the deepest since the Second World War. The inflation rate came down again to below the rates seen in 1976–8, though not right down to the rates of the 1960s. But, everywhere unemployment rose and, on average, stayed up. The first to try to break out were the French. In 1980, output was falling, unemployment rising, as was also inflation. In the election the following year, the result was a socialist President and a socialist Prime Minister. The package of measures in the Interim Plan constituted more than a simple reflation. Welfare benefits were raised; there was a rise of 10 per cent in the minimum wage, an increase in paid holidays, a job creation programme in the public sector, and a start made in reducing the working week. The budget deficit rose by nearly 1 per cent of GDP. However, at the end of 1981, production and trade in OECD as a whole was turning down. French exports fell, the trade deficit widened, and there was a flight of capital. The franc had to be devalued, which helped exports, but worsened inflation, and the retreat from the Interim Plan began in earnest. This retreat was widely trumpeted, not least by the British government, as yet further evidence of the failure of conventional demand management. Once more the formula was repeated: 'You cannot spend your way out of a recession'.

Next to break ranks were the Americans. When President Reagan took office in January 1981, he announced his intention to bring in tax cuts and to raise defence spending. On any conventional calculation this programme entailed rising Federal budget deficits. However, in the early days, the supply-siders were in charge, and they argued that, far from falling, tax revenues would increase because of the incentive effects of lower tax rates on the growth of output. They reckoned that by 1984 the Federal budget would be in balance. (In the event, the deficit, which had been less than 2 per cent of GNP in 1979, was to rise to over 5 per cent in 1984.) Meanwhile, as the supply-side miracle was being planned, interest rates had reached unparalleled heights, and the economy was moving into recession, with rising unemployment. In 1982, the international debt crisis broke and the United States abandoned ship: monetary targets were suspended, the Treasury Bill rate fell from 15 to 9 per cent, and the United States entered the 'longest peace-time expansion' in its history, to use the words of the 1988 Economic Report of the President. In the United States case, over half the rise in output was accounted for by employment, and unemployment fell considerably, unlike in Europe. In Britain, output rose a little more than in the United States up to 1988 but the greater part of it was accounted for by productivity.

It might be objected that the United States case is not the best demonstration that Keynesian demand management still works, because of the size of the Federal structural deficit, that is, the deficit which would have occurred if the economy had been at full employment, and also because of the large deficit in the current account of the balance of payments. It is also worth giving a thought to the effect on business confidence if, instead of lauding the supply-side miracle, President Reagan had announced his intention of giving a Keynesian stimulus to demand, which might well spill over substantially into a large balance-of-payments deficit. But such an objection cannot be raised against the Japanese case. After OPEC 2, Japan joined the others with monetary targets and allowed interest rates to rise. Output growth slowed to 4 per cent per annum, low by Japanese standards, unemployment drifted up, and inflation, though already below the OECD average, slowed down. However, exports continued to grow faster than imports, and Japan came under increasing pressure, especially from the United States, to 'do something about it'. Eventually she did. First, monetary policy was relaxed and interest rates allowed to fall, triggering a boom in residential construction. Then, in May 1987, a fiscal package, including a very large programme of public investment, was brought in. The confidence created by this stimulus, as well as the addition to demand, caused business investment to rise to 19 per cent of GNP, the highest ratio since before OPEC 1. Output growth jumped up, unemployment fell, and consumer prices in early 1988 were no higher than in 1986. Moreover, this was not yet another Japanese export-led boom: on the contrary, between 1984 and 1987 exports rose only 2 per cent in volume, while imports rose 23 per cent. As a result of recent policy, the current account surplus had been reduced by 1½ per cent of GNP by mid-1988, which is what the doctor ordered.

Though a small country, by comparison, Sweden should still be mentioned, because of the strength of its commitment to full employment, and because of the sophistication of its macroeconomic policies. Policy after OPEC 1 was to accommodate the impulse to costs given by the oil price, so that the inflation rate rose and both budget and external deficits increased. The response to OPEC 2 was initially the same, the inflation rate staying at about 10 per cent, much the same as the OECD average, but the external deficit grew. In 1982 there was a change of direction with a substantial devaluation of the krona, combined with a reduction in government expenditure. This sufficed to turn the external account into surplus. Inflation came down, albeit slowly, so that there was some risk of eroding the gain in competitiveness. Sweden seems to have navigated both OPEC storms without experiencing anything like the high unemployment seen in other countries. There has, of course, been for many years an active manpower policy, with work-experience schemes, retraining of older workers and so on, as well as a willingness to expand employment of males, and particularly part-time employment of females, in services provided by local government. It is not easy to separate the influence on unemployment of the microeconomic labour-market policies from that of fiscal and monetary policies, but together they have kept unemployment very low, without involving exceptional inflation.

THE BRITISH EXPERIENCE

British unemployment remained exceptionally low through the 1950s and the first half of the 1960s, despite repeated balance-of-payments crises, but the persistent tendency for British costs to rise somewhat faster than those of principal competitors led to devaluation at the end of 1967. It was necessary to make room for a switch of resources from the domestic economy into the external balance, and to this end Roy Jenkins, the Chancellor of the Exchequer, followed a strict fiscal policy of expenditure restrictions combined with some tax increases, so that the budget balance swung from a deficit of £1,828 million in 1967/8 to a surplus of £662 million in 1969/70, a swing of 5 per cent of GDP.[15] The object was to release resources into extra exports, or to replace imports, but unemployment began to rise more than for nearly two decades, and the question was raised whether too big a hole was being dug. Labour lost the General Election in 1970 but, initially, the incoming Conservative government maintained the restrictive stance of policy. However, when unemployment began to get near to one million at the end of 1971, the macroeconomic engines were put smartly into reverse. The 1972 Budget was intended to raise output in the first half of 1973 by an additional 2 per cent of GDP. The Chancellor of the Exchequer, Anthony Barber, said that his measures, which increased once more the 'weighted full employment' deficit, were intended to get the economy onto a 5 per cent per annum growth path. In the event, the output target for the first half of 1973 was roughly achieved, and by the end of 1973 unemployment was down to half a million. Up to this time, demand management appeared to be working in the normal way on the output and employment variables. But doubts were growing whether the real growth path could be sustained. Sterling was allowed to float in June, 1972, to avoid the need to maintain a fixed rate standing in the way of economic expansion, but the subsequent depreciation, though modest, added its contribution to the re-emerging price inflation.

When it came to power in 1964, the Labour government set up a National Board for Prices and Incomes (NBPI), whose primary aim was to control inflation. The policy, which received the reluctant acquiescence of the TUC, was initially voluntary – and ineffective – and a six-months statutory freeze of wages and prices was imposed in mid-1966. When the Conservatives returned to office in 1970, they soon abolished the NBPI. However, by 1972, the rate of inflation was beginning to increase, and following the floating of the pound in mid-1972, prices were to rise faster still. There was, as yet, no thought of abandoning the 5 per cent growth target. Instead, the Prime Minister, Edward Heath, changed tack and began prolonged negotiations with the TUC to set up a new incomes policy. When voluntary agreement could not be reached, a wage freeze was imposed in November, 1972, the first step in a statutory incomes policy which was to remain in place for the rest of the Conservative administration. The Heath-Barber boom had seen output rise by 10 per cent in two years. Whether in normal circumstances the economy could have slowed down to a sustainable pace without recession is an interesting speculation, but times were not to be normal. At the end of 1973 the economy ran into a double energy crisis. War broke out in the Middle East in October, and the Arab oil producers first cut supplies and then began a sequence of rises which quadrupled the price of oil. At home, the miners began an overtime ban in November, which became an all-out strike in the following February. Mr Heath called a General Election for 28 February, in which Labour was returned as the largest party and took office. Just as the Conservatives had scrapped Labour's incomes policy, so Labour now dropped all wage control, retaining only the threshold agreements, and the Price Commission. Any wage limitation was henceforth to be voluntary, under a social contract with the trade unions.

Initially, demand management was accommodating, and the PSBR was allowed to rise. Unemployment remained low, but wage inflation rose fast, helped on its way by seven percentage points from threshold payments. By early 1975, prices, too, were rising at over 20 per cent a year, and earnings faster still. The social contract proved to be a broken reed and, in July, once more an incomes policy was launched, limiting pay increases to £6 a week, with a zero norm for earned incomes above £8,500 a year. The new policy was set for a year at a time, and operated with the support, albeit increasingly reluctant, of the TUC for three years.[16] There were annual modifications, and the Chancellor of the Exchequer, Denis Healey, in presenting his Budget, twice attempted to trade tax cuts against wage restraint, but the TUC would have none of such bargaining!

The rate of price inflation did come down, getting into single figures between mid-1977 and mid-1978. But, in the first two years of the policy, the reduction was accompanied by falls in real earnings – unique in British postwar experience – and by unemployment which passed the million mark and went on rising. Fiscal policy had been tightened in the wake of the IMF loan[17] at the end of 1976, but the Chancellor felt able, in the 1978 Budget, to relax it again and unemployment began to fall during 1978. However, the incomes policy foundered, in what would have been its fourth year, in the 'winter of discontent' which led to a general election in May, 1979, in which the Conservatives were returned to office with Mrs Thatcher as Prime Minister. It has been suggested that Mr Callaghan's much quoted remark to the Labour Party conference in 1976 that: 'You cannot spend your way out of recession', taken with Denis Healey's virtual adoption of monetary targets in the Letter of Intent to the IMF in December of the same year, denote the abandonment of the aim of full employment and the acceptance of the monetarist critique of demand management. It would be nearer the mark to say that the Labour government was still trying to achieve both full employment and price stability, but was giving greater weight to the latter, and in any case was being defeated by economic circumstance.

The new government's Medium Term Financial Strategy (MTFS), introduced with the 1980 Budget, abandoned full employment as a direct objective of macroeconomic policy. The government believed that such policies cannot alter real variables in the long run. It did argue, however, that if inflation was brought down and kept down, a variety of supply-side measures would improve the division of money GDP between output growth and inflation, thus assisting the creation of jobs. In the first MTFS statement in 1980, inflation was to be brought down by setting bounds on the future growth of the money stock, adjusting the PSBR, the borrowing of the public sector, to support the monetary targets. However, in the following years, while the annual *Financial Statement and Budget Report* continued to contain a special chapter devoted to the MTFS, there were shifts in the objectives of policy, and in the instruments intended to achieve them. Policies were always presented as being consistent with MTFS, in the way that pre-Perestroika policies in the Soviet Union were always announced to be consistent with Marxism-Leninism. In the description of events which follows, therefore, we avoid mention of MTFS (see pages 147–8).

In April, 1979, Mr Healey had brought in a 'care and maintenance' budget. It was Sir Geoffrey Howe's budget in June, after the election, which put down some of the markers of the new administration. The basic rate of income tax was reduced from 33 to 30 per cent, the top rate from 83 to 60 per cent, and there were increases in various allowances. Offsetting these cuts were increases in indirect taxes, the most important being the replacement of the 8 and 12½ per cent rates of VAT with a uniform 15 per cent rate. The National Institute (*National Institute Economic Review*, August 1979) estimated that the budget measures tightened fiscal policy to the extent of nearly £2 billion in the high-employment balance, and that the VAT change would immediately add 3 per cent to the consumer price index. The targets for sterling M3 were reduced from 8–12 to 7–11 per cent. When the budget was introduced, output was still growing slowly and unemployment falling. But the inflation rate, which had dropped into single figures in the previous year, was turning up, as was also the annual increase in money earnings. The rise in VAT gave a kick to prices, quickly followed by a jump in earnings. This accelerating cost inflation confronted a tightened stance of both monetary and fiscal policy, and the economy plunged towards the deepest recession since the Second World War. Though industrial costs in Britain were rising faster than among main competitors, the effective exchange rate, which had started to rise in 1978, continued to rise strongly. Three main reasons have been given to explain the paradox. Firstly, North Sea oil had first come on stream in 1975 and was now reaching the point when the net balance of oil imports would be replaced by a net balance of exports. Secondly, monetary policy had put up interest rates, attracting foreign capital, whose inflow was reinforced by the third – Thatcher – factor, the confidence of financial asset owners abroad and at home that this government would not resort to the kinds of economic regulation attempted by earlier governments. This last could also explain why the abolition of the remaining elements of exchange control in October, 1979, was followed, not by a fall, but by a further rise in the exchange rate.

Several attempts have been made to estimate the contribution of different factors to the recession after 1979. The Bank of England Academic Panel invited the National Institute of Economic and Social Research and the London Business School to 'explain departures of output (GDP) from an assumed non-recessionary trend starting from the year 1978', and set out a number of conventions to govern the studies (Bank of England, 1981). The National Institute identified 60 per cent of the causes of the estimated shortfall of 6.3 per cent of actual output below trend between 1978 and the fourth quarter of 1980. Of this 60 per cent, just over half was attributed to fiscal and monetary policy, and the remainder to the exchange rate rising above the level needed to preserve competitiveness. The London Business School identified less than 30 per cent of the shortfall, of which more than half was policy, with the exchange rate, and a small contribution from too high real wages accounting for the rest. With a number of colleagues Artis undertook a similar exercise for the period from the fourth quarter of 1979 to the fourth quarter of 1982, using conventions similar to those adopted in the Bank of England exercise three years earlier (Artis *et al*. 1984). On this occasion they used the current versions of the National Institute and Treasury econometric models. This exercise asked for an explanation of the shortfall of actual below 'trend' GDP on the alternative assumptions of fixed and flexible exchange rates, the latter being nearer actual history, although floating was not absolutely 'clean'. This time the National Institute model accounted for all the shortfall, attributing two thirds to policy and one third to the world recession (represented by the shortfall of world trade below trend). The Treasury model identified only 60 per cent of the shortfall in output, of which 70 per cent was attributable to policy and the remainder to world recession. Since some of the shortfall in world trade could itself be laid at the door of restrictive demand management in other countries, there seems to be little doubt of the power of demand management to *reduce* real output and hence employment.

The fall in output in Britain came to an end at the turn of 1980–1, and thereafter it began to rise, slowly at first and gathering pace later. In year-on-year terms, output still fell from 1980 to 1981, by 1.2 per cent, but increased by 1.5 per cent in 1982, and 3.4 per cent in 1983. But while it is not too difficult to place the trough in output, it is harder to say when recovery began. When there is a well established upward trend in output, it is customary to speak of growth cycles. When growth, though still positive, is below trend, the economy is in recession, and when it is above trend, it is in recovery. This is unambiguous where the trend is well established and expected to continue, but things become tricky when there is doubt about the trend. We noticed above that the average rate of growth of virtually all major economies slowed down after 1973, and Britain was no exception. But there were large variations in the annual growth rate, both before and after 1973, which make it hard to say what the underlying trend was in 1980. Thus the average growth rate from 1973 to 1979 was 1.3 per cent a year, but for the period 1969 to 1979, which covers two cycles, it was 2 per cent. The rise between 1981 and 1982 was 1.5 per cent, which falls between these two figures. By the one trend the economy was in recovery in 1982, but by the other it was still in recession. Whatever date we settle on for recovery, according to the output criterion, other indicators, such as employment and unemployment, would place it later. The total workforce in employment in 1981 was 24.3 millions, having fallen already by one million below 1979. It continued to fall, by a further 720,000 (3 per cent) until 1983: it got back to the 1981 level by 1985, but it was not until 1989 that it finally surpassed the 1979 level. This measure of employment includes the self-employed. The number of employees in employment in 1989 was still below the level of ten years earlier. For measuring changes in unemployment over a period, the Central Statistical Office advises that the seasonally-adjusted quarterly estimates of the wholly unemployed are the best. Between the second quarter of 1979 and the second quarter of 1981 unemployment rose by over one million to 2.1 million, and it went on rising in every subsequent year until 1986, by which date it had reached 3.1 million. This profile of unemployment is very different from the Great Depression of the 1930s when unemployment began to fall after 1932. Although, in percentage terms, the peak rate of unemployment was lower in the 1980s than in the 1930s, the cumulation of person–years of unemployment was notably higher in the 1980s (Gregg and Worswick, 1988).

The 1981 Budget was contractionary in its impact on aggregate demand, though the scale of the contraction varies considerably according to the measure adopted.[18] Thereafter, fiscal policy was mildly expansionary, especially when we take into account that the proceeds of privatisations were treated as negative expenditure in the public accounts. But the single most important component accounting for the growth of real GDP was consumers' expenditure, which rose slightly faster than total final expenditure, and much faster than output. Very roughly, the annual average increase in consumer spending from 1979 to 1988 was 3 per cent, compared with 2 per cent for GDP. This was in part because, despite high unemployment and a succession of Acts of Parliament curbing the power of trade unions, real wages of workers in employment rose strongly. It was also in part because the containment of the increase in public expenditure made room for cuts in direct taxation. But the main factor seems to have been the remarkable fall in the ratio of saving to personal disposable income from 13.9 per cent in 1980 to 4.5 per cent in 1988, equivalent to adding over 1 per cent a year to consumers' expenditure. Most econometric modellers have found an influence of inflation on the saving ratio, and with inflation coming down from 18 per cent in 1980 to under 5 per cent in 1983, part of the rise in consumption can be attributed to the anti-inflation policy. But the really spectacular falls in the ratio come after 1984, by which time the rate of inflation had levelled off. The contribution of the growth of credit cards and other financial instruments in this period can hardly be doubted: personal credit outstanding, which stood at £7.4 billion in 1979, rose to £10.5 billion in 1983 and £28 billion in 1988 (these figures exclude mortgage borrowing and credit cards).[19]

Nigel Lawson had been the Financial Secretary of the Treasury and a powerful advocate of the Medium Term Financial Strategy in its initial, monetarist, phase. He left for a spell as Minister for Energy, but returned after the 1983 General Election as Chancellor of the Exchequer. It was soon plain that, notwithstanding the parading of an increasing number of alternative monetary aggregates, it was the interest rate which was now seen as the instrument of monetary policy, and the exchange rate as an important target. The sterling rate against all major currencies had risen strongly after 1978 until it peaked at the end of 1980. When Mr Lawson returned to the Treasury, it had already fallen back and he allowed this fall to continue. This, together with the slowing down of wage inflation, kept the competitiveness of British manufacturing exports fairly steady. However, partly as a consequence of the falling exchange rate, import prices started to rise in 1984, and this fed through into the retail price index. To counter this 'blip' in the inflation rate, interest rates rose, and the exchange rate immediately jumped. Import prices fell back, aided by a coincidental fall in world commodity prices. Inspection of the chart of average earnings shows not a tremor of disturbance of its, by then, steady upward march between 7 and 8 per cent a year. This was a clear indication that the *modus operandi* of interest rates as a controller of inflation was *via* the exchange rate. This does not mean, however, that if higher interest rates had been kept for a longer period, they would not have exerted other, direct, effects on the domestic economy.

It was also apparent from this episode that the reduction of inflation no longer had the highest priority: otherwise, interest rates could have been kept up or pushed higher. The Chancellor's view was that it was desirable for Britain to join the Exchange Rate Mechanism of the European Monetary System, whose members undertook to keep their own exchange rate within a narrow band in relation to the rates of other members, and to this end he started in 1986 to shadow the Deutschmark. This meant tolerating an inflation rate of the order of 3 to 4 per cent a year.[20] After the end of 1987, inflation started once more to rise. One way to resolve this dilemma would be to resort to taxation rather than interest rates to restrain aggregate demand. It would have to be direct taxation, since indirect taxes would suffer from the same disadvantage as interest rates of raising prices in the immediate future, while the effects of contracting real demand would only come in later.

The first budget of the Thatcher administration in 1979 had nearly doubled VAT to make room for direct tax reductions, and during Mr Lawson's Chancellorship fiscal policy continued to be seen exclusively from the supply side, the cuts in direct taxation being justified by reference to their supposed influence on incentives to work and to invest. Later budgets included an element of tax reform, removing or reducing a number of tax-breaks, although one of the most important of them, the tax relief on mortgage borrowing up to £30,000, remained in place. Even though it may not be its primary purpose, a budget will nevertheless have effects on aggregate demand. Following the deflationary budget of 1981, subsequent budgets, in the view of the National Institute, were mildly expansionary. The economy was expanding on the back of the growth of consumer demand, fuelled by private borrowing. Public sector borrowing fell, helped by the sale of assets in successive privatisations. The PSBR was about in balance in 1986, and moved into large surplus in 1988 and 1989. The balance of payments on current account, however, was in increasing deficit, reaching nearly 5 per cent of GDP in 1989.

In the 1988 Budget, tax rates on higher incomes were reduced and the standard rate of income tax brought down to 25 per cent. In addition, the policy of reducing interest rates, following the Stock Exchange crash of October, 1987, was continued, the banks' base rate being brought down to 7.5 per cent on 18 May. The Treasury forecast accompanying the budget showed a balance-of-payments current account deficit of £4 billion for the year, but Mr Lawson argued that, since the public sector was in surplus, the external deficit was the consequence of decisions taken in the private sector, and was bound to correct itself eventually. In his speech, Mr Lawson gave an upbeat account of the economy, saying that the six years to 1987 'constituted the longest period of steady growth, averaging 3 per cent a year, for half a century', echoing the expression 'the longest peace-time expansion' used the previous month in the Economic Report of the President of the United States. The question whether the *trend* of growth was exceptional is discussed in the chapter on technology and industrial structure (pp. 31–2). But there was also the claim of greater steadiness, in contrast with the Stop-Go of the earlier postwar years. It is possible that this owed more to circumstance than to policy. The recession of 1979–81 had been the biggest Stop in postwar years, and throughout the first five years of output recovery, unemployment was still rising, fast to begin with and then more slowly until 1986, when it exceeded three million. Even in 1988, it was still twice as high as it had been in 1979. Thus the elasticity of supply of labour must, generally, have been higher than in the years of Stop-Go, even of the 1970s, entailing less danger of the 'overheating' which was one of the occasions for Stops.[21] A second circumstance favourable to steadiness was North Sea oil, ensuring that the balance of payments in the early 1980s would remain in surplus for some years, even if GDP rose. As often as not, it was external deficits, as much as overheating, which triggered the Stops of the past.

Within a few months of the 1988 Budget, it became apparent that the steady growth was not going to be allowed to continue unchecked. The slightly falling rate of inflation in the run-up to the budget was rather sharply reversed soon after. The swing was exaggerated because of the convention of measuring inflation year on year, and ·because of the inclusion of mortgage rates in the RPI. Even so, the index with mortgages taken out started rising, as did the increase in average earnings. In addition the monthly trade figures showed that the current account deficit was widening at an alarming rate, far greater than anticipated. In response to these developments, the Chancellor raised interest rates, usually in steps of ½ per cent, over a dozen times in a period of eighteen months, reaching 15 per cent in October 1989. During this period, there was a lively debate whether the inflation rate could be brought down again, and the external deficit start to diminish, simply by slowing down the growth of aggregate demand, or whether an outright recession, entailing a fall in output would be needed.[22] By the time these words are printed, the answer to that question will be known, but there is a longer-term question raised by the present conjuncture of the economy. The growth since 1981 can now be seen as an unusually long Go, the extension being made possible by North Sea oil, and the depth of the preceding Stop. During this expansion, output grew at well over 3 per cent a year, but personal consumption grew at 4 per cent a year. This was possible because of the restriction in the growth of public expenditure, but even more because of the swing from surplus into deficit in the balance of payments, equivalent to an addition to GDP of between ½ and 1 per cent every year. It seems plain that to get the economy back into balance personal consumption will have for a time to grow more slowly than output. On the face of it tax increases, rather than tax cuts, should be the order of the day, certainly if there is to be an expansion of public capital expenditure, as well as current services, which many believe to be overdue. In maintaining a large budget surplus Mr Lawson was implicitly restoring fiscal policy as an instrument of demand management. He resigned in October, 1989, and it was his successor, Mr John Major, who introduced the Autumn Statement to Parliament, and gave evidence on it to the Treasury Committee of the House of Commons on 4 December. In his remarks on a medium-term framework, his references to the flexibility of the economy and not 'closing options' suggest that he is on the discretionary side of the rules versus discretion debate. Nevertheless, some uncertainty remains. In our view the availability of two instruments of demand management, monetary and fiscal, is better than one only. But, even if the discretionary status of fiscal policy is restored, it still leaves the question how best to reduce inflation.

15

REFLECTIONS ON MACROECONOMIC POLICY

In our review of the evidence concerning macroeconomic policy, we divided the postwar period at 1973, characterising the first part as a Golden Age. Rates of growth of output and productivity were higher, and in some cases much higher, than ever previously experienced. The biggest increases were in Japan and Europe. Unemployment rates were not only far below those of the 1930s, but in most cases lower than in any previous peacetime period of any length. The United States was something of an exception. While the level of its productivity was the highest, there was no spectacular improvement in its growth rate, nor, leaving aside the Depression, was its unemployment unusually low. Britain's productivity growth was less than that of Japan and of its European neighbours, but higher than its own previous best. World trade grew faster than ever before. The view we took was that demand management by governments made a positive contribution to the high levels of employment. There *was* a continuous and persistent inflation, a quite new peacetime phenomenon in the industrial world, and official reports, national and international, at intervals expressed concern. But as Galbraith (1958) observed: 'Where inflation is concerned nearly everyone finds it convenient to confine himself to conversation. All branches of the conventional wisdom are equally agreed on the undesirability of any remedies that are effective'.

Yet it was the first of two bursts of inflation which marked the end of the Golden Age in 1973, and ushered in the second phase of slower growth, higher inflation and higher unemployment. In both of these bursts, the rise in the OPEC price of oil played a major part. In the first case, there was also the wage explosion, starting in France in May 1968, and occurring in the next two years in a number of countries, without any immediately apparent common cause. These were both cost impulses. But there were also elements of demand inflation. In the late 1960s, the dollar was the base currency of the still operating Bretton Woods system, and the gradual rise in the United States price level was demand led, although it should be added that by 1971 and 1972 the United States inflation rate was slowing down. The great rise in commodity prices of 1972/3 could also be attributed to demand expansion in the industrial countries. Our judgement was that the step-up in world inflation rates was initiated by the cost impulses, with some assistance from the demand side. The recession of 1974/5 could only have been averted by a large budgetary stimulus. This might have maintained real output, but it would also have entrenched much higher inflation. Those countries, such as the United Kingdom and Italy, which started off along this road, finished up with much higher inflation in the 1970s than elsewhere. The shift of macroeconomic policy from maintaining employment to combating inflation was almost complete after the second OPEC rise in 1979. On this interpretation of events, there was no need to raise the question whether macroeconomic policy could still work to expand output, since everyone was using it in a contractionary manner, to bring down inflation.

The 1980s recession was, in many countries, the deepest since the war. Though recovery began at various dates, the average growth of OECD output and productivity in the 1980s showed little change from 1973–9. In total output, some countries did better than average, notably Japan, the United States, and Britain.[1] Fiscal policy contributed significantly to the former two, but not in Britain. The main leader of recovery there was consumers' expenditure, assisted, especially in the later years, by a large increase in consumer credit, including mortgage borrowing. Fixed investment also increased in the later stages. By mid-1988, Britain was beginning to show classic pre-Stop symptoms, increasing inflation and emergent deficit in the balance of payments on current account. The question whether the payments deficit mattered in itself is postponed to Part 4 on the International Dimension: here we treat it simply in its role as safety valve for inflationary pressures. Nor do we wish to get involved in the details of how the economy got into the Stop situation. We confine ourselves to a few reflections.

Firstly, many commentators saw the situation at the end of the 1980s as simply one of excess demand, expressing itself in rising prices of domestic output, and partly spilling over into rising imports and a balance-of-payments deficit. If that was all, the remedy in the short run would be equally simple: cut demand. The implication for the domestic economy would be that, either because of shortage of capacity, or because of tightness in important parts of the labour market, demand has to be restrained when unemployment is not far below two million. It would not have got as low as it did if demand had not been allowed to run away. If capacity was the bottleneck, then the sooner it could be increased, the better. From this point of view, interest rates are not the best instrument to reduce demand, since they particularly discourage investment. Tax increases would be better. Direct taxes do not raise costs, but they can only conveniently be changed at annual intervals. VAT could be changed at shorter notice, and is probably speedier and more certain in its effects than interest rates, but its effects on costs is immediate, as was apparent in 1979. In this respect both VAT and interest rates have the dis-advantage of giving apparently contradictory signals to the public, for the instruments intended to bring down aggregate demand and inflation in the medium term have the immediate effect of putting up the index conventionally used to measure inflation – the retail price index – the former through all items subject to VAT, and the latter through the mortgage interest item in the RPI. There is no technical difficulty in constructing an index to exclude such effects: the Treasury already publishes figures for the RPI, excluding the effect of mortgages. But the problem is not technical; it would lie in persuading wage bargainers to switch from the one they know to a new index, especially at a time when they think the outcome of any negotiation will be a lower nominal wage. Other things being equal, interest rate increases raise the exchange rate and, if the effect is expected to last, this reduces import prices. Indeed, this route to lowering inflation may be more certain than the route via reduced aggregate demand. But it will also have an unfavourable effect on the trade balance, an issue we take up later.

In the approach we have just been considering, inflation is a matter of aggregate demand in relation to a supply of output which becomes less elastic as unemployment falls. This may be part of the story. But there is another, which we looked at at some length in Part 2, namely cost inflation and the wage–price spiral. What was really worrying in the mid-1980s was that while the annual rate of increase of earnings had come down quite quickly from the heights of over 20 per cent in 1980 to around 7½ per cent in 1983, it got stuck at that rate thereafter, notwith-standing high unemployment, which was to go on rising for another three years. Moreover, no sooner had unemployment passed its peak of over 3.2 millions in 1986, when it could hardly be said that any rise in aggregate demand was excessive, the annual increase in earnings began to creep up, passing 9 per cent in 1989. The effect on costs was, of course, smaller so long as productivity was rising. But it has been a feature of Stops in the past that productivity growth slows down and costs jump up correspond-ingly. This appears to have happened again in 1989. The question is whether a gradual squeeze on the economy, which will keep output growth below trend for a year or two, will suffice to reverse the increase in earnings, or will we experience one or more rounds of high wage increases, high cost increases, and so on. In that case will another 1981-type recession be required to break the wage–price spiral?

One way out of the dilemma would be to set up an incomes policy framework, starting off, perhaps, with a moratorium on wage and price increases in order to give a jolt to expectations. Some have seen joining the European Exchange Rate Mechanism as having a similar salutary effect. The argument is that the commitment to maintain the exchange rate of sterling with other European currencies, especially the D-mark, within a narrow band would force wage-setters, employers and trade unions alike to reappraise their positions fundamentally, for they would realise that excessive wage and cost increases would now drive firms out of business and workers out of jobs. However firms and workers engaged in exports, or directly competitive with imports, are not the majority, and it may be doubted whether wage-setting in High Street banks, retail distribution or local government would be much influenced by exchange rates. If joining ERM did succeed in bringing Britain into line with the rest of the Community, well and good. But what if it did not? Once financial markets come to believe that sterling will in fact stay within a narrow band of fluctuation against other European currencies, large movements of interest rates will be precluded, such movements as do occur being confined to keeping sterling within the ERM range. Interest rates will no longer be available to reduce, or for that matter to revive, aggregate demand. If, indeed, the situation was one of excess demand, the best way to reduce it would be to raise income tax, which does not have the disadvantage of putting prices up.

THE SUPPLY SIDE

The idea that there could be circumstances in which the best policy was to raise income tax goes against the supply-side doctrines which have influenced both the United States' and British governments in the 1980s. High income taxes, it was argued, reduce the incentives to save and to work. The claims of the supply-siders in the United States were, perhaps, the more extravagant, and certainly President Reagan believed that the way to reduce the Budget deficit was to cut taxes. In this country, the claims were more moderate but still definite. The Medium Term Financial Strategy statement of 1980 spoke of the government's intention 'to strengthen the supply side of the economy, by tax and other incentives and by improving the working of the market mechanism'. Sir Terence Burns (1988), the government's Chief Economic Adviser, believed that lower income tax was an important factor in better performance, but acknowledged that there was no hard evidence to this effect.

During the ten years from 1978/9 to 1988/9 the share of income tax in total taxation came down from 45.9 to 34.8 per cent, while that of VAT went up from 12.0 per cent to 21.9 per cent. The reductions in income tax took the form of eliminating all progressivity beyond 40 per cent, with successive reductions in the standard rate, bringing it down to 25 per cent. There are few serious advocates of the very high marginal rates of over 80 per cent at the top end of the scale, which prevailed throughout the postwar period: their main incentive was towards tax avoidance. In his Presidential Address to the American Economic Association, Pechman (1990) noted that, as long ago as 1938, Simons had argued in favour of a broad-based income tax, with a graduated rate schedule, rising to a maximum of 50 per cent, and he added that: 'Curiously, the world appears to be moving towards a consensus on the Simons' view ...' As regards the incentive effects of income tax, Pechman observed that: 'The reduction in the personal saving rate in the United States in the 1980s confounded most economists, in view of the reductions in marginal rates ...' British income-tax payers, whose personal saving ratio was steeply falling during the 1980s, appear to have been equally unresponsive to the incentive of tax reductions. As regards work, Pechman observed that: 'Historical trends in US labor supply are not consistent with the finding that taxes have reduced work effort'. Attempts to measure the incentive effects of income tax are, of course, difficult, because the income effects and substitution effects work in opposite directions. Certainly, no convincing evidence of any significant work-incentive effect has been found in Britain, although a good case can be made for trying to get rid of the very high marginal rates of income tax and national insurance contributions, of 80 per cent or more, which can be found at the bottom end of the income scale. Our conclusion is that the supply-side argument should not preclude higher direct taxes, should the state of the economy require the restraint of aggregate demand.

THE POLITICAL ECONOMY OF ELECTIONS

Besides running the country democratic governments wish to get themselves re-elected. They will try to avoid unpopular decisions in the run-up to elections, preferring to store them up for the months after the election when they can either take them themselves, or else leave them for the opposition in the event of their losing the election. That there is scope for manipulation of the timing of prosperous Goes and corrective Stops is partly the consequence of uncertainty. Knowledge of how the economy works is incomplete, forecasts are fallible, and one can never be sure when expansionary or contractionary changes in instruments will take effect. As a counter to these uncertainties, there is the advantage that, under the British constitution, the Prime Minister of the day can choose the date of the general election at quite short notice within a period which normally could well be more than a year. An early example of the influence of electoral considerations on macroeconomic policy was the sequence of events in 1955. In February of that year, bank rate was raised and credit controls were tightened, with a view to taking pressure off the balance of payments. In the April Budget, nevertheless, the standard rate of income tax was reduced. In the General Election in May, the Conservative government was returned with an increased majority. Then, in October, a second budget was brought in, raising profits tax and the (indirect) Purchase Tax by amounts which almost cancelled out the revenue lost from the income-tax cut in April.[2] It is not always easy to establish whether a particular Budget was influenced by non-economic factors. Thus Roy Jenkins' Budget of 1970 was widely criticised by Labour supporters for being insufficiently reflationary, while some Conservative critics accused him of 'letting wages rip'.[3]

Other than causing pain to high-minded economists who think it is not cricket, does the electoral manipulation of macroeconomic policy matter? The answer turns first on whether the average performance of any variable over a period is the same as it would have been but for the change in timing. If the pre-electoral Goes cause adverse movements in the balance of payments, for instance, which are easily reversed when the election is passed, all may be well. But if the Goes start up a cumulative process, for instance, of inflation, which requires a prolonged recession to reverse, a non-partisan observer would criticise pre-electoral manipulation. The second issue is whereabouts the average of Goes and Stops lies in relation to the steady potential which is feasible. In his famous essay on the *Political Aspects of Full Employment*, Kalecki (1943) was somewhat pessimistic on this score. If full employment were to be maintained permanently, by the kinds of method he was himself to expound a year later (Kalecki, 1944), the discipline of the sack would be removed, and workers might put forward increasing demands which capitalists would be unwilling or unable to meet. Consequently, between elections, unemployment would be allowed to rise to restore industrial discipline and only at election times would governments yield to pressures to follow full employment policies.

So far as Britain was concerned Kalecki's prophecy appeared to be falsified. The first test came at the end of the postwar reconstruction period, when Labour was replaced by a Conservative government in 1951. It is true that, for a brief spell, there was some unemployment, associated with the switch to rearmament in the Korean War, but it did not last long. Within a year or two, it became apparent that the Conservative government was going to follow policies which would keep unemployment very low. A case could be made that in the quarter century after the war, Keynesian macroeconomic policies were as willingly adopted by Conservative as by Labour Chancellors, if not more so. If true, this ought not to cause too much surprise. Outside macroeconomic questions Keynes did not have radical prescriptions: in deciding what should be produced, as distinct from how much, he found private markets generally adequate, albeit he did advocate a 'somewhat comprehensive socialisation of investment'. Full employment was a programme to make capitalism work better, not to undermine it, or destroy it.

The bi-partisan agreement on objectives was not confined to the use of the budget for employment. It extended to planning for faster growth and incomes policy. Planning is often associated with the 1964 Labour government and the National Plan, and incomes policy with the National Board for Prices and Incomes. But in both cases the seeds had been sown by the preceding Conservative government, which established in 1962 the National Economic Development Council, with a remit to study measures to improve the longer-term growth rate, and the National Incomes Commission. After 1964, there began a period in which Labour and Conservative governments alternated at shorter intervals of between four and seven years. Given the apparent similarity of economic aims, the modern student may be surprised by the sharp changes in direction which occurred between administrations. The most conspicuous case was incomes policy, in which each incoming government swept away the machinery of its predecessor, only to set up new machinery of its own, which was duly dismantled after the next election, and so on. Some will justify Box and Cox in economic policy as a necessary price to be paid for political democracy. But it does not strike one as a very sensible procedure. Some see the solution of the problem in some version of proportional representation to replace the present single member, first past the post, electoral system, which can throw up alternative governments with radically different policies on the basis of quite small swings in the overall vote. Others believe that constitutional changes are needed to prevent the emergence of an 'elective dictatorship', which the present system allows.

While it is still possible to regard the alternations of economic policy following government changes in elections up to 1974 as differences in degree, the change in 1979 looks like a difference in kind. Incomes policy was to go, and did, except for the public sector where the government was the employer. NEDO was kept alive, but only just. The direct objectives of macroeconomic policy were reduced to the single aim of bringing down inflation, by means of one instrument – the money supply – with fiscal policy entirely subordinate. It was expected that the process would take time, as indicated by the emphasis on the medium term. As political events were to transpire, the government was twice re-elected, so that there were to be over ten years to give the method of economic management a chance to show its paces. In the form originally presented, the method did not succeed. The inflation objective has not been achieved, the sustainability of the growth of output and employment has been put in question, while the control instrument of the new policy – the gradual reduction of the money supply – has long been abandoned, in favour of the discretionary manipulation of interest rates. There has been an intellectual gain. The argument that there was an effective monetarist way to get rid of inflation has been tried out in practice. At some considerable cost to all those unemployed in the 1980s, we should all be wiser. But the failure of the monetarist experiment has left a vacuum at the centre of policy formation. There is an urgent need for a new statement of economic policy aims which could receive support across the political spectrum. This would undoubtedly be hard for the present government, not merely because it would mean admitting some error on their own part, but also retracting some of their comprehensive dismissal of all their predecessors. If we turn to the Labour Party, we find many things which might receive widespread support, but on the central issue of how to control inflation, there is an ominous silence. Again, the reticence is understandable. It was over the issue of incomes policy that the last Labour government was brought down by the Winter of Discontent, and it is a question that Labour politicians would rather not talk about. It would indeed be comic, were its implications not so serious, that it is hard to imagine a rational conversation on the subject of wages and prices between Treasury ministers and their opposition shadows.

A possible way out of this difficulty would be to set up a Council of Economic Advisers, which would report to the public rather than just to the Chancellor of the Exchequer. It could be given, as a routine task, much of what is already done inside the Treasury, preparing regular analyses and forecasts of the likely trends in the economy, as well as studies of particular questions, for example, the pros and cons of alternative exchange rate regimes. Its first job would be to cover all of macroeconomic policy, which we have discussed in previous chapters, as well as issues of international economic policy, which we have yet to consider in Part 4. Consideration should be given to extending its remit in two directions. The first is the range of factors bearing on future economic growth, such as research and development, vocational training, industrial structure and so on, the kinds of questions, in short, which NEDO deals with. The second concerns environmental issues, an area in which there is a body of economics familiar to economists but not to the general public. These are both areas in which the government of the day needs research done and advice given, but in which the public also needs to be informed. It is not being suggested that government be obliged to follow the recommendations of the Council. It would, as it already does with reports of Parliamentary Committees, indicate the extent to which it accepts the analyses and recommendations of the Council. The secretariat of the Council would be civil servants, permanent or temporary. The members of the Council itself would be economists, some academic and some with experience in industry, finance, government or international organisations.

There is the difficult question whether membership of the Council would change with a change in administration, on the American model, or be appointed in such a way that clean sweeps at elections would be avoided, for example, for six years at a time. My own preference is for the latter. The postwar economic policy consensus was not created from scratch. It emerged from the shared experience of the politicians in the wartime coalition, and of administrators, including many academics brought in during the war, coinciding with the Keynesian revolution in economics. One senses that the public is becoming disenchanted with conviction policies, and would prefer a consensus. Whether a new consensus can be constructed remains to be seen.

PART 4

THE INTERNATIONAL DIMENSION

16

THEORY AND INSTITUTIONS

In Part 3, notwithstanding occasional excursions abroad, we were essentially considering a closed economy and all the conclusions reached about the scope for policy were provisional. We must now deal explicitly with the various linkages between the British economy and the rest of the world. First of all there is the way in which changes abroad impinge on the British economy and, in particular, on employment. Then there is the fact that Britain is party to agreements with other countries, as well as being a member of a number of international economic organisations whose decisions affect the British economy. Do these agreements, and the international framework within which the economy operates, improve, or worsen, the prospects for employment? In particular, can such prospects be improved by the coordination of the economic policies of groups of countries? These are complex and difficult questions. This is partly because, just as we found in the macroeconomics of a closed economy, there are doctrinal differences. But it is also because judgements about policy are closely bound up with the particular institutional setting at the time. To give but one example: when the Bretton Woods monetary system of fixed, but adjustable, exchange rates was in operation, it was generally accepted that, as an act of policy an adjustment of the exchange rate could help resolve conflicts between the domestic and external balances of the economy. But, in the era of floating rates which followed, question marks were placed both against the ability of governments to alter the course of exchange rates and, supposing that they could, the assistance, if any, such alteration would give to resolving conflicts between internal and external balance.

In the first part of this chapter we begin with a general account of external linkages: the migration of labour; the movement of capital; the foreign exchange rate; and the movement of goods and services. In the second part we provide a brief historical sketch of the postwar years, cutting it up into periods chosen to bring out the connection between institutions and the dominant ideas about policy. Then, in the following chapter, we will consider the impact of openness upon employment prospects, starting with the existing institutional framework, but looking also at alternatives, notably 'going it alone' and participating in various forms of international cooperation. We continue in this vein in the following chapter which focuses on the European dimension.

THEORETICAL CONSIDERATIONS

Migration

Throughout history there have been migrations of people seeking land and a better living, or escaping from oppression. In the nineteenth century the industrial development of Europe greatly increased the demand for labour, but populations grew faster still and emigration to the Americas, to Australia and to a lesser extent to Africa and Asia was a characteristic feature which continued into the early decades of the twentieth century. But in the present century the natural growth of population in Europe has everywhere slowed down, while at the same time the newly developing countries have matured and increasingly restricted immigration.

After the Second World War the emigration from most European countries ceased and with the very high demand for labour the employment of foreign workers was encouraged. Table 16.1 shows recent figures for the three largest economies in Europe. Some smaller countries, such as Switzerland, have had even higher proportions of foreign workers.

In Britain, net emigration was still averaging around 50,000 a year in the early part of this century, but in the 1930s the movement was reversed by the influx of refugees from Nazism. After the war, the balance of migration continued to be inwards, with large contingents arriving from the West Indies and later from India, Pakistan, and Africa. But restrictions on this flow were tightened and, by the 1980s, net migration had become very small. In the years 1980–6 an average annual outflow of 208,000 was almost offset by an inflow of 202,000. And, while barriers to movement within the European Community have been coming down, the

Table 16.1. *Foreign employees as a percentage of total employees in employment*

	France	Germany	United Kingdom
1975	11.2	10.0	3.5
1980	6.9	9.4	4.1
1985	7.0	7.0	3.8

Source: Eurostat

average annual inflow into Britain of 25,000 was exactly balanced by an outflow of the same size.

The economic consequences of migration depend not only on the number of migrants, but also on their attributes. An immigrant who arrives penniless, speaks no English and possesses no skills, will, in one way or another, make calls on resources to feed and house him. In times of acute labour shortage, he may find low-paid employment in an unskilled job. But, if there is already considerable unemployment, he may just add one to the total. An immigrant who is highly qualified and brings with him capital enabling him to buy or build a house is likely to raise productivity and, indirectly, raise employment. Similar considerations apply to emigration.

At the time when there was considerable immigration from the New Commonwealth in the 1950s and 1960s, those from India and Pakistan were more likely to bring capital than those from the West Indies and were more likely to provide a stimulus to investment. But in neither case was there a threat to employment, since the demand for labour was high throughout these decades. Indeed, many of the immigrants from the West Indies were recruited by enterprising firms and bus companies to fill jobs left vacant by the indigenous labour force.

Zero *net* migration does not mean that there could be no effects on productivity and employment. If, for instance, the emigrants were all highly qualified and took their private capital with them, while the immigrants were all unskilled, with little capital, the effects might be disadvantageous. But it may be doubted whether the two-way movement so far has been lopsided on this scale. Moreover the *gross* annual flows have recently constituted less than 1 per cent of the labour force and, were this to continue, we do not think it would be necessary to take migration explicitly into account. However, the virtually zero *net* balance may not persist.

Legal obstacles to movement within the European Community have been coming down and, by 1992, a citizen of any EC country will have the right to work and to reside in any other. Emigration from the United Kingdom is likely to continue to be limited by British reluctance to speak other languages but this particular barrier is much lower the other way, as English has become more and more the common language. Lower British real incomes may deter immigrants from France, Germany and the Netherlands, but there could be some increase from the poorer parts of the extended Community. Conceivably, there might also be some overspill from the renewed movement from East Germany to West Germany, since the destruction of the Berlin Wall. The movement, so far, is not on the scale which followed the Second World War. In 1953, 22 per cent of the resident population of West Germany were 'incomers', $8\frac{1}{2}$

million 'expelled persons' from all parts, and over two million refugees
from the newly established GDR. With the aid of a massive building
programme, West Germany succeeded in absorbing this huge immigration, although unemployment was not eliminated until the mid-1950s.
The West German authorities are clearly anxious for the GDR emigration to stop, in order to avert a complete collapse of that country's
economy. Nor, one imagines, would they discourage those who have
already arrived from moving further on. That may turn on whether these
new incomers acquire EC citizenship. The great postwar wave of
displaced persons and refugees had largely spent its force by the time it
reached the English Channel, and British immigration was comparatively small and short-lived. Taking into account that unemployment in Britain is much higher than it was in the late 1940s, it does not
seem likely that any large new influx should be expected from this source.

We already know that 50,000 entry permits are to be given to British
passport holders in Hong Kong, but we also know that the purpose is to
enable the people concerned to stay in Hong Kong until at least 1997. But
much may happen in the next few years and it may be that, eventually,
some hundreds of thousands will find their way here. A similar question
mark stands against holders of British passports in South Africa, who
might, at some point, wish to exercise their present right to reside in this
country, because they are not prepared to put up with whatever new
constitution emerges from negotiations which are expected to begin quite
soon.

Thus, if the zero *net* balance we have described is to alter, it is likely to
be in the direction of larger immigration into this country, in circumstances where, with the possible exception of the Germans, the initial
consideration will be political rather than economic. Many of the
immigrants from Hong Kong and South Africa would bring capital with
them, if it were not confiscated on the way: some from the former have
already started to acquire assets in this country. And one would expect
the *average* level of qualification and skill to be above the average level
already here. These are circumstances which are favourable to increasing
employment, at least to match the immigration, if not to surpass it. There
are so many unknown factors that it is not possible to say more than that.

The movement of capital

The migration of people is comparatively straightforward, but the
movement of capital can take many forms. Physical assets can be
transferred from one country to another: furniture and pictures are
examples, and the old London Bridge was shipped, stone by stone, to
Arizona. The more common case, from the economist's point of view, is
where the assets stay put, but their ownership is transferred from a

British household or firm to a foreign household or firm, or *vice versa*. One vehicle for such a change of ownership is the purchase or sale of company shares. The asset may be purely financial, for example, a bond or treasury bill, a bank deposit or even bank notes. Also coming under the heading of the movement of capital is the case where a British firm undertakes direct investment abroad, for example, the building of a new factory, or office: or a foreigner sets up a plant in Britain. The motives for the movement of capital may be primarily financial as, for instance, a British pension fund buying shares or bonds in the United States or Germany because it hopes to get a higher or safer return than from British shares. In the case of direct investment wider industrial and commercial considerations may come into the picture. The British company may locate a subsidiary production unit in Belgium, because it has closer access to the intended market for its products than if it exported them from a British factory. A large multinational may be influenced in its choice of location, by the availability of particular materials or of labour.

Most movements of capital involve an exchange of currencies. To buy shares in an American company, dollars must usually be acquired, though if the present owner is already British, a buyer could pay in sterling and no crossing of the exchanges would be needed. Similarly, with direct investment, the parent British company might need to use pounds to buy dollars to pay for the construction of a plant in the United States, or it might finance the new investment out of its profits, which are already in dollars. Nevertheless, even in cases where no immediate exchange of currencies is required, present and expected future rates of exchange will be important background factors influencing the investment decision.

Our primary concern is with the impact on employment of different kinds of capital movement. Take, first, the case of direct investment. A common view is that such investment abroad will make jobs for foreigners, both to build and work the plant, while investment at home makes jobs for us. There is one case where the first part of the above statement could well be true, namely, when a developed country invests in industrial plant in a hitherto underdeveloped country. The likelihood in such cases is that the financial investment will be accompanied by management and qualified labour, to build and run a railway or a textile mill, which could not be undertaken by the underdeveloped country out of its own resources. In this case the investment creates jobs for foreigners. But it does not necessarily follow that these jobs will be at the expense of jobs at home. A developed country may generate savings more than sufficient to cover its own investment, and have a surplus for investment abroad. At the same time, the case where overseas investment crowds out domestic investment is not inconceivable. This might not affect employment so much as the future productivity of the domestic labour force. Some economists have taken the view that the great surge of British overseas investment at the end of the nineteenth century had adverse effects on the growth of productivity in British industry. In a recent survey of British manufacturing investment overseas, Shepherd, Silberston and Strange (1985) sent questionnaires and visited a small sample of firms. Several of them reported that, had they not invested abroad, they might have been able to sell exports from their home factory instead, but only on a much smaller scale – 10 to 20 per cent of the production of the overseas plant. Thus, in the absence of the overseas investment, there might have been some small compensating increase of investment and employment at home, though the authors reckoned this effect would only be temporary, even in the absence of full employment. Presumably, this small effect would have further reduced, to the extent that there was inward direct investment of foreign firms in Britain.[1]

Even if one has qualms about the unfavourable effect on employment of net overseas direct investment, the remedy does not lie in attempting to interfere with that flow. We wrote above as though direct investment consisted of a British firm setting up a plant abroad to make much the same things that it already makes at home – the object being to get nearer the market, or behind a tariff barrier. Such cases exist. But there are also cases where the plants in different countries form part of an integrated production plan of a single parent company, with different plants specialising in different components which they exchange with one another. What governments can do is to create conditions favourable to investment generally, whether undertaken by British or foreign firms. This is one of the issues we will discuss later, especially in the context of EC 1992.

Foreign exchange rate

There remains the question whether portfolio investment and, more especially, the movement of short-term funds, can exercise any influence on employment. At first sight, the answer would seem to be no. What difference does it make to employment in Detroit whether shares in General Motors are owned by Americans, Canadians, or Englishmen? But perhaps it is not so simple. In the case of direct investment, the exchange rate will be taken into account, but only as one of a great many factors bearing on the decision whether or not to build a plant of such and such a capacity. But, for short-term capital movements involving the acquisition of short-term bonds, bills, bank deposits or even bank notes, there are only three main factors, the exchange rate and the interest rate in the two countries; their present values, and their expected future movements. If interest rates in London are expected to stay where they are and there is a rise in the United States, it would pay an investor to buy dollars and take the higher United States interest, provided he or she expects the differential to remain over the planning period and *also* that the exchange rate of the dollar against the pound is not expected to fall: otherwise, when the time comes, at the end of the planning period, to buy back pounds, the investor may lose some or all of the intended interest gain. It is not only speculators who are concerned with these matters. They affect every exporter or importer who places an order now, but may have to wait weeks, or even years, before taking delivery and making or receiving payments. In a world of free exchange rates, which go up and down daily, there is scope for specialists to provide 'hedging' facilities to producers and traders. And there is room for pure speculators.

The volume of short-term capital movements across the exchanges between various pairs of currencies is huge, far greater than the amounts which would be needed simply to finance trade in goods and services between countries. This means that, in free exchange markets, and in the absence of intervention by governments, central banks or international banks, fluctuations in exchange rates can be frequent and large. The rate of exchange may often be carried beyond the levels which would be compatible with the requirements of trade and long-term capital movements. The fear is that they may overshoot to such an extent that governments are forced into excessively deflationary policies, to the detriment of employment. Intervention can take two forms. First, there is exchange control. Governments, or central banks acting as their agents, may prohibit or restrict the purchase by their own residents of foreign currencies except for a range of permitted transactions, for example, to buy authorised imports of materials or manufactured goods, or for travel abroad. The restrictions may be confined to capital transfers, leaving current transactions free. The alternative to restricting demand is to supplement supply. The central bank intervenes by buying or selling foreign currencies in order, for instance, to keep the exchange rate at a steady level. For it to use pounds to buy dollars or yen presents no problem. But to use dollars or yen to buy pounds to prevent the exchange rate falling requires that the bank has previously acquired a sufficiently large stock of foreign currencies. Obviously the scope of this kind of intervention is increased if governments agree to support one another, and one of the most important forms of international cooperation we will wish to discuss is where governments agree to intervene in exchange markets so as to confine the movement of any particular rate between upper and lower limits, which could be wide apart or so close as to constitute virtually fixed exchange rates. We need also to discuss whether there is a conflict between the desire of the financial institutions for the maximum freedom of exchange transactions, in order to build up the City of London as a centre of employment, and the needs of industry. And what limits does exchange freedom impose on fiscal policy? If a government were to announce the intention to impose a sizeable tax on wealth, would that lead to a flight of capital, causing the exchange rate to fall steeply?

The movement of goods and services
The benefits to be obtained from trade are often presented in terms of exchanges between pairs of countries. Country A exports those things in the production of which it enjoys a comparative advantage, and imports those things in which country B has a comparative advantage. Such abstract models tell us a good deal about the motivation for trade and, even in the twentieth century, there are practical instances of barter agreements between countries, in which a specified list of goods and services produced by A is to be exchanged for another list of amounts of items produced by B. But such barter arrangements are not the norm for major trading countries today. Employment, as such, does not usually appear in any significant way in the abstract models. It is commonly assumed that each country has its endowment of labour and other factors of production, and it is implied that all the labour is employed in producing something, whether for the home market or for export, and the problem to be solved is the deployment of the given amounts of labour and other factors among different industries in the two countries, so as to get the maximum gain from trade between them.

Employment comes into the picture significantly when we look at exports and imports separately. Starting from an initial position where there is some unemployment in Britain, suppose that the overseas demand for British exports rises. This will give rise to additional British production, and create jobs. There will be a feedback into additional imports of raw materials and semi-finished products to be incorporated in the exports. There will be further multiplier effects on British employment, from the extra spending out of higher incomes generated by the increased exports and, of course, further increases in imports generated by this spending. In this example, the increase in imports will be less than the rise in exports which set things going and the balance of trade will increase. Suppose instead that, starting from the same initial position, the increase in demand originated in Britain from, let us say, an increase in private or public investment, financed by borrowing. This will create jobs, and there will be additional multiplier effects on employment: but there will also be additional imports, to supply materials and semi-finished products for the investment, as well as for the additional output induced by the multiplier. This time, total imports will increase, with a spillover effect on jobs abroad. As to exports, there may be no effect, unless the rise in investment begins to compete for labour against production for export, or some of the income generated abroad in supplying additional British imports is used to buy imports from Britain. In this example, the balance of trade will decrease, or become negative.

When they are inputs into later stages of production, for example, raw materials, imports are largely complementary with the level of activity in Britain. Not entirely, since British manufacturers may have a choice between overseas and domestic suppliers of inputs, such as steel. In macroeconomic terms we can think of the volume of imports being determined by two principal factors: real national income and the competitiveness of British and foreign suppliers of raw materials and semi-finished products. From the standpoint of a British consumer, it is competitiveness of British and foreign suppliers of finished goods which appears to dominate, though changes in the real income of consumers are likely to affect imports as well as domestic production. Similar factors influence the volume of British exports. If principal trading partners experience growth of real income, it is likely that British exports will rise correspondingly. At the same time, at any given level of real income abroad, there will be competition between British and other exporters, as well as domestic producers in overseas markets. In the 1950s the ratios of imports and exports to total final expenditure (GDP *plus* imports) were both rather less than one fifth: the ratios fell a little in the 1960s, but since then they have risen again and in the 1980s were both near to 21 per cent. These are ratios of values and so are affected both by changes in relative volumes of domestic output and trade, but also by relative prices at home and in traded goods. The fall in the import ratio in the 1960s was influenced by the exceptionally low relative prices of commodities. But the upward trend in the ratios reflects increasing openness, the consequence of the removal or lowering of barriers to trade.

The classical model was about the exchange of exports for imports. The question of their balance never arose: implicitly it was zero. But when exports and imports are looked at separately, the outcome of a myriad of independent decisions of households and firms, at home and abroad, the balance comes into its own. From what we have said so far, it will depend on world trade, domestic output, or employment, and the international competitiveness of British producers with their overseas counterparts. If we suppose, first, that competitiveness does not change, we can set up a model of exports and imports that brings out some of the main issues. In this model, exports are determined by world trade, while imports depend on total domestic expenditure, or GDP. When world trade increases by 1 per cent, we suppose that British exports will grow by e per cent: e is the world trade elasticity of exports. Similarly, when British GDP goes up by

1 per cent, imports rise by m per cent: m is the GDP elasticity of imports. If world trade is rising by q per cent a year, exports will be growing at an annual rate of eq per cent. Similarly, if British output grows at r per cent per annum, imports will grow by mr per cent per annum. If we start from a year in which imports and exports are already in balance, it follows that if the balance is to remain zero, $mr = eq$, or $r = q \times e/m$.

From this simple equation, a number of interesting results follow. If e and m remain constant, then $r = kq$, where k is a constant equal to the ratio of the two elasticities. If k is greater than one, British GDP must rise faster than world trade to keep balance: if it does not, a rising surplus in the balance of trade will emerge. If k is less than one, British growth must be slower than world trade: otherwise a growing deficit will appear. We set the model up in terms of British GDP and world trade. We could have used other variables, such as world GDP; or the world could be narrowed to those countries which had a substantial trade with Britain. The choice of variable depends on three factors: does it make any sense, are there data to measure it, is there, in fact, a good fit?

The first conclusion then is that, if e and m are constant and trade has to balance, in the long term the British growth rate has to conform to the rest of the world and, if k is less than one, the British growth rate may have to be low. In the shorter run, this means either slower productivity growth, or rising unemployment. Our initial assumption was unchanged competitiveness, and to escape from the trap of slow growth or unemployment it is necessary to improve the competitiveness of British producers, so that they will sell more exports and, at any given level of demand, sell more British goods in substitution for items hitherto imported. Improving competitiveness means lowering relative prices,[2] and this can be achieved by taking lower profits, paying lower wages, or improving efficiency. Assuming that all that is feasible in these directions has been done, there remains the lowering of the exchange rate – either altering the parity in a regime of otherwise fixed rates, or allowing a floating rate to fall. What both these routes end up with is offering a lower price than before in overseas markets, while in the domestic market it is the price of the foreign supplier which is raised by the exchange rate change. What the ultimate effect of lower British prices will be on the trade balance depends on many factors. On the export side, allowing for quality, their lower price should increase the volume of sales, so long as there is spare capacity to produce the extra output. The revenue from export sales is likely to fall initially, as the price fall comes in at once, while it takes time for the volume of sales to grow. On the other side of the account, some imports are complementary to British GDP and their cost will rise at once, of which more in a moment. The sterling price of other imports will rise, and should choke off demand, provided there is British capacity available to produce substitutes. In this case, the sterling outlay on imports will rise at once, but will gradually fall back to the extent that home production is able to substitute for goods previously imported. In the short run then, the trade balance of the value of exports *minus* the value of imports will deteriorate, but will start to improve again once the volume effects begin to come through, with an eventual improvement, which will be larger the larger are the price elasticities of supply and demand for British exports and import substitutes. These price elasticities may be high for homogeneous products, such as oil, and lower for manufactures where product differentiation is extensive. However, this account is incomplete for the case of a fall in the exchange rate. We noticed that there would be an immediate rise in import prices and, if nominal wages remained unchanged, real wages would fall. If wage earners pressed for and secured higher nominal wages in an attempt to restore their real wage, they would start a process which would only end when the British wage and price level had risen fully to offset the initial fall in the exchange rate, thus eliminating the competitive advantage gained. Whether, and how quickly, the competitive advantage would be eroded in this manner is a question of fact and may well vary between different countries and at different times. We shall have occasion to return to this question.

The policy implications of the classical model are usually that free trade is best. It is, of course, acknowledged that a tariff or other protection can secure more employment in the protected industry. But it does not increase total employment, since the model assumes that all labour is employed on something. What it does do is to divert employment into the protected industry, but only at the expense of a loss of real income to consumers. There is, it is true, a valid argument that one country can improve its terms of trade (the relative prices of exports and imports) by the imposition of an appropriate general tariff. But the country only gains so long as trading partners do not retaliate.

A quite different argument for protection emerges when it appears that balance between exports and imports can only be secured at a low level of activity with considerable unemployment. Any increase of imports would mean a loss of reserves, which would require deflationary measures to bring them down again. There is the alternative route of attempting to achieve balance by improving competitiveness, by lowering wages or by devaluation. However, if the trade elasticities are very low, neither method might be effective. Moreover, devaluation might be followed by a wage–price spiral, nullifying any gains. These difficulties might be avoided by imposing tariffs, or other restrictions on imports with the object of reducing the propensity to import, that is the amount of imports brought in at any given level of domestic expenditure or output. In this way, an increase in domestic output and employment could be achieved, which would offset the reduced import propensity, leaving the absolute amount of imports unchanged. Thus trading partners should have no valid grounds for retaliation.

CHANGING INSTITUTIONS

During the twentieth century, there have been oscillations in the degree of freedom of migration and trade in the wider world and, more specifically, in the degree of openness of the British economy and the extent of government regulation of overseas transactions of all kinds. At the beginning of the century, there existed the rudiments of a world economic system, with Britain the largest trading economy and London the major financial centre. Britain put no barriers in the way of imports, nor of the migration of people and, more especially, capital throughout the world. There were still many countries giving protection to their own industries, by tariffs and other means. But the overall tendency at the turn of the century was towards a freer system of trade and payments, in which also movements of people and capital would be increasingly free. This tendency was twice interrupted by world wars. In the first case, it looked as though the interruption might only be temporary. By the mid-1920s the runaway inflations of Germany and Central Europe had been overcome and the gold standard had been restored throughout the greater part of the world. It seemed that the World Economic Conference in 1927 had checked any tendency for tariffs to increase. The world economy was back on the rails leading to economic liberalism. But within a very short time the whole system had broken down. The prime cause was the prolonged depression in the United States. Between 1929 and 1932, United States industrial production fell nearly 50 per cent and with it the volume of imports by 40 per cent. Equally important was the virtual cessation of United States lending, especially to European economies recovering from the war. The supply of freely available dollars was cut by over three-quarters. The threat to the reserves of gold standard countries was immediate. Some, like Britain, were driven off gold. Others resorted to drastic import restrictions. We need not embark on any detailed account of the fragmented trade and payments arrangements which were made in the 1930s, for the world system was still in disarray when the Second World War broke out. One comment only needs to be made about this period. Some economists have suggested that protection was a principal cause of the prolonged unemployment of the 1930s. However, in the main, the wave of import restrictions, preference agreements, bilateral agreements and exchange controls of the 1930s was a response to depression and not the cause of it.[3] The volume of world trade in 1937 was still nearly one quarter below the level of 1929 and it was not until 1950 that the peak level of 1929 was to be surpassed. Meanwhile, during the war, the volume of trade was to fall still further and the many restrictions already in existence in 1939 were intensified and extended.

When the war ended, the victorious allies set about establishing a liberal world economy of free multilateral trade and payments. On the monetary plane, this process was to be assisted by the International Monetary Fund, and there was to have been a complementary International Trade Organisation. In the event, the former was set up but the latter was restricted to the General Agreement on Tariffs and Trade (GATT), an organisation which has supervised a succession of rounds of negotiation for the simultaneous reduction of tariffs and other departures from free trade. In retrospect, the period from 1945 until the early 1970s can be seen as a fairly steady movement along the road from the tight controls of the immediate postwar years towards a liberal trading system and we can take advantage of this historical trend to examine, one by one, the impact of different aspects of openness on employment. During this period the Bretton Woods (IMF) system of fixed, but adjustable, exchange rates was in operation. That system broke down finally in 1972, and was superseded by floating exchange rates. In the years since then unemployment has re-emerged on a considerable scale, at times comparable with the 1930s. There has been a further liberalisation of capital movements throughout the world, but there have also emerged massive problems of international indebtedness, as well as persistent deficits and surpluses in current balances. There has also been a resurgence of protectionism, very often in disguised forms.

1945–52: Reconstruction
For several years after the war, there was excess demand for British goods at home and in most export markets. Britain had sold many of its overseas assets to pay for the war, so that in future it could no longer rely on income from them to pay for a sizeable fraction of imports: exports would have to rise to close the gap. For many years the limit to exports was supply and priority was given to them by controls and rationing which kept down domestic consumption. Unemployment was low throughout. Convertibility of sterling was restored in 1947, as a condition of the United States Loan Agreement, but the reserves were quickly drained and convertibility abandoned after five weeks. This experience demonstrated that at ruling relative price levels, British markets in traded goods were still far from balance. Sterling was devalued in 1949. The rate against the dollar was reduced from 4.02 to 2.80, a fall of 30 per cent. But at, or near, this time, most of the rest of the world also adjusted their parities with the dollar and the trade-weighted devaluation of sterling

was only about 9 per cent (Cairncross, 1985, p. 209). From the mid-1950s to the mid-1960s an index of the unit values of world exports of manufactures rose at an annual rate of less than 1 per cent, while United Kingdom export prices edged up at about 1 per cent per annum faster. It seems that, following the rise and fall of prices across the Korean War, the 1949 devaluation had left United Kingdom export prices highly competitive: in the later 1950s and the early 1960s, United Kingdom export prices were about right: they then began to be over-priced.[4]

Setting the people free: the 1950s
During the 1950s, many physical controls, such as the quantitative allocation of steel, were wound up and, where government regulation remained, it tended to be financial rather than physical. If government wished to hold back domestic car sales, it used purchase tax, or hire purchase restrictions, rather than steel allocations. A similar process of decontrol occurred with imports. Exchange control remained in force, though it became gradually easier to obtain foreign exchange. Full convertibility for current transactions was reached in 1958. There was not the complete freedom of markets for goods and services such as existed in the 1980s, but there was significant movement in that direction. The first instance of demand, rather than supply, being a limiting factor for exports was in textiles in the mild recession following the Korean War.

While exports and imports became increasingly a matter of demand, supply and price, this did not apply to capital transactions. Tight exchange control still operated, requiring British residents, for example, to secure official approval to obtain funds to finance overseas investment. The frontier of exchange control, however, was the whole sterling area, and not just the United Kingdom. When reserves were lost, this could have been caused by a deficit in the United Kingdom current account: but it could equally have been caused by a deficit elsewhere, Australia, for instance, and there were intermittent grumbles that British belts were being tightened to permit excessive Australian investment. Whatever the specific origin of a sterling crisis, remedial action was usually concentrated on the United Kingdom economy. There was usually a package of measures, which might include raising bank rate, imposing a ceiling on bank advances, stiffening hire purchase restrictions, cuts in public investment and suspension of investment allowances to private firms. Normally, the package did not include tax increases in the 1950s, but in the budget of 1960 powers were taken to vary most indirect taxes by 10 per cent, up or down, at any time – the Regulator.[5] The Regulator was used for the first time in the following year. The government also replenished the reserves, on occasion, by making use of its drawing rights in the International Monetary Fund. These packages stopped the drain on reserves; but they also stopped the economy. For a while the growth of output slowed right down, or in one case became briefly negative. After a sufficient period of Stop, the deflationary package was removed, taxes might be cut in a subsequent budget and the economy could Go again.

In retrospect, it seems remarkable that in successive Stops, induced by balance-of-payments crises, unemployment never rose by more than an additional percentage point. Fluctuations in employment were much smaller in relation to output than before the war, because, in recessions, employers held on to labour, in anticipation of swift recovery. The exchange rate fixed in 1949 seems to have been well chosen. Nevertheless, though Stops could be succeeded by Goes, the idea gained ground in the later 1950s and early 1960s that the underlying trend in the balance of payments was unfavourable, and there was growing advocacy among economists for devaluation in order to improve competitiveness, an argument strengthened by the apparent success of French devaluations. It also seems remarkable that, although unemployment was generally well below 2 per cent, the average annual inflation was below 4 per cent.

1964–72: The era of devaluation
The possibility of devaluation had already become a live issue when the Labour government was returned in October 1964 with a tiny majority. During 1964, the balance of payments had been moving into deficit at what was then thought to be an alarming rate.[6] The decision was taken at once by the incoming government not to devalue, but to impose a surcharge of 15 per cent on all imports. This measure appeared to do the trick, but by 1967 the current account was moving sharply into deficit again, and in November the parity of sterling in the International Monetary Fund was changed from $2.80 to $2.40, a fall of 14.3 per cent. The central questions much debated at that time, and since, were: to the extent that devaluation gave a competitive edge to British producers, especially manufacturers, in export markets and in the home market competing with imports, how big would the improvement be in the current balance, bearing in mind that to achieve it the volumes of exports and imports would have to change enough to offset the accompanying deterioration in the terms of trade? Secondly, could any competitive advantage be maintained, or would it be eroded by accelerated increases in money wages, in an attempt to offset the worsening of real wages implicit in the devaluation?

On the face of it, the devaluation was a success. From a deficit of 0.75 per cent of GDP in 1967 the current balance moved into a surplus of 1 per cent of GDP in 1969 and nearly 2 per cent in 1971. However, it would be wrong to attribute the whole of this change to devaluation. On the export side, world trade in manufactures was rising exceptionally fast in 1968

Table 16.2. *Percentage change in annual average over preceding year of weekly earnings and various price indices*

	Weekly earnings	RPI	Unit values	
			Imports	Exports
1964	7.1	3.3	4.0	2.0
1965	7.5	4.5	0.0	1.9
1966	6.4	4.2	2.9	3.8
1967	3.3	2.5	−0.9	0.9
1968	8.0	4.7	11.3	8.2
1969	7.8	5.4	4.2	4.2
1970	11.5	6.4	4.1	7.2
1971	11.1	9.5	3.1	8.3

Source: *National Institute Economic Review*, August 1972.

and 1969, between one and a half and two times the previous average rate; and in 1971 unemployment in the United Kingdom by previous standards was exceptionally high, so that actual imports were well below full employment imports. When allowance is made for these and other special factors the pure devaluation effect on the current balance was estimated by the National Institute to be of the order of +1 per cent of GDP, of which one third was contributed by the visible and two thirds by the invisible balance.[7]

What about the expected acceleration of inflation? In table 16.2 we show the annual rate of change of average weekly earnings, the retail price index, and the unit value indices of imports and exports, for the years preceding and following devaluation.

It will be seen that the rates of increase of both earnings and the RPI were exceptionally low between 1966 and 1967. This was undoubtedly the consequence of the wage and price stop imposed in mid-1966 and followed by a very tight prices and incomes policy in 1967. The effect is to exaggerate the jump brought about by devaluation. If we compare the three years 1965–7 with 1968–70, we find that the earnings rise jumped from an average of 5.7 to 9.1 per cent, and the RPI from 3.7 to 5.5 per cent. Thus, although erosion began at once, it would have taken some time, perhaps four or five years, before the competitive edge gained had been completely blunted.

At this time some economists were arguing that devaluation could trigger a virtuous circle of export-propelled growth, whereby the balance of payments surplus would instil confidence in businessmen that a new

Stop was not around the corner; they would raise investment; productivity would rise and costs fall; exports would be further stimulated; and so on and so on. A great leap forward of this kind did not, in fact, occur. The scale of the pure devaluation effect seems to have been too small to have such great consequences.[8] At the same time the message from this period remains that, in a regime of fixed, but adjustable, exchange rates, devaluation was a valid instrument of demand management, though possibly less powerful than some of its advocates had hoped. This was a lesson, however, which before very long had to be put in cold storage, for by 1972 the Bretton Woods system had finally broken down.

1972–9: Floating and inflation
The outstanding features of the period after 1973 until the end of the decade in most industrial countries were high unemployment, high inflation and slow growth of productivity. The last traces of the Bretton Woods adjustable peg system of exchange rates dissolved in 1972, and the era of floating rates began. In 1973, after many hesitations, Britain joined the European Economic Community.

In 1972 and 1973 booms occurred in the industrial countries with unusual simultaneity, inducing an exceptional rise in commodity prices, which was followed by the quadrupling of oil prices at the end of 1973. In 1971, the British balance of payments had been in surplus, but unemployment had risen to the highest rate since the war – about one million. The 1972 budget aimed to increase the growth rate to 5 per cent per annum over the next eighteen months, and to bring unemployment down to half a million by the end of 1973. As it happens, both targets were achieved. The government hoped that this expansion would be the beginning of several years of high growth, and to that end, the Chancellor announced in his budget speech that a fixed exchange rate would not be allowed to stand in the way of expansion: the pound was, in fact, allowed to float in June 1972. Thereafter, the major currencies floated against one another, though the EC countries, including Britain, attempted a loosely knit joint float – the Snake[9] – followed later in the decade by the European Monetary System, which however, Britain did not join.[10]

As things were to turn out, it was not immediately the balance of payments which was to call a halt to growth, but inflation. We have described elsewhere (p. 160) the problem presented to governments by OPEC 1, namely whether to accommodate the rise in oil and other costs, by loosening nominal fiscal and monetary policy, or to adhere to the existing nominal framework at the risk of precipitating a recession. The response to OPEC 1 was mixed, with Britain initially accommodatory, but coming out in the mid-1970s with higher inflation than most other major countries. The consequential collapse of the exchange rate in 1976 was only overcome by recourse to a loan from the International Monetary Fund, accompanied by severe reductions in public expenditure.[11] Meanwhile, from 1975 onwards, North Sea oil began to flow in increasing quantities, bringing relief to the balance of payments, and in 1978 and 1979 renewed expansion became possible, with employment rising and unemployment falling.

Besides raising costs, the oil price rise brought about huge current account surpluses for the producers and deficits in oil-importing countries. The producers deposited unspent funds in London and New York. Vigorous 'on-lending' by banks to LDCs brought about a financial recycling of the oil surpluses, which at the time was hailed as a remarkable vindication of the working of private markets. (It was not until the next decade that the magnitude of the debt problem of LDCs was to become fully apparent.) Sooner, in some countries, or later in others, the inflation rates subsided, though they did not fall back to the levels of pre-1972. Monetarist ideas were gathering strength, and many governments adopted monetary targets. Output recovered, but it did so at a slower rate than before, and unemployment remained high. The persistence of stagflation led to the proposal at the Bonn summit meeting in 1978 that countries with balance of payments surpluses, notably Germany and Japan, should reflate and act as a 'locomotive' for the others, while the United States promised to allow its domestic fuel price to rise. Though this initiative was soon to be swamped by OPEC 2 (see p. 161), its significance lay in the acceptance of asymmetry, that is, only *some* countries should act on the level of demand.

Sterling had been allowed to float in 1972 in order that the policy of expansion should not be frustrated by a balance-of-payments crisis, the presumption being that the exchange rate would fall to whatever level was needed to maintain external balance. The stronger version of the argument would have been that a lower exchange rate would trigger export-propelled growth. Towards the end of this period a quite new virtuous circle was advanced in a Green Paper (HM Treasury, 1978) only this time it was to be started off by *raising* the exchange rate. Such a rise would, it was admitted, initially make British goods appear dearer to foreigners, but this would put pressure on British exporters to increase efficiency and to reduce costs. The rise would also make imports cheaper; but this, it was argued, meant that smaller rises in nominal incomes, including wages, would be needed to preserve living standards. 'Once a virtuous circle of exchange rate stability, lower costs, greater stimulus to efficiency has been established, the effects of any initial loss of price competitiveness may be removed (*Ibid*, para. 39). That a higher exchange rate might help to reduce the rate of inflation was not disputed, but the Green Paper offered no hard evidence about costs and efficiency.[12]

No very clear lessons concerning the impact of the rest of the world on British macroeconomic policy emerge from this period. In terms of economic performance, it was the most turbulent and, on average, the least successful for most countries since the war. Many of the difficulties could be laid at the door of OPEC 1. There is no reason to think that they could have been any better handled within the fixed rate system of Bretton Woods. At the same time, the actual experience of floating proved to be less liberating than its more enthusiastic advocates had led one to expect. Many thought that floating might have contributed to higher inflation. Be that as it may, there was agreement in 1979 among the leading nations that getting inflation down should have the highest priority.

1979–88: World recession and halting recovery
The recession of the early part of the 1980s affected all major industrial countries and was the most severe since the war. The rise in unemployment in some countries invited comparison with the 1930s and there were also large falls in food and commodity prices. Nevertheless, for OECD as a whole, there was no absolute fall in output – only a slowing down to an annual rate of growth of less than 1 per cent for three years, while the fall in the volume of world trade was of the order of 3 per cent, compared with over one sixth in the Great Depression. The growth of output was resumed for OECD as a whole after 1983, albeit at the rather modest rate of $2\frac{1}{2}$ per cent per annum, and in many countries unemployment remained obstinately high. The annual rate of inflation in OECD as a whole had been running at 8 or 9 per cent in the late 1970s; it jumped to 15 per cent at the end of 1979, and thereafter subsided to 3 per cent or less in 1985 and 1986, but it rose again to over 5 per cent at the end of the decade.

In table 16.3 we show the changes in output, productivity (output per

Table 16.3. *Output, productivity and consumer prices: 1979–89*
$$1979 = 100$$

	Output	Productivity	Inflation
United States	128.9	108.6	170.8
Japan	150.9	132.1	128.2
France	123.6	122.7	202.2
Germany	120.9	118.5	133.0
United Kingdom	124.7	126.0	203.3

Source: *National Institute Economic Review*, August, 1990.

Table 16.4. *OECD standardised unemployment rates*

	1979	1983	1985	1986	1987	1988	1989
United States	5.8	9.5	7.1	6.9	6.1	5.4	5.2
Japan	2.1	2.6	2.6	2.8	2.8	2.5	2.3
France	5.9	8.3	10.2	10.4	10.5	10.0	9.6
Germany	3.2	8.0	7.2	6.4	6.2	6.2	5.5
United Kingdom	5.0	12.4	11.2	11.2	10.3	8.5	6.9

Source: OECD *Economic Outlook*, June 1990.

person employed) and prices for five major countries over the whole period 1979–89. In general, the slower growth of output and productivity which had set in after 1973 persisted through the 1980s: only the United Kingdom got back to its pre-1973 growth rates. But accompanying this improvement relative to other industrial countries was a worsening in the relative unemployment picture, as is shown in table 16.4, which records the OECD standardised unemployment rates for the same group of countries.

What is striking is the persistence of the high rates of unemployment once reached. When recession occurs in all countries at about the same time, one looks for common causes. The proximate causes for the 1980s recession were OPEC 2 coming up against the renewed determination of governments to bring down inflation, which had never fallen right back after OPEC 1. Once started off, the recession in any one country leads to lower imports, which pass on the contraction to trading partners. When questioned about rising unemployment in 1980, British government spokesmen very often simply referred to the world recession. This could not have been a satisfactory answer. In the first place, the recession in Britain started six months to a year before it did elsewhere. Secondly, whereas the British recession in 1929–31 was fully accounted for by the reduction in British exports of one third, in line with the similar fall in world trade in manufactures, and the recession of 1974–5 was preceded by OPEC 1, which induced a very large balance of payments deficit, the decline in 1979–81 originated entirely at home.[13]

Instead of importing all its oil, as it did in the early 1970s, by 1979 Britain was rapidly becoming self-sufficient, and then a net exporter of oil. Consequently, the current balance moved from a small deficit in 1979 to a surplus of 2½ per cent of GDP in 1981. Ironically, Britain experienced in the early 1980s the highest unemployment in the postwar years, when, for the first time in that period, it had become completely free from any balance of payments constraint. The 1981 surplus proved to be a maximum and thereafter there was a gradual decline to balance in 1986 and growing deficit thereafter. Whether, and to what extent, the external balance has once more become a constraint on domestic macreoconomic policy, are questions which we leave for the next chapter.

If we regard the European Exchange Rate Mechanism as loosely tying the currencies of EC members (other than the United Kingdom) to the D-mark, we can say that the 1980s began with the four major currencies, the dollar, the yen, the D-mark and sterling, all floating freely with respect to one another, the official attitude in all major centres being that the exchange rate was best left to the market. But this attitude did not last. First of all, the British government became increasingly alarmed by the extraordinary rise in the value of sterling through 1979 and 1980, which was having a most damaging effect on British manufacturing industry. By allowing interest rates to fall, the government succeeded in bringing the effective rate down by 20 per cent in the next five years. Together with the reduction in inflation this brought competitiveness back towards, though not the whole way, the level prevailing in 1978. It had been possible to rationalise the rise in sterling in terms of tight monetary policy, North Sea oil, and the 'Thatcher' confidence factor – in various proportions. But no satisfactory rationalisation was found for the remarkable rise in the dollar in 1985. Its effect on the world economy was more disruptive than had been the earlier rise in sterling and there was a dramatic change in international policy when the Finance Ministers of the major countries, meeting at the Plaza Hotel in New York, agreed to appreciate their currencies against the dollar. This was followed by an agreement to stabilise exchange rate levels (Louvre, 1987). Meanwhile the EC countries have been edging towards a closer monetary union.

The experience of the 1980s confirmed doubts which some had already begun to express in the 1970s, that free floating was not ideal. By the end of the decade, all major countries agreed that an exchange rate policy was desirable, although there was less agreement about what it should be. As for Britain, it began the decade clearly freed from the external constraint, but when oil earnings fell, output was allowed to grow above trend, and unemployment began to fall rapidly, the old question re-emerged whether, after all, employment would have to give way to the external constraint.

17

THE EXTERNAL CONSTRAINT

The questions we explore in this chapter are whether openness – especially in trade and capital movements – prevents, or makes more difficult, the achievement of policy objectives to which there might appear to be no obstacle in a closed economy. If we conclude that there are such constraints, the next question is whether there exist measures which might mitigate or even counter their influence. In Britain, in the interwar years and for many years since, the current balance of payments[1] has been seen as a problem, in particular leading to unemployment or blocking policies for full employment. But this is not the only possibility. Indeed, some countries, such as Germany and Japan, which have run large surpluses for long periods, might not see it so much as a constraint, but as an opportunity to maintain employment through increasing exports. But they might see in openness a possible threat to their own policy of domestic price stability. And, of course, the same country might find openness presenting different opportunities and different constraints at different times in its history. But it is British employment which is our subject and it is with that problem that we begin.

Table 17.1 shows the five-yearly average of the United Kingdom current balance from 1950/4 to 1985/9. As causes of intermittent crises in the 1950s and 1960s, these ratios seem small beer. Only in the 1980s, when the doctrine that the current account does not matter began to receive currency, do we encounter figures above 1 per cent. But this is to mislead. In the first place, a lot may happen in five years: thus, in 1985 there was a surplus of 1 per cent but in 1989, a deficit of 4.6 per cent.

Table 17.1. *Average ratio of the current balance to GDP, United Kingdom, from 1950/4 to 1985/9*

per cent

1950/4	1955/9	1960/4	1965/9	1970/4	1975/9	1980/4	1985/9
+0.4	+0.7	−0.2	0	−0.4	−0.3	+1.8	−1.7

Secondly, the actual surplus or deficit is not what we really need, but what the position would have been if domestic objectives, for example, full employment, were being achieved. Policy may not be to achieve a surplus, but balance at full employment.

DOES A CURRENT ACCOUNT DEFICIT MATTER?

In a period of fixed, but adjustable, exchange rates, the mere appearance of a current account deficit would not necessarily call for immediate action: reserves were held to finance normal fluctuations in trade. Nevertheless, as we saw in the previous chapter, it was the prospect of continuing deficit which was the most common trigger for Stops and no-one, at home or abroad, seriously questioned the need for action of some kind. It is only in recent years, when Britain has been running exceptionally large deficits, that some have asked whether deficits matter at all. First of all, we have been reminded that periods of persistent deficit have constituted a feature of the normal historical development of many countries. Lindbeck (1988) points out that Australia, Canada and Sweden all had annual average deficits of 3 per cent of GDP for 40 years prior to the outbreak of World War I without causing concern, partly because the loans were used for investment and 'partly, perhaps, because hardly any current account statistics were published at that time'.[2]

However, these were all cases of countries in the earlier stages of economic development, when it made perfectly good sense to supplement their own savings with savings borrowed from advanced countries, so long as the investment made possible the growth of national income and, in particular, developed exporting capacity.[3] On the face of it, it seems odd that Britain, the first to industrialise, should, two centuries later, find itself in need of additional capital. However, for a while, ministers said that all was well, since the exceptionally large imports included a great deal of equipment for investment in British industry. This argument, however, did not last very long when it soon became apparent that the balance of direct investment, far from being inward, was heavily outward.[4] The argument from historical precedent is not convincing.

A line of argument which some have found more persuasive is that if the external deficit arises from private borrowing, of individuals or firms, it will correct itself in time, because their borrowing power is not unlimited, whereas, it is said, governments can go on borrowing indefinitely. Thus the United States government ought to take action to reduce its external deficit, since there is a simultaneous budget deficit, whereas the British government (in 1988 or 1989) need not, since the budget is in surplus. This implies that markets are able to distinguish between different kinds of balance of payments deficit, according to their origins, and will react to them in a different way. But, if this is the case, what constitutes sound budgetary policy? If money national income is growing, balancing the Budget would mean that the ratio of national debt to GDP would be falling. Is that necessary, or is policy still sound if there is a budget deficit, but not more than would keep the debt/GDP ratio constant? One may rather doubt whether markets engage in quite such deep analysis. It seems more plausible to suppose that, to the extent that they take a long view, it will be whether or not to expect the deficit to come down within a reasonable time span.

Setting aside, for the moment, the question whether a British balance of payments deficit in fact constitutes a problem for the government, we ask a different question. If it were a problem, by what means could it correct itself, and what measures are open to government to assist or speed up the process? We begin by asking how the deficit could arise in the first place, to which there are two principal answers. The one is in terms of the balance of aggregate demand and domestic output, and the other in terms of competitiveness. To simplify matters, assume that initially all prices of domestic output, as well as of imports are fixed, so that only quantitative changes take place, in the volume of output (with employment corresponding) and imports. We start the system off with exports, E, fixed, while the volume of imports, M, is proportionate to domestic output, Y, so that $M = mY$. To achieve trade balance, we must choose Y so that $mY = E$. It would be a fluke if this permitted output corresponded to full employment. If it corresponds to a lower level, so that there is some unemployment, then raising demand so that there is full employment will mean that imports will exceed E, and there is a deficit. The way to restore balance is to reduce demand so that output falls back to Y, and we have unemployment again. If demand were to increase beyond full employment, the whole of the further increase would have to go on imports, domestic output being assumed to become completely inelastic at full employment. Once again, to correct the deficit, demand must fall back to the original level. To refer briefly to the real world, the kind of situation where domestic output (in this case of manufactures) reaches a ceiling (again, in this case a rising one) was encountered in the 1980s. Between 1983 and 1987, the volume of United Kingdom exports of manufactures rose by 6.6 per cent a year, and of imports of manufactures by 8.2 per cent a year, 1.6 per cent in excess. In 1988 and 1989, domestic output of manufactures was running up against short-run capacity limits. Exports in these two years grew at 8.6 per cent a year, but import rises leapt to 14.5 per cent a year, 5.9 per cent a year in excess. If demand were the only change involved, then the original balance of exports and imports would be restored, when demand fell back. Could this be expected to happen of its own accord, or is government action needed to give it a push?

If the deficit originated from an increase in borrowing by consumers who included imports in their additional purchases, it will unwind itself when consumers decide that it is no longer prudent for their debt to increase, and start to pay it off. But it is against historical evidence to suppose that the contraction phase will always be orderly: there have been many financial collapses. Nor, if the deficit is attributable to public borrowing, will it never be reversed. So far, we have supposed that simple reversibility will be possible: but that may not always be the case. In our illustration we kept prices fixed. A slightly more realistic scenario would allow for an increase in monetary demand (primed by private or public borrowing) to be split between output and price increases. As the expansion gets near to domestic capacity, there are two leakages, not just the one into imports, but also another into higher domestic prices. If the import leakage was blocked, the whole of the excess demand would be dissipated in higher prices. In this sense the external deficit is a safety valve for inflation. Now the question becomes whether, when demand is reduced, either by the prudence of private borrowers or of the state, reversibility still prevails. If imports have established themselves in the British market, it may be harder to displace them when demand falls than it was easy to pull them in when demand rose. And inflation, once set going, may acquire a momentum of its own, so that restoring the original rate of price increase may entail larger unemployment than when we started off. Whether or not the deficit is a problem depends on whether the authorities are convinced that it will reverse itself sufficiently quickly so that no dynamic processes are set going.

If a deficit mattered, how could it be corrected?
If the decision is taken that intervention is necessary, the options are fiscal and monetary policy. The *modus operandi* of both is through the reduction in the flow of monetary expenditure, which should reduce both domestic price rises and imports as well as, most probably, domestic output. The disadvantage of relying entirely on monetary policy is that, if the exchange rate is floating, it will be pulled up. This helps to reduce inflation, by keeping down the sterling prices of imports, but it also encourages the substitution of imports for home production. Tighter fiscal policy and lower interest rates might be more appropriate.

Whether or not correction of a deficit is achieved by natural causes, or is assisted by macroeconomic policy, the level of GDP corresponding to external balance may prove to be well below full employment. This means that the economy is, to that extent, uncompetitive. Competitiveness is commonly *measured* in a number of ways, such as relative export prices, relative unit labour costs, relative profitability of exports, or import price competitiveness. These indicators do not always point in the same direction, and there is plenty of room for debate about which measure is best. There is some danger that this debate obscures a fundamental conceptual issue, namely that competitiveness is not an absolute attribute of an economy, but has to be taken in conjunction with the macroeconomic balance. If, for instance, our chosen indicator of competitiveness shows no change between one period and another but, in order for the current balance to be zero, the level of unemployment has to be higher in the second period than the first, then competitiveness has deteriorated. This is of vital significance in any decision about the level of the exchange rate at which it would be right to join any fixed exchange rate system.

What means are available to improve competitiveness, and what are their chances of success? The largest item in domestic production costs is wages and salaries, and a measure commonly advocated to improve competitiveness is to raise productivity. This would certainly reduce unit costs: nevertheless we do not regard this as a relevant suggestion in this context. If untapped productivity improvements are available, they should be harvested anyway, whether or not there is a balance of payments deficit. The other way to get costs down is to secure lower wage and salary increases, but recommendations to this effect are empty, unless there is some form of incomes policy in place. If nominal wages and salaries were lower than they would otherwise be, then, indeed, costs would be lower and British goods that much more competitive in overseas markets and at home in competing with imports. If capital movements are also free, then, *ceteris paribus*, firms, whether British or foreign, would find it cheaper to locate plants in Britain than before. All these are developments favourable to British employment. But this is all hypothetical. For it to become real, there would have to be some sort of political concordat for a voluntary incomes policy, or else some previously established machinery for enforcing a lower norm. This emphasises, once again, the importance of incomes policy but, in the absence of such a policy, the appeal to moderation is a statement of the problem, and not a contribution to its solution.

The alternative is to lower the exchange rate. This was possible under the fixed, but adjustable, exchange rate system of Bretton Woods and, as we saw earlier, had positive effects on the trade balance. When the exchange rate is floating, it is less certain that the path of the rate can be lowered in any very precise way, but there is a presumption that lower interest rates will bring about the desired result. The fear in the cases both of fixed and floating rates is that a lower nominal exchange rate will raise import costs, which will cause prices and then wages to rise, reducing and ultimately extinguishing the competitive gain of the initial depreciation. The question then is whether the gain in competitiveness lasts long enough to make a significant improvement in the trade balance averaged over a period of years. To recommend tighter fiscal policy to contain demand, and lower interest rates to bring down the floating exchange rate, may strike some readers as old fashioned. If it does, it is partly because we have retained an explicit employment objective, whereas contemporary British policy has no specific employment objective, but only one, of reducing inflation; and partly because we have retained the notion of the exchange rate as an instrument of policy. We shall have more to say about whether this notion is still tenable in a world of free capital movements but first we turn aside for a moment to consider the argument that, as an instrument, the exchange rate was simply too weak or too easily trumped by inflation, to be effective in controlling the trade balance and that something stronger, in the form of protection, was needed.

PROTECTION

In the 1950s and 1960s barriers to trade were brought down throughout the world, beginning with the dismantling of quantitative restrictions, and followed by multilateral reductions in tariffs negotiated in a succession of GATT rounds. The success of freer trade seemed to be manifested in the extraordinarily high elasticity of world trade with respect to world output: from 1953 to 1973 world trade grew at an annual average rate over 1.7 times that of world GDP. During those years the predominant view was that free trade was good for the economic performance of advanced economies, although it could not escape notice that the most successful of all the industrial countries – Japan – was, by any standard, highly protectionist. Among the fast-growing European economies, French *dirigisme* was much admired. Since the mid-1970s there appears to have been a resurgence of protectionism, mainly in the form of non-tariff barriers (NTBs). Page (1987) points out how difficult it is to identify NTBs and to measure their intensity. However, she quotes a number of studies suggesting that the range of NTBs was on the increase in the 1980s. The sectors most often controlled by both developing and industrial countries are: food, textiles, clothing, steel, cars, electrical machinery and electronics. The best known arrangements are the Multi-Fibre Agreement, which is directed primarily against the textile exports of developing countries, and which has undoubtedly sustained employment in those industries in the advanced countries, and voluntary export restrictions (VERs) such as those operated to limit Japanese car exports. Boltho and Allsopp (1987) suggested that the decline in the world trade–output elasticity, to 1.5 in 1973–9, and further still to 1 in 1979–85 – 'a figure ominously reminiscent of that in the interwar period', confirms the growth of protectionism. The period 1979–85, however, is rather short and coincides with the deepest part of the recession. In the later 1980s, the world trade–output elasticity seems to have recovered sharply. Be that as it may, so long as unemployment persists in significant parts of the industrial world, protectionism is likely to remain on the agenda.

An argument developed in the late 1970s by the New Cambridge school (Neild, 1979) took the case of an industrial country facing unemployment and argued that whereas devaluation immediately caused a rise in prices and a reduction in real wages, protection could secure an immediate fall in prices, a rise in real wages and possibly a reduction in inflation. The price reductions came from cuts in indirect taxes designed to expand employment, an expansion made possible by the immediate cut in the propensity to import brought about by the tariffs or quotas. The New Cambridge argument was subjected to detailed criticism (Lal, 1979), but the controversy lapsed in face of the new monetarist policies of the Thatcher government and the large balance of payments surpluses (products of recession and North Sea oil) which emerged in the early 1980s. It is possible that such arguments might be revived, if the post-1988 squeeze were to tip the economy into a second serious recession. Other protectionist arguments are likely to continue, for example, for an industrial strategy, or for government support for high-technology industry. Such proposals cannot be dismissed out of hand as infringing the tenets of classical free trade, since that model never dealt with dynamic issues in the first place. They can be considered on their merits. One general caution is, however, justified. Policy moves of any kind, whether protectionist, or exchange-rate changes which improve the situation of one country, will invite retaliation if the improvement is at the expense of others and, possibly, even if it is not. The better strategy may, therefore, be to look for areas of cooperation, a subject to which we shall return.

THE SCOPE FOR POLICY

The previous discussion was conducted on a hypothetical basis. If the balance of payments constituted a constraint on domestic macro-economic policy, what measures were available to ease or remove this constraint? Before we go on to a more detailed consideration of policies, we should come clean on whether we think a deficit is, in fact, a constraint. We take the view that it certainly can be. This first reason is one of general principle. We cannot see why a comparatively rich nation should, year in year out, consume more than it produces, leaving aside just wars. We can see the force of the argument that richer nations might run surpluses to assist the economic development of poor nations, but not the other way round. If this argument of principle is too moralistic, there is a pragmatic argument. Whether or not markets are rational in the technical economic sense, they have tended to take a poor view of the current British trade deficit. Bad monthly balance of payments figures have often been followed by falls in the exchange rate. In the 1989 squeeze, Chancellors have spoken of 'bearing down on inflation', but in many cases it was these exchange rate falls which triggered the rises in interest rates.[5] A third reason is political. If the economy has a period in which it consumes more than it produces, as happened in 1986–9, when consumers' expenditure, in real terms, grew at 5¾ per cent a year, compared with the 4½ per cent of GDP, to correct the external balance requires a period in which consumers' expenditure growth must be below the GDP growth rate. Projections of the economy for the next decade have output running at 2¾ per cent, with consumers' expenditure running at around 2 per cent. This will not be popular and, accordingly, a start to reducing the deficit should not be too long delayed. Our answer to the question whether openness is a constraint on policy, particularly with respect to employment, is that the current balance has been such in the past, and we think it will continue to be. We have to ask whether there are policies to achieve improvement in the balance without implying higher unemployment.

Any policy decisions in Britain take place within an international framework of institutions and agreements. The framework, which is normally subject to a process of continuous change, has been shaken by the remarkable political developments in the Soviet Union and Eastern Europe. The effective, but enormously expensive, nuclear stalemate between NATO and the Warsaw Pact is rapidly dissolving, with enticing economic prospects from the 'peace dividend'. A year or two ago, the central questions facing the EC were monetary union and the possible development of a federal government. To such questions are now added the prospective relation between East European countries and the Community and, in particular, the role of East Germany. There are many possible outcomes and we cannot conceivably discuss all alternatives. We shall examine just three cases. In the first, Britain goes it alone: it remains a member of the EC but stays out of the Exchange Rate Mechanism. In view of the commitment to join ERM when the conditions are right, this is a most unlikely case but it enables us to concentrate on the role of the exchange rate. We shall take the view that completely free floating generates instability. For our second case, we consider various forms of international cooperation in the management of exchange rates, as well as in macroeconomic policy. In the next chapter, we take the third case, in which Britain joins ERM, and we discuss the pros and cons of a common currency.

In the broadest terms, the case for floating exchange rates has always been that it enables countries to pursue their own domestic macro-economic policies, without being frustrated by international commitments. However, the national autonomy which was to be protected was not exactly the same for everyone. For some, it was a question of monetary control and inflation. Under the fixed exchange rate regime, low inflation countries, such as Germany, complained from time to time about importing inflation. With floating rates, it was argued, this problem could be averted by allowing the D-mark to appreciate, relative to the currencies of the higher inflation currencies. Other countries had a different worry, that their policies for expansion of output and employment might be frustrated, since these policies entailed some increase in prices relative to competitors. This could be taken care of by allowing their currency to float down. In a frictionless world, exchange rates would be determined by purchasing power parity (PPP). If prices are constant in country A, but are doubled in B, the exchange rate of B should be one half of what it had originally been. The link was to be maintained automatically through trade.

If British prices rise more than elsewhere, exports will fall and imports rise. The demand for sterling will fall and for the currency of suppliers will rise, giving rise automatically to the required adjustment of the exchange rate. There is plenty of scope for argument about which measure of purchasing power is appropriate: consumer prices, the GDP deflator, export prices, for instance; or, alternatively, not a measure of prices at all, but of costs, for example, labour costs. The choice of measure would be especially important if there exists a significant and persistent difference in productivity growth between the tradeable and non-tradeable sectors of the economy (see p. 150).

Whichever measure of PPP is chosen, it is apparent that in the past two decades there have been prolonged periods during which exchange rates were moving away from the direction which would be indicated by PPP. For instance, between 1980 and 1985, albeit it was decelerating, the actual rate of inflation in the United States was higher than in all major countries and, additionally, there was an exceptionally large deficit in the balance of payments on current account, factors which on PPP grounds would indicate a fall in the dollar, whereas it rose strongly against other major currencies, by as much as 60 per cent in the case of the D-mark. In Britain, the inflation rate rose sharply from 1978, exceeding the weighted average for seven major countries by 1.3 per cent per annum in 1978 and 5.7 per cent in 1980. Yet the effective exchange rate rose by 18 per cent. In the end, after 1980, sterling did fall and, after 1985, so did the dollar.

What these episodes show is that, though current account imbalances and divergent purchasing power changes may give rise to equilibrating effects, they are not so strong, or so fast moving, that they cannot be outweighed, for quite long periods, by capital flows.

There are three issues. The first is whether floating increases the volatility of exchange rates and gives rise to movements which are contrary to those which might be indicated by long-run factors, such as the need to maintain competitiveness at a high level of employment. We believe that they have done.[6] The second question is whether, in a world full of uncertainty, one additional uncertainty matters. Up to a point, traders can hedge against exchange rate changes. This is bound to be an additional cost, but it can be argued that trade has continued to grow under floating. The third issue is whether, notwithstanding the volatility and intermittent perversity of the movement of the exchange rate which floating delivers, it is still possible for the authorities to retain the exchange rate as a policy instrument. The answer, in the light of recent British experience, is a qualified affirmative. Base rate, which was 12½ per cent in early 1986, was brought down to 9 per cent over the period from May 1987 to April 1988, over which period sterling tracked the D-mark quite closely. Thereafter, base rates (after a dip to 7½ per cent in May 1988) were raised and sterling rose against the D-mark. It happens, and this may be a source of confusion, that in this last period, when base rates rose from 7½ per cent to 15 per cent in less than eighteen months, the government's stated purpose was not to raise the exchange rate , as such, but to 'bear down on inflation'. This it does in two ways. The first is precisely through a higher exchange rate reducing import costs: this comes through quite quickly. The second is through its effect on domestic investment and consumption expenditure: this comes through much more slowly, and when it does, it may bear on output and employment as much as on prices. Dow (1988), has argued persuasively that, in Britain, monetary policy is inappropriate for regulating demand, for which, as we discussed in Chapter 14, fiscal policy is more suited. It is conceivable, but exceedingly improbable, in the foreseeable British future that the management of demand and the need to change competitiveness would both point to a movement of the interest rate in the same direction. But the case where they point in opposite directions is more likely.

It must be acknowledged that in bearing down on inflation, while it may operate more quickly and more certainly than monetary policy, fiscal policy can also bear just as much on output and employment as on the price level. Moreover, if it is being used in conjunction with a lower exchange rate whose purpose is to improve competitiveness, the reduction in the nominal rate, which is all that monetary policy can achieve directly, may have raised import costs: and if these are followed by higher nominal wages, the gain in competitiveness may be reduced or cancelled. Back, yet again, to the importance of the nominal wage level. Given the volatility and intermittent perversity of floating exchange rates, even the proper mix of monetary and fiscal policy just described may not make going it alone a very attractive prospect.

INTERNATIONAL COOPERATION AND THE COORDINATION OF POLICIES

So far, the only objection we have raised against lowering the exchange rate to relieve the external constraint is the fear of inflation. But there is also the possibility of retaliation.[7] If this makes us cautious about unilateral action, it also points to the potential of international cooperation and the coordination of policies.

The postwar era began with the creation of new international institutions. These organisations were supplemented at various times by others such as OECD, and by regional bodies such as the European Community. All major countries outside the communist bloc accepted, and still accept, that in matters of trade policy they no longer have complete autonomy, but are subject to rules and to the decisions of supranational bodies. This does not mean that all is sweetness and light: on the contrary, one can read almost daily allegations of unfair trading made by one country against another. But all still accept that these matters should be regulated by appropriate institutions. Overt trade wars are comparatively infrequent.

In exchange rates the story has been different. For a quarter of a century after the Second World War exchange parities were fixed by the Bretton Woods agreement. They could be changed but only, in principle at any rate, in accordance with the rules of the IMF. The fixed rate system crumbled and was succeeded in the 1970s by floating. Initially floating was hailed as a step forward, removing any external constraint on the freedom of countries to choose their own macroeconomic policy. But as we have seen, experience did not live up to these hopes, and this led to renewed interest in the possibilities of coordination of policies. We mentioned in Chapter 14 (page 161) the summit meeting in Bonn in 1978, which aimed to reduce unemployment by getting the surplus countries to act as locomotives to pull the world economy out of stagflation. Cooperation for the stabilisation of exchange rates began in the Plaza Accord of 1985. We shall not go into detail about this and subsequent meetings. What we shall attempt is to indicate the potential for cooperation of this kind, and then we shall try to determine how far it is sensible and realistic to bank on achieving a significant degree of cooperation in the future.

ALTERNATIVE SCHEMES

(i)   Restore controls on capital movements

When the International Monetary Fund was set up its clear purpose was to provide funds to assist central banks in financing current transactions. Members could not use the Fund's resources to meet a large or continuing outflow of capital, and to this end, members could, if they wished, exercise controls over international capital movements. When the Fund started, most members had inherited exchange controls from the war period, or else introduced them as they re-started normal trade. Over the years, these controls became weaker or were abolished. The last vestiges of sterling exchange control disappeared in 1979 and the remaining controls of the major European Community countries will have gone by the end of 1990. Meanwhile, for some time, there has been no control over capital movements, which can take place freely, and on any scale, between New York, Tokyo, London and Frankfurt.

One consequence of this, which we have already seen, is that exchange rate movements are dominated by market expectations about future asset prices in the various countries, as well as the future exchange rates themselves, factors altogether swamping such longer-run influences as differential inflation rates, or surpluses and deficits in the current trade balance. In principle, one way to restore the influence of the long-run factors would be for all countries to agree to operate controls over capital movements. It is arguable, however, that such a proposal is no longer practicable. In Britain, for instance, exchange control was operated by a central office in the Bank of England, which used the main British commercial banks as agents to deal with individual applications. The central office has been disbanded and, since 1979, there has been a large influx of foreign banks in London. Even if British banks were willing again to act as agents, it is doubtful whether foreign banks would be very keen. But, apart from any practical obstacles to the reintroduction of exchange controls, the attempt would run counter to the tide of financial deregulation which has been running very strongly in the 1980s. Control over capital movements could only reappear on the agenda after a major breakdown of the present system and we shall not pursue the matter any further here.

(ii)   A new fixed exchange rate system

There has not, so far as I am aware, been any suggestion of reviving the Bretton Woods system in all its original detail, but McKinnon has proposed the fixing of the exchange rates between Japanese yen, the German mark and the United States dollar. There is no theoretical obstacle against such a system. All that would be required is for the three central banks to be willing to purchase one another's currency in indefinite amounts, according to how the private capital markets swing between one centre and another. Given the large volumes of such movements under floating, no doubt the central banks would have to be prepared to make huge purchases of currencies before the markets became wholly convinced that they meant business, and quietened down. The nominal exchange rates to be established would be on the basis of purchasing power parity, which would align the price levels of internationally tradeable goods, as reckoned by producer or wholesale price indices. McKinnon (1988) rejects what, he says, is 'now a false academic doctrine' – the idea that a once-for-all devaluation of a country's currency can reduce that country's trade deficit. Such deficits should be addressed by fiscal policy. The United States deficit, he says, 'merely reflects the saving–investment gap in the American economy created by the not coincidentally equally large United States fiscal deficit'. This remark seems to postulate the one-to-one correspondence between the budget deficit and the balance of payments deficit, which was a striking feature of the New Cambridge doctrines which enjoyed a brief life in the early 1970s. Neither McKinnon nor New Cambridge would stand up well in the Britain of the late 1980s, when the two balances have been seen marching strongly in opposite directions!

The fortuitous nature of any one-to-one correspondence between Budget and trade deficits is one of the points made in criticisms of the McKinnon proposal by Dornbusch (1988) and Williamson (1988). While both authors accept many of McKinnon's criticisms of floating exchange rates, they both reject his view that real exchange rates have no effect on the current account. Both state the need for employment targets as well as inflation targets, and assert the need for both fiscal and monetary policy, and the importance of changes in the real exchange rate.

(iii) Target zones

In theory, the old Bretton Woods scheme, which fixed parities but allowed adjustment in the case of fundamental disequilibrium, would seem to be superior to permanently fixed rates. But it was open to the objection that when a fundamental disequilibrium was emerging, speculation against a currency became a one way bet. This difficulty is overcome in Williamson's proposal for target zones.[8] The first requirement of this scheme is that each participating country announces a target for the growth of nominal national income. This is to be built up from the growth of productive potential, an allowance for inflation (a little below recent experience so as gradually to bring inflation down) and a term reflecting the deflationary gap. Each country would also have a target for its real exchange rate, chosen with a view to reconciling external and internal balance in the long run. The system would operate under three rules. First, the average level of world interest rates would be raised or lowered according to whether the aggregate of nominal incomes exceeded or fell short of the aggregate of the target nominal incomes. Secondly, differences in interest rates between countries should be revised to prevent exchange rates from deviating from the target levels by more than a certain amount, say 10 per cent. Thirdly, fiscal policy would be used to keep countries on the track of their target nominal incomes. The importance of this scheme is that it recognises that correction of trade deficits normally requires a combination of a reduction in the real exchange rate and a fiscal adjustment to prevent the improved competitiveness from being wiped out by increased inflation.[9]

Two questions immediately suggest themselves about such schemes. Assuming, first of all, that all major countries are prepared to play according to the rules of the game, would this kind of economic cooperation make all that much difference? And, secondly, how realistic is it to suppose that important countries would keep to the rules?

A beginning towards one kind of answer has been made by Currie and Wren-Lewis (1989), using the method of policy optimisation, for the G3 countries, the United States, Japan and Germany. For their model of the world, they use the National Institute's Global Econometric Model (GEM), which includes sixteen countries altogether and in which the G7 countries are modelled in some detail. The principal arguments of the objective function, whose value is to be minimised, are capacity utilisation and inflation. But there is also a term in nominal interest rates, designed to penalise very low or negative rates, and a term which penalises departures in government expenditure from trend. The procedure is to compare the value of the objective function provided by the actual history of 1975–86 with what it would have been had a version of the target zone scheme been in operation. In this exercise the parameters of the objective function were taken to be the same for each of the three countries, though experiments with variations were tried. The results suggested that policy cooperation using the 'Williamson' rule would have led to a substantial Pareto improvement, that is, all three countries would have been better off, as measured by the objective function. The results also suggested that fiscal, rather than monetary, policy should play the major role in stabilising global output and inflation. If policymakers had followed the optimal rules, the main difference would have been the absence of the sharp increase in United States interest rates around 1980. These conclusions have a commonsense appeal, but they should be treated with caution. Currie and Wren-Lewis themselves draw attention to the Brookings model comparison exercise, which used six international models to represent possible states of the world (Bryant et al., 1988). Two 'countries', the

United States and the Rest of the World could subscribe to any of the six models, and each one in turn was taken to be the true model. (In fact, of course, none of them might have been true.) Cooperation was found to give benefits to both 'countries' in only 60 per cent of the cases, and in nearly one third of cases cooperation made matters worse in at least one country. It may well be that differences between models in the view of how the world works, as well as differences between countries in the relative value of different objectives, such as higher employment, or lower inflation, make it premature to attempt to embody Williamson type rules in a revitalised IMF and that, for the time being, it would be better to build on the meetings of G3 and G7 countries, putting on their agenda the results of macroeconomic policy analysis,[10] and leaving them to make suggestions to meet specific situations. But here also a further word of caution is necessary.

In a series of lectures and articles, Feldstein has been arguing that although international coordination of macroeconomic policymaking sounds like a way to improve international relations more generally, there is a serious risk that it will have the opposite effect.[11] People may form exaggerated expectations of what such policy coordination can achieve. He fears that governments might use the meetings to avoid taking difficult domestic decisions and make foreign governments scapegoats for their own delinquency. In his sights are primarily the G3 countries, the United States, Japan and Germany, but he criticises also G5 and G7 meetings. He approves the 'quiet exchange' of macroeconomic forecasts and policy plans which occurs between government officials within the framework of BIS, OECD, and the various Groups. But that is as far as it should go. Feldstein has based his argument firstly on the divergence of the subsequent course of the dollar–yen–D-mark exchange rates from what the 'summiteers' were hoping to see. Secondly, he argues that other countries should not rely upon the United States to deliver on any undertakings given at such meetings. This is not a reflection on the integrity of American Presidents or Secretaries of the Treasury, but a statement about the separation of powers in the United States constitution. The first argument is open to debate. One could argue, for instance, that the spectacle of leading countries agreeing about their hopes for exchange rates is itself a factor making for calmer seas than might otherwise be encountered. As to the second, the point is perhaps already more familiar to the representatives of other countries than Feldstein gives them credit for.

Be that as it may, the policy coordination with which Feldstein is primarily concerned is that between the G3 countries – the United States, Japan and Germany. It is in Britain's interest that the exchange rates between the major currencies should not be subject to violent fluctuations and that the domestic policies of these countries should not be in obvious conflict. But Britain may be wise not to bank too heavily on the successful coordination of policies between them. The situation is different, however, so far as the European Community is concerned. Britain is already a member, and the issue is not whether there should be policy coordination or not, but how the existing coordination should develop.

18

THE EUROPEAN DIMENSION

Since Britain joined the European Community in 1973 the share of her trade with the rest of the Community has risen from around one third to over one half, with imports rising rather more than exports, partly because of the increase in EC membership, and partly because of the rise of the United Kingdom share with individual members. During the remainder of the 1970s, employment edged upward, but so did unemployment. In the recession employment fell by two million and unemployment rose by almost as much. In 1989, employees in employment were still below 1973, though if the self-employed are added in, the total surpassed the previous peak. But unemployment was still nearly a million more than in 1973. On the face of it, it would seem easier to mount an argument that joining the European Community had been bad for jobs than that it had been good. But, in truth, so many other things were going on that one doubts whether any more definite statement can be made. In any case, it is the future which concerns us. Of the many possible influences on British employment, we shall look at only two policy areas: the development of the European Monetary System, and the single market to be completed by 1992.

THE EUROPEAN MONETARY SYSTEM

The European Monetary System was set up in 1979 with the object of limiting the extent to which the currencies of the participating countries fluctuated against one another. Only Britain, of the then membership of the Community, stayed outside the Exchange Rate Mechanism. The participants undertook to maintain their exchange rates within bilateral limits of $\pm 2\frac{1}{4}$ per cent, with Italy negotiating a wider band of ± 6 per cent. The system was organised around a composite currency – the ECU – in terms of which the central rates of the members are expressed.[1] Realignments of the central rates are permitted. Between 1979 and 1987, there were altogether eleven realignments, two of them involving all participants, and the remainder on a more limited scale. The D-mark was altered seven times, always upwards, to a total of $25\frac{1}{4}$ per cent; the French franc went up once, and down four times, to a net total of $-12\frac{1}{4}$ per cent.[2] The formal purpose of EMS was to stabilise the nominal rates of exchange between members. One aspect of stabilisation is to reduce the, often substantial, day-to-day fluctuations: another is to keep steady the relative competitive positions of the members. The former, the reduction of volatility, is primarily a matter of nominal exchange rates: the latter concerns relative *real* rates of exchange, since competitiveness involves, besides nominal exchange rates, the relevant rates of inflation of the parties. It should be noted, in passing, that because different members have different proportions of their trade with non-EC countries, ensuring a level competitive ground between members does not necessarily ensure that the overall competitiveness of any one country remains unchanged. This was one of the considerations which led Britain, with large trade with non-EC countries, to stay out of the ERM.

The first question is whether the ERM has succeeded in reducing the volatility of exchange rates. Taylor and Artis (1988), produce evidence that it has. They found 'unequivocal evidence' of a reduction in the volatility of exchange rates: moreover, far from getting this at the cost of increased volatility of interest rates, there is some evidence of reduced interest rate fluctuations as well. This, say the authors, is attributable to the growing credibility, with markets and with governments, of the exchange rate policies of members. When ERM was started in 1979, inflation was rising in all EC countries, and the average increase in consumer prices peaked at 12.8 per cent in 1980 for the Community as a whole. In that year, Italy had the highest rate, of 21.2 per cent, and Germany the lowest, at 5.5 per cent, a difference of 15.7 per cent per annum. By 1988, the average rate for the EC as a whole was down to 3.4 per cent (which includes an above average 4.9 per cent for the United Kingdom), and the gap between the highest and lowest rates was down to 4.3 per cent. Thus, besides reduction, there has also been convergence of rates. So great were the initial differences that, as we noted above, realignments of central rates were necessary. The net effect of these realignments was that the French franc was devalued with respect to the D-mark by 43 per cent in eight years. Over the same period, consumer prices in France rose nearly 50 per cent more than in Germany, that is, by the same order of magnitude. It has been argued that the policy of frequent, but discrete, realignments, was only possible because of the capital controls exercised by some countries, notably France and Italy. Without them, the markets might have forced the hands of those governments which were using temporary over-valuation of their currencies as weapons against their own inflations. Taylor and Artis reserved judgement on this point. The remaining capital controls are due to be liquidated in 1990 and it remains to be seen whether the ERM can continue to operate successfully.

Apart from the technical question whether ERM could work at all, original British objections were essentially concerned with alignment.

According to one set of protagonists, joining ERM would prevent, or hamper, the engineering of a lower exchange rate,[3] as part of a policy to retain external balance at a higher level of employment. Joining ERM, argued the other set of protagonists, would prevent, or hamper, the engineering of a higher exchange rate, with a view to damping down British inflation. Whatever may be said for either of these lines of argument, they cannot both be pursued at the same time. What the experience of ERM to date appears to show is that neither set of protagonists would have been severely handicapped by joining. If the issue for Britain in 1990 were whether to join an ERM which was to continue to operate as it has done so far, the economic arguments for or against cannot be overwhelming. Even the gap between Britain's 1990 rate of inflation and that of the average of the rest of the EC is less than that between Italy and the rest in 1979, so that if the United Kingdom started off with the ±6 per cent wider band, it would not be tying its hands unduly.

But that may be to put the issue in too narrow a perspective. In the eyes of some Community members, the ERM is a staging post on the way to a common currency. For such a currency to exist, there would have to be a European central bank. What would its objectives be? And who would control it? To ensure stability at a high level of employment, there would have to be Community command over a significant volume of fiscal resources. How could that be arranged? These are big questions. But, before we consider them, it would be best to look first at the implications of the single market in 1992 and beyond.

THE SINGLE MARKET

The driving force behind the single market is liberalisation, intended to remove as many as possible of the hindrances to the free movement of labour, capital and goods and services among the members of the European Community. In practice, it is more than likely that, at the end of 1992, there will still survive a variety of obstacles in particular cases, whether open or disguised. It is important always to bear in mind that we are concerned with liberalisation among EC members, which will not necessarily extend to non-members. The European Commission has stressed the need for the EC not to look into itself and to remain open to third countries. From time to time, there have been rumblings of protectionist wars between big trading blocs. The United States and Japan is a current instance and, agricultural protection frequently raises the temperature between the United States and Europe. More recent events in the Soviet Union and Eastern Europe have not only broken down the Comecon trading bloc, but have opened the question of trading relations between individual countries of Eastern Europe and the West. It is unlikely that the Community itself will continue to develop as though none of these events had taken place. We will nevertheless confine ourselves to the Community. It will suffice to bring to the fore a number of questions which will have to be answered within the present EC, or within some broader association including new countries. The single market concept, as such, does not entail any commitment to create full economic and monetary union by 1992, or any other specific date. Nevertheless, it will highlight certain fundamental problems if we assume initially that there is a single currency throughout the Community.

The enduring argument used by supporters of the Common Market concept since its earliest days has been that a large market will promote competition, efficiency and growth. An enduring counter to this argument has been to cite the instance of the United States. With some exceptions concerning interstate commerce, this was and still is the largest single market among the leading industrial countries. Until lately, it had the highest real income *per capita*. But it has also had, for much of the past half-century, the slowest rate of growth of output per person employed. One is more inclined to attribute the high standard of living in the United States to abundant land and other natural resources, especially cheap energy, and to waves of immigrants whose very arrival often signified enterprise above the average, than to the size of the domestic market, as such. Doubtless, there are industries, like aircraft production, which benefit from the largest domestic market. Denison (1974) attributed 0.19 of the average annual growth of 1.36 per cent of national income per person employed in the period 1929–41 to economies of scale. For the years 1964–9 he attributed 0.54 out of growth in national income per person employed of 1.57 per cent. Perhaps the single market will bring gains of a similar order of magnitude, although it should be borne in mind that international companies, such as Ford, by concentrating production of different components in plants distributed throughout Europe, and delivering these components to plants which specialise in the assembly of single marques of car, may not have left much scope for further gains from scale economies. Nevertheless, it is not unreasonable to hope that the single market will bring some efficiency gains, even if they are not spectacular. But what about employment?

It does appear that, in the Great Depression of the 1930s, the United States, among the larger industrial countries, had the hardest time economically. Civilian employment, rising through the 1920s, peaked at 46.2 million in 1929, a figure which was not to be reached again until 1940. Meanwhile the numbers unemployed jumped from 1.5 million in 1929 to nearly 13 million in 1933, and were still over 8 million in 1940.[4] In Britain, the rise in employment was briefly interrupted, but then resumed in the mid-1930s. In Germany, though unemployment was initially very high, full employment was reached by the end of 1936. The exact nature of the shock which brought about the Great Depression is still the subject of controversy, but the point being made here is that sheer size of market did not provide any insurance. In the recession of the early 1980s things were different. In the United States, the interruption of employment growth was small and short-lived, and the increase in unemployment no greater than elsewhere, notably Europe. Moreover, the United States is the one major economy in which the prevailing contractionary policy was quickly reversed, and unemployment fell back from its peak in a more or less normal cyclical fashion, whereas elsewhere, in Europe especially, it was to remain stubbornly high.

Both in the 1930s and the 1980s the States of the Union had a common currency, the dollar. And they had a Federal Government. In the 1930s the government produced the New Deal, an amalgam of policies, of which some were expansionary and some not: in the 1980s, when the authorities abandoned the tight monetary stance which had contributed to recession, increased defence spending and lower tax rates combined to lift the economy out again. But in Europe after 1992, on the assumptions we are making, stabilisation policy would, for practical purposes, be confined to the monetary arrangements of the European Central Bank. It must be questioned whether, if a shock on the scale of the 1930s were to occur, monetary policy alone would be enough to dig the economy out. But what of the scope of national governments for stabilisation policy? If there were a common currency, there would be little possibility of raising or lowering interest rates against the Central Bank rate. It would be limited to such imperfections as remained in capital markets, which it would, in any case, be the object of the single market to remove. But could not national governments increase their own public expenditure, or cut taxes, financing the deficit by borrowing? Some light on this can be obtained by looking at existing federations. The comment of the Padoa-Schioppa Report (1987) prepared for the European Community was: 'In the predominant model, the effective restraint on the borrowing of states is the sanction of the capital market, under conditions in which the state authorities have no power for monetisation of the public debt' (Report page 85). It is possible that this observation may have been influenced by the case of Italy, which has the largest budget deficit, in relation to GDP, of the major Community countries. If Britain were to be placed, as now, with a budget surplus, it could reduce that surplus without difficulty. It would not be limited as to the amounts that it borrowed, but it would no longer be able to control the terms on which it borrowed. It would have to accept the – internationally determined – rate plus any margin the market might begin to require if it thought the borrowing were becoming too great.

If one country did go it alone, there would be considerable leakages abroad, including a large share to other community countries. If several, or all members acted simultaneously, a given proportionate increase in output and income could be achieved, with a smaller budget deficit than if one country had acted alone. The members of the EC would be attempting the policy coordination which we discussed earlier. A logical development from this would be the creation of a fully fledged Community government, with a command over sufficient resources to make Community-wide fiscal policy realistic.

A COMMUNITY GOVERNMENT

The *raison d'être* of government in the economic sphere is the provision of public goods. Adam Smith's list included defence, law and order, and public works which it would not pay individuals to produce for themselves. Since then, the list has extended, to include regulation, stabilisation and income redistribution, and there is a grey area which includes such goods as education and health. At present, most public expenditure consequential upon Community regulatory decisions is borne by national governments. If a Community government were to be established, no doubt some of these expenditures would be shifted from the national to the Community level. For a Community government to come into being, there would have to be much prior discussion about the proportion of various functions to be transferred to the centre, but with such details we are not concerned. Our interest here is stabilisation and redistribution of income and employment. To be effective, the Community government would have to handle some minimum percentage of Community total income so that, by varying its expenditure or taxation, it would be able to exert significant leverage on the Community economy. In existing federations, such as the United States or Germany, federal public expenditure is of the order of 20–25 per cent of GNP, which compares with the average share of all forms of public expenditure in GNP of present members of the Community of over 40 per cent.[5]

We imagine, then, that a Community government exists, with a scale of revenue and expenditure, in proportion to GNP, similar to that of the United States. As regards stabilisation, we have little to add to what was said earlier in the discussion of macroeconomic policy. Since more than half of the foreign trade of EC members is with other EC members, any external constraint on macroeconomic policy will be proportionately smaller. Otherwise the problems of macroeconomic policy remain the same.

Something more, however, may be said on the subject of redistribution. We earlier established the importance of the regional element in employment policy within Britain itself. The main factor giving rise to the problem there is the decline of once flourishing industries, so that either new industries must replace them, or the people choose between staying at home unemployed or going elsewhere. There are similar areas of industrial decline in other EC countries. In addition, the Southern countries have regions which have never developed beyond agriculture, but with populations surplus to their needs, which have migrated to other parts of Europe or to North America or Australia. Mass tourism has come to the rescue of some of these regions in the matter of employment, though, from another point of view, the lining of the Mediterranean and southern Atlantic coastlines with concrete blocks may not be the best solution. The European Commission already makes regional grants, and the problem is discussed at some length in the Padoa-Schioppa report, mentioned above.

The MacDougall Report (EC Commission, 1977) examined the inter-regional redistributive power in terms of income and output and we will give a brief account in these terms of what they say, going on to draw inferences for employment. The Report studied five existing federations, including the large United States and the smaller Switzerland, and three unitary states, France, Italy and the United Kingdom. They distinguished 72 regions within the Community, which at that time had nine members. They found that average *per capita* incomes were as unequal between the nine countries as between the 72 regions. They calculated Gini coefficients of inequality for all regions and countries. These are the weighted averages of *per capita* income differences between regions, where relative populations were used as weights. A value of 0.0 means exact equality. The highest coefficients came out at 0.15, which indicated substantial inequality. As an example, among the nine members of the EC, Ireland had the lowest average personal income of 51 per cent of the average for the whole Community, with Denmark the highest, at 140 per cent of the average.[6] Similar differences were encountered between regions within Italy, but the range between highest and lowest in other countries was usually smaller: the coefficient for the United Kingdom was 0.06, personal income in Northern Ireland standing at 69 per cent of national average, and of the South-East at 119 per cent.

Public expenditure and taxation, in the nine countries studied by the Report, reduced the regional inequality in *per capita* income by, on average, about 40 per cent. In the wealthier regions *per capita* taxation is higher. On the expenditure side, social security systems and public expenditure programmes, such as health and education, also have substantial redistributive effects. In addition, there are specific regional aid programmes, though these normally constitute a minor part of the redistribution. Poor regions have continuing balance-of-payments deficits with the rest of the country, and rich regions surpluses. Net flows of between 3 and 10 per cent of regional product are to be found for both rich and poor regions, with even higher flows for the poorest. These redistributive flows have an obvious impact on employment. Education programmes, for instance, may provide more jobs for teachers in poor regions than the region could afford if it were self-sufficient. Inasmuch as taxation is redistributive, personal expenditure out of net income will sustain more employment than would be possible with self-sufficiency. Of particular interest is the conjunctural aspect. If a region, be it poor or rich, experiences a recessionary shock, the result, say, of a fall in exports to other countries, workers unemployed will draw benefits which flow from the Community government, and those remaining in employment will pay less taxes and employers with smaller profits the same. Thus the multiplier effects of shocks are damped down, although, of course, they are not reversed. If the decision were taken to go for integration and a Community government, an early candidate to start the process would be a Community Unemployment Fund. In order to make clear the principle we first assume that the conditions and amounts of contributions and benefits are the same in all Community members. If unemployment rises in Britain and nowhere else, funds will flow from the centre (Brussels) to pay the benefits. The automatic stabilising element is just the same as if the unemployment fund were exclusively British. The difference is that the deficit opens up in the Community Fund in Brussels and not in a British fund in London. Of course, if Britain were to fall into continuing recession, the more prosperous members would find themselves, automatically, giving long-term support to the depressed country.

In practice existing contributions and benefits are not uniform among EC members. One could nevertheless set the *European* contributions and benefits at the level of the lowest existing national scheme, allowing each member to add a top-up national scheme which will bring the total of contributions and benefits for a worker in any country to the levels already prevailing in that country. In this case the Community stabilising effect will be smaller than with uniform contributions and benefits at a higher level. The automatic redistribution of an Unemployment Fund could not *eliminate* the unemployment of a depressed member. For that, new capital, whether private or public, would need to flow in. We discussed some of the possibilities in the national context earlier on (Chapter 6) and need not repeat the proposals here.

If a Community government were to be established, deploying, let us imagine, between one third and one half of total public expenditure of the member countries, then it would be possible, in principle, for both the

Community government and the national governments to engage in stabilisation and redistribution, raising questions of coordination and possible conflict. When British regions secured aid under a Brussels programme, the British government used to cut their own aid *pro tanto*. This practice has now been abandoned, but it illustrates the scope for discussion whether there should be only one Community regional aid programme or, if there were complementary national programmes, how the central and national programmes should be related.

It is not our purpose to consider the wider aspects of a Community government. Our interest is confined to stabilisation and regional redistribution. If there were a common currency *and* a Community government with adequate fiscal leverage, they should, in principle, be able to perform in these respects as well as under present arrangements, or if Britain joined the ERM. However, a federal government of the kind envisaged is not an immediate prospect. The unification of the two Germanies will present monetary and fiscal problems for the larger Germany. It will also require budgetary readjustments in the Economic Community. And there is the further possibility of some kind of Community association with other East European countries. Perhaps, one day, a Federal Europe will emerge, but it seems a distant prospect.

Meanwhile, a common currency without any substantial central fiscal leverage may be pressed hard by some Community members. What would it augur for British employment prospects? Of late, British fiscal policy has been used in a moderately restrictive manner, to supplement high interest rates also intended to reduce demand. But what of a situation which called for an increase in demand. A common currency would leave no scope for reducing interest rates. But it still leaves fiscal policy. However, imagine that the Central Bank has raised interest rates to a high level in order to subdue inflation and that, as a consequence, there was widespread unemployment. National governments would still be able to run national budget deficits to raise demand, but if they did, they would have to pay high interest rates. It is difficult to judge how far governments would be prepared to go in such circumstances. The most one can say is that governments may feel themselves more constrained than they have done in the past. This is a state of affairs which might be welcomed by some economists in what I earlier called the classical stream. Workers should get the message that the Central Bank meant business and cut their wages accordingly, thereby pricing themselves back into jobs. We questioned whether differential wages constituted the whole of the North–South story within Britain, though it is part of it. If Britain had entered the currency union at too high a rate of the pound to the ECU, or whatever, it could find the whole economy becoming a 'North' to the rest of the Community. We should also remind ourselves that while one half of Britain's trade is with the Community, a half of it is not. Britain is still open to cost impulses coming from overseas. Given her propensity to generate rather too much nominal wage inflation, this could easily lead to higher price inflation. If there were an incomes policy in place, to keep a curb on that propensity, one might view a common currency with greater equanimity.

CONCLUSION

We began this group of chapters on the International Dimension by asking whether the openness of the British economy put any constraints upon domestic policies to maintain employment. This was a central preoccupation in the era of fixed exchange rates. With free, or qualified, floating and free capital movements, the old verities appear no longer to hold. There is no need for immediate concern about current account deficits, but it is still the case that there should be a sustainable balance in the longer term. There is a serious question whether freely floating exchange rates are equilibrating, that is, always pointing the economy towards a long-term equilibrium. Exchange rates have not only shown excessive volatility, but also perversity, leading the economy away, sometimes for long periods, rather than towards such benchmarks as Purchasing Power Parity would suggest. There is therefore need for government to have an exchange rate policy. Monetary policy should be assigned to exchange rate management, leaving inflation and demand management generally to fiscal policy. (We had, of course, reservations in the macroeconomic chapters whether fiscal policy would be enough, without the support of incomes policy.) It should not be thought that the exchange rate is an autonomous instrument, to be changed at will at the sole discretion of government. Governments can only make a lasting difference to rates if they act in concert.

As regards the European Community, we thought that any employment objectives which could be achieved under present arrangements, could also be achieved if Britain joined ERM in its present form. We thought the same would be possible with a common currency, provided there was a Community federal government with significant fiscal leverage. But we have serious doubts about the potentially adverse effects of a common currency on its own.

19

CONCLUSION

THE SCALE OF THE PROBLEM

Whereas employment in the United States roughly doubled between 1950 and 1989, employment in Britain stayed much the same. In between, there were ups and downs, the highest figures occurring in 1966 and 1979, and the lowest in 1950–3 and 1983. The story of unemployment was different. The average number of unemployed between 1948 and 1968 was 350,000; in the 1970s it was just short of a million; in the 1980s it was higher in every year than it had been in any year prior to 1979; it exceeded three millions in the middle of the decade and was still 1.7 million at the end. The workforce in employment (which includes, besides employees, the self-employed and HM forces) kept close to the working population until the early 1970s, but thereafter a gap opened up.

The Department of Employment has made projections up to the year 2001 of civilian activity rates for men and women, on the assumption of a constant pressure of demand for labour (roughly speaking, constant unemployment), which imply a small rise in the total labour force of 67,000 a year, most of whom are women, who are expected to make up 45 per cent of the total in 2001. If unemployment were to come down by one million below the level at the end of 1989, which would still leave it twice the average of the years 1948–68, the increase in the labour force would be higher, but still less than the average increase between 1971 and 1989. We are dealing with comparatively small changes in the totals. Within the totals, the fall in the number of workers in the lowest age groups, which will become increasingly apparent in the early 1990s, has important implications for training. The unknowns are the scale of the potential immigrations from Hong Kong and South Africa and, possibly, from Eastern Europe.

THE CAUSES OF THE RISE IN UNEMPLOYMENT

The stagflation after 1973 was widespread among the major industrial countries and in explaining it we put much weight on the change in the public's attitude towards inflation. There *was* sustained inflation in Britain in the 1950s and 1960s – for the first time in peace for over 300 years – but it was, if anything, slightly declining. Most other countries also had inflation, though the profile was not always the same: the United States, very important in this context, had smaller price rises in the 1950s but a gradual but distinct acceleration in the 1960s. Since, in most cases, the real economies were performing extraordinarily well, in terms of output, employment and productivity, the inflation was generally tolerated. We attributed the jump in price rises in the early 1970s to three factors; the synchronised expansion of demand in industrial countries triggering an exceptional leap in primary product prices; and two cost impulses – the wage explosions which occurred in several countries at different dates following May 1968 and the quadrupling of the price of oil engineered by the OPEC countries at the end of 1973. At the peak of the upsurge of consumer prices in 1974–5, the lowest rate among sixteen OECD industrial countries was that of Germany, with 7 per cent and the highest Britain and Japan, with nearly 25 per cent. Contractionary demand management, aided in some cases, including Britain, by incomes policies, brought inflation down. By 1978–9 there were six countries with rates below 5 per cent but in the remaining ten rates ran from 6.6 to 13.5 per cent. At this point OPEC gave renewed impetus to costs, countered once more with contractionary demand management policies. This time there was more success in getting inflation down but at the cost of obstinately high unemployment, especially in Europe. Finally, at the end of the 1980s, albeit without any external cost stimulus – primary product prices are relatively low – a new cycle of inflation, to be followed by contraction, seems to threaten. A crude generalisation might be: so long as inflation stays below 5 per cent other objectives are not seriously threatened, while, when it gets over 10 per cent, stopping it gets the highest priority. Between 5 and 10 per cent, different countries respond differently. That was the picture which we formed for mature industrial countries[1] and we shall return to the specifically British role within it. But, before we do so, we turn aside to state our conclusions from examining other explanations for the rise in unemployment.

Spectacular changes in technology, displacing large numbers of workers, are frequently reported and we considered whether the speeding up of technical change might have been responsible. But the facts do not fit. When productivity growth was becoming faster in the decades after the war, unemployment remained exceptionally low: when productivity growth slowed down, unemployment rose. Even so, it could be argued that the full impact of information technology (IT) has yet to be felt and, although we were not able to identify especially vulnerable sectors, we made the obvious, though none the less valid, observation concerning the importance of technical education and training.

The other structural explanation of the rise in unemployment, at any rate in the 1980s, was the impact of the discovery of North Sea oil, whereby Britain had become self-sufficient at the beginning of the decade, when only five years earlier it still had to import all its needs. The consequence was that, to secure any given overall trade balance, the balance among other tradeable goods and services could be allowed to deteriorate to the amount of the gain on oil account. In turn, the share of these tradeables in total GDP could fall, to make room for oil output. The biggest item among these tradeables was manufacturing. But while the enjoyment of the benefits of North Sea oil entailed this 'structural' change, of a relative fall in the output of tradeables, what would happen to the absolute output in these sectors depended on what was happening to the total non-oil GDP. If, for instance, the opportunity had been taken of the relief given by North Sea oil to the balance of payments constraint to expand non-oil output, the absolute fall in manufacturing and other tradeables would have been smaller than if non-oil output was stationary or falling. By a stroke of ill-fortune, self-sufficiency in oil coincided with the first monetarist phase of financial policy of the new Thatcher administration, imposing a tight monetary squeeze, which, reinforced by the effect of North Sea oil itself, drove the real exchange rate up far too high. Within two years manufacturing output had fallen by 15 per cent while employment, already declining, plunged at an alarming rate. The fall was eventually stemmed in the recovery after 1987 but, in 1989, the five million or so employed in manufacturing were 28 per cent fewer than ten years earlier. If much of the unemployment in manufacturing in the early 1980s can be laid at the door of macroeconomic policy, some of it gradually became structural, in the sense that equipment was sold or became obsolete, so that the chances diminished of displaced workers being re-employed in their own industries when output recovered. This is the gloss I would put on the world picture sketched earlier to account for the British recession starting earlier, and going deeper, than in most other countries. A particular consequence of this was the intensification of the North–South divide.

THE WAGE QUESTION

Another alternative explanation of unemployment is that wages are too high. The argument is deceptively simple. Wages are the price of labour: if the price is raised, less labour will be demanded. But, our critique of an Open Letter to the Prime Minister of 1984, whose signatories included some well-known economists, showed the simplicity to be deceptive. Are we concerned with money wages or real wages? If the latter, should we divide money wages by the cost of living to obtain a consumption real wage, as seen by the wage earner, or by some indicator of the prices of the things he sells, to yield a product real wage, which is the cost of labour as seen by the employer. We reported the results of three different approaches.

In the first, the movement of the share of profits in value added in British (non-oil) industrial and commercial companies and in manufacturing since the early 1970s was studied, and the conclusion reached that the considerable movements could be adequately accounted for by demand fluctuations and international competitiveness. The latter, of course, includes the influence of British wages, *vis-à-vis* the rest of the world, which was not in dispute. There was room for a direct influence of wages on the profit share: but, if it was there, it was small. The other studies were all international, addressed to the argument that the high unemployment in Western Europe in the 1980s was the result of real wages being rigid and too high by contrast with the alleged greater flexibility of real wages in the United States. We can best sum up all this work, which is reported in Chapter 8, in the words of Pencavel, the author of one of the most elegant studies, namely that the results 'lean in the direction of rejecting' the classical (that is, high real wage) unemployment hypothesis.

Although the results were not conclusive, we stopped pursuing real wages any further, partly on the grounds that the variable directly involved in wage bargains is the nominal, or money, wage. What determines the level of money wages and what are the consequences of the levels which get established? We looked at three models which have exercised considerable influence on economic policy, in two of which unemployment plays a prominent part. The first, the Phillips curve, did not survive long in its original (1958) form, which made the change in money wages depend on the level of unemployment. The fault, it has always seemed to me, lay not in the general idea that pressure to raise money wages would be weak or non-existent when there is high unemployment and strong when labour is scarce, which is a perfectly sensible idea, but in the attempt to impart spurious precision. The second idea was that of the natural rate of unemployment, which implied that while a Phillips-type trade-off between unemployment and inflation might exist in the short run, the attempt, by means of monetary policy, to push unemployment below the natural rate, could only entail accelerating monetary expansion and inflation. Among my objections here was the extremely wide range of estimates of the natural rate, or NAIRU, which rendered it of little use for practical policy. In the third model, unemployment did not enter the picture at all: instead we were to envisage workers, or their trade unions, having in mind a target real wage when they came to the bargaining table. If, since the last settlement, prices have risen by so much, the first step is to ask for a money wage increase to cover this and then to go for more, for various reasons, for example, productivity, or relativity with other workers. The ideas of the annual wage round and that, at the very least, past, or expected future, price rises should be covered, have become deeply embedded in the British wage-bargaining system. This model can capture the idea of a continuing spiral of wages and prices, which can be damped if productivity rises faster, or if import prices fall relative to domestic costs and with potentially explosive consequences if productivity falters, or import prices rise sharply.

It appears that over most of the postwar period, in times of full employment and in times of high unemployment, the British system of wage and price determination has delivered an annual average rate of wage inflation which has tended to make us lose competitiveness with respect to other major economies. Apart from unemployment itself, we have attempted to check this weakness by means of a succession of incomes policies, or to compensate for it by devaluation during the period of fixed exchange rates, or by allowing the exchange rate to fall in the period of floating which succeeded it. Before coming to broader macroeconomic policies, we examined three types of modification to the wage system. Wage subsidies were suggested by Pigou in the 1920s, as a device to offset the tendency of trade unions to set wages too high. They have been revived in recent years in a marginal form with a variety of objectives in view, for example, to get a lower level of unemployment than the natural rate; to re-employ the long-term unemployed; or to get the benefits of devaluation without intensifying the wage–price spiral. Next we looked at profit sharing, for which Weitzman has made strong claims as an antidote to stagflation, examining the theoretical arguments as well as the lengthy experience of profit sharing in Britain. Unemployment is too serious and persistent for us to wish to reject any proposal which might have even small favourable effects. But we did notice that the historical evidence of the working of profit-sharing schemes in Britain tended to contradict the theoretical claims being made for it, while the wage-subsidy schemes seemed to have in common an element of subterfuge, of getting round various obstacles in the way of sensible objectives. Why not then attack the problem frontally of reforming the system of wage fixing in such a manner as to ensure that the aggregate output of individual wage settlements would be kept in line with what the economy could afford? This discussion of incomes policies included an account of the experience of other countries as well as proposals for this country. This is an issue to which we returned in our consideration of macroeconomic policies.

MACROECONOMIC POLICY IN AN OPEN ECONOMY

The last two parts of the book consider whether the prospects for employment can be improved by macroeconomic policy and how such policy will be affected by the international commercial and financial system within which we shall be living, in particular by developments within the European Economic Community. The analysis of these questions has been made more difficult by doctrinal disputes in economics. Whether these are more acute than in other periods I am not sure, but certainly there was a wave of monetarism which swept in from the Atlantic in the late 1970s. It probably won least support among professional economists, but it undoubtedly captured the imagination of some of our ablest and most influential economic journalists. Most important of all, the macroeconomic programme of the first Thatcher government could reasonably be regarded as a full-scale experiment in monetarist economics. Is it possible, then, to examine the issues objectively? The view we took was that it is very often possible to put one's finger on differences of assumption which lead to differences of policy prescription. This applies to the broad distinction we made between the classical and Keynesian strands of thought, between those who believe that, when subjected to some shock, a market economy will always find its own way back to an optimal configuration and those who believe that, at times, the adjustment mechanisms may fail to work leaving the economy some way off its best, for example, stuck with high unemployment. We illustrated this for the relationships between money, output and prices, with the aid of the famous Fisher equation for the quantity of money, $MV = PT$. By making alternative assumptions about which variables were fixed and which free, one could tell different stories about causality: with one set of assumptions one got the monetarist position, while another set fitted a Keynesian model. Drawing heavily on Brown's study of world inflation (1985), we looked at the historical evidence, noting how in some countries and at some times the inflationary pressure has come from the side of demand and at others from cost impulses, and we supplemented the statistical evidence with case studies of episodes in the postwar period, especially of the British case.

Our survey showed that, when not constrained by other considerations, expansionary fiscal and monetary policy could raise output and employment. The most common 'other considerations' were the fear of inflation and of balance-of-payments deficits. Equally, when exercised in a contractionary manner, demand management could reduce inflation, but it could also bring down output and employment. The fact that the monetarist phase of the Medium Term Financial Strategy was an experiment that did not go according to plan might be regarded as a scientific advance. But any intellectual satisfaction to be derived from this has to be tempered by two considerations. The authors of the strategy had certainly envisaged 'some losses of output initially', but the cost in terms of persistent and prolonged unemployment was inordinately high.

Secondly, while inflation did come down, wage inflation got stuck at around 7½ per cent per annum and, when demand began to grow fast enough to start eating into unemployment, wage inflation began to creep up again.

Whether or not a particular rate of nominal wage inflation is too high depends, of course, on the behaviour of productivity, the increase in competitors' prices and, finally, on the exchange rate. The theory behind floating exchange rates was, precisely, to allow different countries to choose their own inflation rate, which would be reconciled with the others by the appropriate movement of the exchange rate. Unfortunately, experience has shown that free exchange rates can be dominated by capital movements in such a way that for long periods they can move away from the direction indicated by any measure of purchasing power parity. Governments, individually and collectively, have been moving back towards managed exchange rates. We argued that, insofar as interest rates bear on inflation, they do so primarily by raising the exchange rate. But this may, and in the present conjuncture does, go against the need to keep the real exchange rate down in order to improve competitiveness and reduce the excessive deficit in the current balance of payments. The control of aggregate demand should, therefore, be transferred to fiscal policy. It could be that a cut in demand achieved by an increase in income tax will be split between output and prices in the same way as a cut of an equivalent amount achieved by higher interest rates. There is, of course, less likelihood of a money wage response in this case than with higher interest rates which have the initial effect of putting up the retail price index. But the truth is that neither separately, nor together, may fiscal and monetary policy suffice to bring down inflation to the desired extent, without a substantial rise in unemployment. If an incomes policy could be made to stick, it might make all the difference.

ALTERNATIVE TRADE AND PAYMENTS REGIMES

We considered what effect different trade and payments regimes might have on employment. We looked briefly at protection. Without doubt, in the past, such measures have helped employment in particular industries and countries. But their success is heavily dependent on the absence of retaliation. One might be driven to such measures in a crisis as happened in the 1930s. But so long as the free trade and payments system is functioning reasonably well the better policy is to strive for improvements in that system. A similar argument applies, though perhaps with less force, against the reinstitution of some control over capital movements. One reason for the variability and perversity of exchange-rate movements has been the wave of financial deregulation which has been going round the world. Would not the restoration of some control over capital movements help stability? We doubted whether the unilateral introduction of such controls was now feasible. It would have to be done by international cooperation. It is not on today's agenda, but the idea may be revived if other improvements meet no success. What are on the international agenda are schemes for establishing target zones within which countries would undertake to maintain their currencies. Research has suggested that if such a scheme had been operated by Germany, the United States and Japan between 1975 and 1986, all three countries could have been better off. Other theoretical models have demonstrated the potential gains from international cooperation in monetary and fiscal policy. At the same time, it would be prudent not to bank too heavily on the successful coordination of national policies. These schemes are still on the drawing board. More urgent, perhaps, are decisions which must be taken in relation to the European Economic Community.

THE EUROPEAN DIMENSION

Britain, with other members of the European Community, is already committed to the Single Market in 1992. It is also committed to join the Exchange Rate Mechanism of the European Monetary System as soon as the time is right. There is an ambiguity about 'joining the ERM'. There is the ERM as it has been operated by its members since 1979 – and there are the next stages intended to culminate, in the not too distant future, in a common European currency. Under present rules of ERM, realignments of the central rates of the different currencies are permitted and in the period 1979–87 eleven such realignments occurred. We took the view that, if it was that kind of ERM we were to join, the British would not be tying their macroeconomic policy hands in any significant manner. But we should also consider where the ERM is intended to go, and the way to do this seemed to be to assume the Single Market (which is, of course, a separate matter) in full operation, with freedom of movement between members of all goods and services, as well as of capital, including the location of enterprises. We also assume a Eurobank issuing the common currency. In such a world interest rates would no longer be a significant instrument of macroeconomic policy at the national level, though they would still operate for the whole Community. There might still be differences in retail bank deposit rates in Bolton and Bologna, without causing an instant transfer of all accounts from one to the other, but arbitrage would prevent the emergence of differences between rates in the major financial centres. Thus, if there is to be an instrument of demand management at the national level, it has, by default, to be fiscal policy which I have recommended anyway. However, it may be less readily available than in the past. Suppose that the Eurobank has decided to rein in demand and has raised interest rates. But suppose that member A already has higher unemployment than the rest of the Community, in the way that Scotland has more than the United Kingdom as a whole. The government of A might want to increase public expenditure, or cut taxes, to avert even higher unemployment. It can do so by borrowing, but only at the lately increased interest rates.

However, suppose that besides the Eurobank there is also a European central government, or rather a Community agency with significant fiscal leverage. Then, either in a discretionary manner, or automatically, it can channel funds in the direction of country A. We referred to the suggestion of pooling part, or all, of the unemployment insurance funds of Community members. Then, if the conjuncture is such that some members have falling while others have rising unemployment, some of the increased contributions from the former will *automatically* be transferred to the latter. This will not reverse, but will certainly soften the impact of unemployment and loss of income, as already happens between the more prosperous South and less prosperous North within the United Kingdom. Such a scheme would not give any additional discretionary power to the European Commission. At the same time it does not exclude the further development of Community government functions.[2] Already the Commission can make regional grants to underdeveloped parts of the EC, or areas adversely affected by industrial decline. But beyond observing that we do not think that a Community government, with significant fiscal leverage, would be detrimental to British employment prospects, we need pursue the matter no further. In any case, the time scale for any such developments is longer than that involved in joining the ERM or a common currency.

In early 1990, the United Kingdom inflation rate was above that of other major EC economies, and the strategy was to bring the rate down before joining the ERM. What matters in the medium term is the rate of wage inflation, rather than a price index which is abnormally high or low because of the inclusion – *via* mortgage rates – of the influence of interest rates themselves and of the practice of measuring inflation in terms of prices now, as against the same month a year ago. The instrument for reducing inflation has been the interest rate, and it works on the import component of costs through the exchange rate and on the wage component through reducing demand and higher unemployment. To the extent that realignment within the ERM in the future may be made harder and, *a fortiori* with a common currency, the high exchange rate means of reducing inflation is cut out, leaving only the effect on wages *via* unemployment, which may be small, and long drawn out. Fiscal policy is a more predictable instrument for regulating demand, but in reducing wage inflation, it too works *via* unemployment. Our fear is that we may be in for a long grinding process, with slow growth and unemployment rising again.

Some commentators believe that the announcement that Britain is about to join, or has joined, the ERM will, of itself, bring an immediate moderation in wage increases, since wage-earners are served notice that, from now on, excessive wage increases will not be accommodated by a fall in the exchange rate, but instead would mean workers pricing themselves, or others, out of jobs. One has to be sceptical. Only a minority of workers perceive themselves to be directly involved in producing for export, or to compete with imports. High wage increases have by no means been confined to manufacturing: there have been spectacular rises in retail distribution. And even when exports, or competing with imports are directly involved, while half our trade is with the EC, half is not. Even if we become pegged to the D-mark, we shall not be pegged to the dollar, or the yen. There may be times when exports to non-EC markets are exceptionally profitable; workers may want a share; and their rises may have knock-on effects elsewhere. The habit of having rather too much wage inflation is very deeply engrained, and it is wishful thinking that employers and workers will give it up simply in response to an announcement. If excessive wage inflation persists after we have joined, then, of course, the pressure will be on the sectors of the economy most exposed to trade with the Community. But this too may be a long-drawn-out process. Hence our fear that getting wage inflation down before we go into the ERM, and keeping it down when we are in, by means of monetary and/or fiscal policy alone, means that unemployment will be rising for a while, from the 1.6 millions as measured in 1990, or from over two millions, using the measurement methods of 1980. There is very little prospect of it going on down to the levels of the 1960s.

FUTURE POLICY

In the first two parts of the book we discussed a number of measures which might be taken which need not push up costs. There is, first of all, the regional disparity between North and South, which existed even at times of low national unemployment in the 1950s and 1960s. Developments in the North meant, in some degree, putting less pressure on costs than in the South. If the balance of job creation could be tilted towards the North, all the country might benefit. It would give a little relief to the traffic congestion in London and other parts of the South, and would reduce the amount of new development in the South, which is often strenuously resisted by those who live there already. Putting aside euphemisms this means taxing the South, not just for the benefit of the

North, but for the benefit of both. Secondly, schemes for re-employing the long-term unemployed seem to exert less inflationary pressure than re-employing the same number of persons by conventional reflation, and they are good in themselves. Finally there is training, in which, in the past, Britain has been notoriously backward. Recently much attention has been paid to the education and training of the young. They are going to become scarce in the 1990s. The better they are trained, the better the outlook in the long term. Meanwhile, the retraining of workers in the middle age group, who become redundant, or who have left the labour market and wish to return, assumes greater urgency.

But the biggest question mark hanging over future employment and unemployment prospects in the coming decade is nominal wage inflation. In Chapter 11, on Incomes Policy, we argued that such policies had succeeded in some countries and, indeed, had some success in Britain. But such an opinion would not be universally accepted. At the end of the 1970s monetarists could argue that it did not matter anyway, since control of the money supply would suffice to bring inflation down, without any such unnecessary interventions in the labour market. Now, ten years on, one has to say that the experiment was tried, but it failed. It failed on its own terms. It is not that restrictive monetary policy had no effects. It did: but what was worrying was that even three million unemployed appear to have had limits in bringing down nominal wage inflation. Possibly memories of the severity of the 1980 squeeze will make wage-bargainers more responsive to ministerial appeals for wage restraint in the milder 1990 squeeze. One hopes this will be so, but does not believe it. In my view the time is ripe to reopen the question of incomes policy, to see whether some mechanisms can be set up which will allow renewed expansion of demand and employment, without reigniting inflation. Neither incomes policy, nor, for that matter, exchange rate policy, fall easily along the lines of division which the major British political parties have set for themselves. It was as an antidote to unhelpful partisanship that I suggested setting up a Council of Economic Advisers. Others would go further and advocate changes in voting methods, or more far-reaching constitutional changes.

With the economy poised as it is at the outset of the 1990s, the fear is that with interest rates the sole instrument to manage demand – even if supplemented, or replaced, by a more active fiscal policy – unemployment may remain high for many years ahead. There are no economic laws which say that this must be so. There would be nothing 'natural' about such an outcome. We could have much lower unemployment than we have had, even at the end of the 1980s, but the way there requires political leadership as much as economic inventiveness.

As an interest group, the unemployed are among the weakest in society. The great majority of them, men and women, young and old, have a powerful common aim – to get a job. But, when they succeed, they become, at once, members of another interest group. Unemployment is not a reflection on the unemployed – it is a reflection on all of us.

Appendix to Chapter 8

THE PUZZLE OF THE APPARENT FALL IN UNITED STATES REAL WAGES

To simplify matters we will concentrate on two periods of ten years before and after the peak in weekly earnings in 1973. From 1963 to 1973 an index of real weekly earnings rose from 101.1 to 114.7 (1980=100) and in the next ten years fell back to 98.8, leaving a net drop of 2.25 per cent. The first things to suggest themselves as an explanation are hours of work. They dropped from 38.8 in 1963 to 35 hours a week in 1983, so that average real hourly earnings rose over the whole period by 5.9 per cent. To the extent that this fall was voluntary, the reduction in weekly earnings does not denote a loss of economic welfare. The next line of investigation is suggested by the fact that over the whole period real weekly earnings in manufacturing rose by 9.25 per cent, compared with the fall of 2.25 per cent for the whole economy. We know that most of the increase in employment in the United States has taken place in the service sector, in many parts of which, for example the retail trade, weekly and hourly earnings were lower than average in 1963 and were growing more slowly thereafter. Was the overall average being kept down by a relative shift in the labour force towards lower paid jobs?

   Table A1 gives details of hourly and weekly earnings (in 1975 dollars) for eight industrial groups in the non-agricultural private sector of the United States economy, as well as figures for employment of wage and salary earners, for the years 1963, 1973, and 1983. Both real hourly and real weekly earnings were higher in all groups in 1973 than in 1963. Hourly and weekly earnings in mining continued to increase between 1973 and 1983, but in all other groups they fell, in quite widely varying proportions.

   Total employment increased throughout the period, by 33 per cent in the first ten years, and by 17 per cent in the second. Employment rose much faster than average in both periods in Retail Trade; Finance, Insurance and Real Estate; and Services, in all of which hourly and weekly earnings were initially lower than average in 1963 and increased less than average until 1983. In the other five groups earnings, both hourly and weekly, were above average in all three years. The facts suggest that we should calculate averages of hourly and weekly earnings in the three years weighted respectively with employment in 1963 and 1983. The results of this exercise are shown in table A2. The figures in table A2 for the unweighted average of 'total private' differ from those in table A1. The main reason is that the employment figures in table A1 are for wage and salary earners, which includes non-production workers as well as production workers. As was observed earlier the ratio of non-production to production workers was changing, but we are only using the employment figures as weights and the error would be systematic and unlikely to alter much the *relative* changes in real earnings.

Table A1. *United States hourly and weekly earnings in 1975 dollars and employment of wage and salary earners*

	Hourly earnings $1975			Weekly earnings $1975			Employment (000s)		
	1963	1973	1983	1963	1973	1983	1963	1973	1983
Total private	4.01	4.77	4.33	155.5	176.0	151.6	47,427	63,059	74,287
Mining	4.83	5.75	6.09	201.1	243.8	259.0	635	642	957
Construction	5.99	8.25	6.45	223.5	285.6	239.3	3,010	4,097	3,940
Manufacturing	4.32	4.95	4.77	175.1	201.6	191.3	16,995	20,154	18,497
Transportation[a]	5.08	6.08	5.83	208.8	246.1	227.3	3,903	4,656	4,958
Wholesale trade	4.31	4.94	4.62	174.8	194.1	177.8	3,248	4,279	5,259
Retail trade	2.95	3.52	3.10	110.1	116.6	92.4	8,530	12,329	15,545
Finance, Insurance and real estate	3.95	4.27	3.94	148.3	156.4	142.6	2,830	4,046	5,467
Services[a]	3.41	4.54	3.95	123.1	152.5	129.1	8,277	12,857	19,665

Source: *Employment and Earnings Report of President, 1985.*
[a] 1964 figures for 1963 earnings.

Table A2. *United States hourly and weekly earnings in the non-agricultural private sector in 1975 dollars: average and weighted with employments of 1963 and 1983*

	Hourly			Weekly		
	1963	1973	1983	1963	1973	1983
1963 weights	4.07	4.89	4.48	158.9	184.1	165.7
Unweighted	4.07	4.85	4.31	158.9	180.7	155.4
1983 weights	3.91	4.75	4.31	150.9	173.9	155.4

Comparison of the simple average figures of real earnings with the two employment weighted averages, shows the importance of the changing composition of the labour force. The rise in earnings between 1963 and 1973 is slightly accentuated, and the fall between 1973 and 1983 diminished with fixed employment weights. Overall, real hourly earnings in 1983 were 10 per cent higher than 1963, compared with the 6 per cent rise of the simple average, while the real weekly earnings were up 3–4 per cent, instead of over 2 per cent down.

Parallel with the changes in the industrial composition of the labour force, there have also been important changes in its personal characteristics. For instance, in 1963, 34.1 per cent of civilian employees were women and by 1983 this had risen to 43.7 per cent. Similarly the percentage in total employment of black and other ethnic minorities rose from 10.5 to 11.8 per cent, according to the

1989 Economic Report of the President. The presumption is that women and ethnic minorities are, on average, lower paid than men and whites, but these demographic changes in the labour force are, to some extent, correlated with the changes in industrial composition and we shall not attempt to estimate independently their contribution to resolving the paradox of falling real wages.

These calculations make the overall picture of the past twenty or so years more credible. They show that the typical annual increase of earnings continued up to 1973. It was there that the break occurred. With fixed weights, the average fall in hourly earnings in the next ten years was 9 per cent, and in weekly earnings over 10 per cent. This still seems to call for explanation. The first question is to ask what were the respective contributions to this fall of changes in nominal earnings and changes in the price level.

Table A3 shows the annual percentage changes in United States hourly earnings, the Consumer Price Index, and the real wage obtained by dividing the former by the latter.

It is apparent that the changes in nominal earnings fluctuate comparatively little – between 6.5 and 9 per cent in the 1970s, and dropping to between 2.25 and 4.5 per cent in the 1980s. An index adjusted for overtime (in manufacturing only) and interindustry employment shifts shows even greater stability. By comparison the fluctuations in the CPI are quite large and it is these changes which dominate in determining the changes in real wages. We shall return to this phenomenon later.

Table A3. *Percentage changes in hourly earnings, prices and real earnings in the United States since previous year*

	Nominal hourly earnings	CPI	Real earnings
1971	6.8	4.4	2.3
1972	7.2	3.2	3.9
1973	6.5	6.2	0.3
1974	7.6	11.0	−3.1
1975	6.8	9.1	−2.1
1976	7.3	5.8	1.4
1977	8.0	1.7	6.2
1978	8.4	7.6	0.7
1979	8.3	11.3	−2.7
1980	8.1	13.5	−4.8
1981	8.9	10.3	−1.3
1982	5.9	6.2	−0.3
1983	4.4	3.2	1.2
1984	3.7	4.3	−0.6
1985	3.0	3.6	−0.6
1986	2.2	1.9	0.3
1987	2.5	3.6	−1.1
1988	3.3	4.0	−0.7

Source: *Economic Report of the President, 1989.*

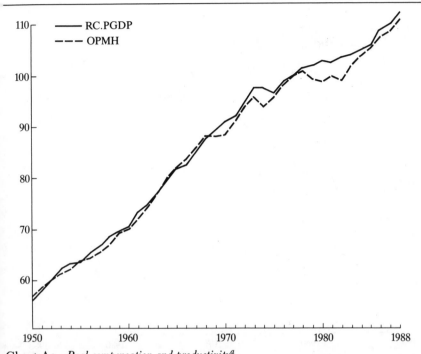

Chart A1   *Real compensation and productivity*[a]
Source: *Economic Report of the President, 1990*, Tables C44 and C46
[a]RC.PGDP is nominal hourly compensation divided by the implicit GDP deflator for the non-farm business sector, and OPMH is output per manhour in the same sector.

The concept of the real wage we have been considering so far relates the nominal earnings of a worker to the prices of the things he buys – it is a measure of the consumption wage. But the concept which would bear upon employment is the product wage: what matter are the costs of labour to the employer, set against the value of his product. One such measure is real hourly compensation,[1] which we show in chart A1 for the non-farm business sector for the period 1950 to 1988, together with productivity – output per manhour – in the same sector. Unlike the graph of real hourly earnings (chart A2), this chart springs no surprises. Over the whole period from 1950 to 1988 real compensation and productivity both nearly doubled, and they follow one another quite closely on the way. One can discern the productivity slowdown, starting around 1968, which is in accordance with Denison's more subtle diagnosis (Denison, 1979) and there is a corresponding slowdown in real compensation. But, apart from one fall, from 1973 to 1975, real compensation is rising all the time. Whereas, between 1963 and 1983, there was a rise of a mere 8 per cent in real hourly earnings, there was a rise of 34 per cent in real hourly compensation, and while the former *fell* by 9 per cent between 1973 and 1983, real hourly compensation rose by a further 6 per cent. What the signatories of the open letter appeared to be

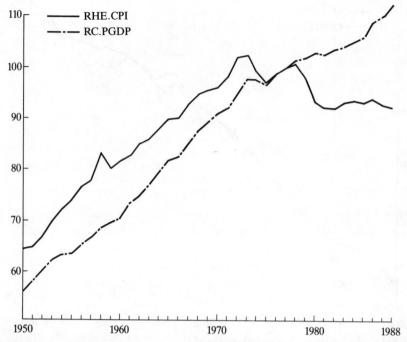

Chart A2 *Consumption earnings and product compensation*[a]
Source: *As Chart A1*
[a]RHECPI is nominal hourly earnings divided by the consumer price index, and
RCPGDP is nominal hourly compensation divided by the implicit GDP deflator,
all for the non-farm business sector.

doing was to praise the real wage restraint of the United States, which they
believed contributed to the growth of employment in the longer run (twenty
years). What is being said here is that when the appropriate concept of real
wages is used, and related to productivity, the alleged restraint disappears. To
turn the issue inside out in this manner may be correct, but one suspects that
many readers may not find it altogether convincing.

There is still left unresolved the gap between real hourly earnings and real
hourly compensation which opened up in the mid-1970s and appears to be
widening (chart A2). Can one offer any explanation of this remarkable difference? The greater part of the arithmetical answer is quickly given. Compensation
is earnings *plus* supplementary payments, that is, employers' contributions to
social insurance and private benefit plans for their employees. These supplementaries were 5–7 per cent of the wage and salary bill in the 1950s; rose to 12 per
cent in 1970; and reached nearly 20 per cent in the mid-1980s. Secondly, real
compensation was obtained by dividing the nominal amounts by the implicit
GDP price deflator, while real earnings were obtained by deflating nominal
earnings with the consumer price index. Throughout much of the postwar

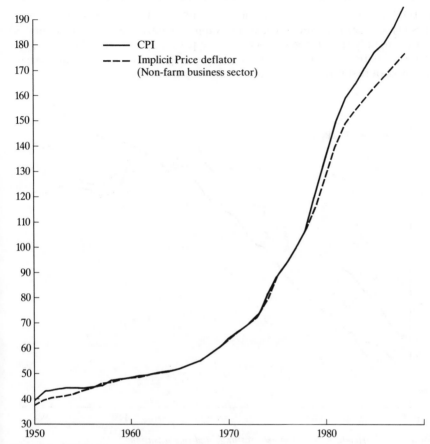

Chart A3 *Two measures of price change*
Source: *As chart A1*

period, these two indexes kept close together, but after 1978 they began, increasingly, to part company (chart A3). The main reasons for this divergence would appear to be the exceptional rises in the items of 'shelter' and 'energy' in the CPI, the former being heavily influenced by the rate of interest, until the estimation of this item was changed in 1983, so that between 1977 and 1984 the increase in the CPI was 8 per cent more than in the implicit GDP deflator. These items also tend to fluctuate more widely than other items in the index. There are some other small differences between real hourly earnings and real hourly compensation, but supplementaries and the differing price indexes are the main ones. In chart A4, line (1) is real hourly earnings, which fell 9 per cent between 1977 and 1988. Line (2) is nominal hourly compensation divided by the CPI: there is still an initial fall after 1978, but by 1988 we have an overall rise of nearly 2 per cent. Line (3) is nominal compensation divided by the implicit GDP deflator. The initial fall has now been reduced to a barely perceptible pause and, by 1988, real compensation is 12 per cent higher than 1977. The gap between lines (1) and (2) is mainly the growing supplementaries, and between lines (2) and (3) mainly the divergence between the price indexes. Together with some smaller differences, they open up a gap of 20 per cent between the extreme measures of real wages, in a matter of eleven years.

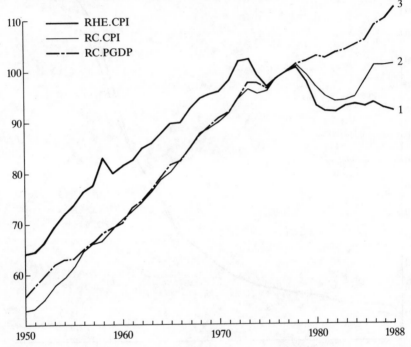

Chart A4 *Different measures of real earnings and compensation*
Source: *As chart A1*

NOTES

NOTES TO CHAPTER 2

1 Trends through the year are obtained from samples of employers.
2 Though figures are published by the Department of Employment for the whole United Kingdom, the Labour Force Survey covers only Great Britain. Tiresome as it is, one should always note when only Great Britain is involved.
3 This refers to people without a job who were available to start work within two weeks, and had either looked for a job in the last four weeks, or were waiting to start a job already obtained. The labour force refers to those aged sixteen and over, which includes men of 65 and over and women of 60 and over, and is thus not co-extensive with the population of working age. In 1989, there were 0.8 million over retirement age in the labour force.
4 Participants in the black economy may do one or more of the following: evade direct taxes; not collect taxes (such as VAT) when, by law, they should and/or not pay over the proceeds; not pay insurance contributions for their employees. Estimates of the scale of the black economy run from the order of 3 per cent of GDP to much higher numbers. As regards policy, the view taken here is that since what defines blackness is law-breaking, the only proper policy is to reduce it at every opportunity.
5 Those participants in government training programmes and schemes who in the course of their participation receive training in the context of a workplace but are not employees, self-employed or HM forces.
6 Dicks and Hatch (1989) have made a careful econometric study of the relationship between employment and unemployment. They found that a simple rule-of-thumb model, which took into account the fact that any rise in employment would, besides drawing on claimants, also draw on those hitherto economically inactive, and they built up a more sophisticated model which took into account special employment measures and Restart interviews. Their results suggested that, although unemployment had been falling because there were more jobs, it was also true that much of the decline in claimants since 1986 was due to a shift in the employment–unemployment relationship, as a result of Special Employment measures – especially the introduction of more rigorous availability-for-work tests and the rapid growth of Restart interviews. Their Restart variable alone contributed 0.75 million to the fall in unemployment, which is about one half of the fall between 1986 and mid-1989, which seems to be consistent with Gregg's estimate of 0.5 million up to early 1988.

NOTES TO CHAPTER 3

1 These concepts turn out to be not as simple as they sound, but we will not pursue the matter here.
2 For an exposition of this kind of model see Worswick (1959).
3 This case is of special interest, for it corresponds to the revised opinion of Ricardo (1821) in the third edition of his *Principles of Political Economy* that, while the introduction of machinery would always be of benefit to landlords and capitalists (in the present example, the Planner) it could often be injurious to the interest of the class of labourers by putting men and women out of work.
4 See also Nabseth and Ray (1974) and Ray (1984). Both works study the first introduction and subsequent diffusion through industry in different countries of new industrial processes. The time lags are often long.
5 A further reason for sticking to labour productivity is that the conceptual problems in measuring capital are very great, and, in the view of some, insurmountable.
6 See the comments by Matthews on a version of the catch-up hypothesis presented by Marris to a conference on Slower Growth in the Western World in 1982 (Matthews, 1982, pages 12 and 13).
7 We treat the energy cost rises as, in the main, the result of decisions taken by OPEC, when they got their act together. The shock came from the supply side. The primary product price increases of 1972–3 are not so straightforward. They can be seen as the consequence of the synchronisation of booms in a number of advanced countries, and were thus endogenous. However, for any *one* country, the raw material price rises could be regarded as in the main exogenous cost increases, to which domestic policy then had to respond.
8 There was a lesser recovery in productivity growth in the United States, but there unemployment started to fall even earlier.
9 During the 1980s there was a notable rise in self employment, and the equation was re-estimated to include self-employed as well as employees in employment.

NOTES TO CHAPTER 5

1 Brown (1972). See also the chapter on 'UV Analysis' by Brown in Worswick (1974).
2 Layard and Nickell (1987) also calculate this index for occupations, industries and regions.

NOTES TO CHAPTER 6

1 It hardly needs to be said that not all regions in the North and South share a common experience. The former includes, for instance, the East Midlands,

whose unemployment rate, to mention but one economic indicator, has been below the national average throughout, while the South West includes Cornwall, parts of which could claim to be honorary North. But the North–South distinction is commonly made in discussions of this question, and it seemed sensible to draw an uncomplicated dividing line.

2 Until the 1970s, the West Midlands region could be bracketed with the South East for high growth and low unemployment, but in the 1980s it had joined the North with high unemployment. (A less marked switch was made by Yorkshire and Humberside.) If the chart is redrawn with West Midlands taken out altogether, the downward slope is somewhat reduced before 1971 and after 1979, but the intervening pause remains.

3 For a fuller discussion of this point see page 17–18.

4 They are: Agriculture, forestry and fishing; Energy and water supply; Metal manufacturing and chemicals; Metal goods, engineering and vehicles; Other manufacturing; Construction; Transport and communication; Wholesale distribution, hotels, and catering; Retail distribution; Banking, insurance and finance; Public administration and defence; and Education, health and other services.

5 Egginton was, in fact, unable to find firm evidence of the influence of the housing variables he tried, but Jackman and Kan (1988) had more success.

6 Figures for unemployment have been revised many times since 1979, almost always downward. These figures are taken from the *Employment Gazette, Supplement*, April 1989.

7 Brown (1972) reckoned that in the 1960s the effects of all forms of regional policy was to create jobs in manufacturing at the rate of around 30,000 a year, and in total employment around 50,000 a year in the Development Areas. Moore, Rhodes and Tyler (1986) estimated that over the period 1960–71 regional policy created 336,000 (gross) and 309,000 (net) jobs in manufacturing, and from 1971–81, 268,000 (gross) and 221,000 (net). The 1960s estimates are very close to Brown's.

8 Apart from varying parts of the South-West Region, all the Development Areas or Districts come within the North of our North–South divide.

NOTES TO CHAPTER 7

1 These figures are taken from Prais (1976).

2 Small multiples have 2–9 outlets and large multiples 10 or more.

3 We include public corporations in the market sector. Their output is mainly determined by market considerations – qualified to a limited extent by government regulation. Also in this period a number of public corporations were privatised, for example, British Telecom, British Gas. By including public corporations in the market sector already, no modifications of employment numbers are needed when privatisation occurs.

4 It is not an absolute requirement that the extra jobs should be given by the government. The extra jobs could be made to appear in the private sector, for example, by deficit financed tax cuts. But the points we wish to make can all

be made with the example of government as employer. It is also assumed that their net contribution to GDP is useful. In most national accounts all government employment contributes to GDP, whether it is useful or not.

5 A more exact statement would be: When there is a net addition of one to the total employed in the public sector. The question of positive discrimination in filling posts in the public sector in favour of particular groups, for example, the long-term unemployed, is a separate issue.

NOTES TO CHAPTER 8

1 I have been unable to reproduce exactly the figures quoted in the open letter, and there are some ambiguities, for example, are we concerned with labour costs or wages? But I would not dispute the broad picture.

2 The United States figures are total employees on non-agricultural payrolls: the United Kingdom figures are employees in employment. Both series exclude the self-employed. If hours of work were taken into account, both lines would be tilted a little downward.

3 The difference continued. In 1987, real weekly earnings were nearly 5 per cent below the level of 1963, while real hourly compensation and productivity were up by 39.1 per cent and 38.4 per cent respectively.

4 Paper delivered at the Centre for Economic Policy Research, March 1985.

5 According to the wage-gap approach, United States real wages were believed to be more flexible than Western Europe's in the 1970s and less afterwards. Pencavel's calculations show that the standard deviations over the period 1960–84 (with and without removal of trend) of both money and real wages were less in the United States than in the other seven countries.

6 The danger of a vicious spiral of wages and prices was discussed by Beveridge (1944); and economists in the Economic Section of the Cabinet Office who were engaged in studies leading to the 1944 White Paper on *Employment Policy* were preoccupied with the threat of excessive wage increases under conditions of full employment (see Cairncross and Watts, 1989, p. 324).

7 Alternatively, 5½ per cent unemployment would deliver zero wage inflation. Since productivity was rising, some wage inflation could occur without prices rising.

8 Friedman (1968). Phelps had formulated the idea earlier.

9 Introduction to Cross (1988).

10 See Laidler (1975), page 45.

11 See Bean, Nickell and Layard (1988) page 158.

12 See the figures quoted by Solow in Bean, Layard and Nickell (1988), page 32.

13 Hysteresis, a concept taken into economics from electromagnetism, in which a variable is influenced by its own past values, needs to be handled with caution. One can understand how, all other things being equal, a larger number of unemployed will exercise a bigger downward pressure on wage settlements than a smaller one. One can further understand that, if the unemployment is prolonged, more and more unemployed will become 'unemployable' and cease to exercise downward pressure on wages. But will

this work in reverse? Starting from high unemployment, we embark on a vigorous expansion. Initially, wage inflation may accelerate while total unemployment is still high. But, provided we stick to our guns, more and more 'unemployables' rehabilitate themselves and take jobs. Their absorption into employment exercises no additional pressure on wages. It is a nice idea, but would a responsible economic adviser put his shirt on it?

14 This compensated in full on gross earnings of the average wage earner. The threshold was, in the event, triggered eleven times in some agreements.

15 If this seems strange to a modern reader, it may be added that the inflation differential in export prices was quite small, of the order of 1 per cent per annum, and many thought that, following the 1949 devaluation, sterling was undervalued.

NOTES TO CHAPTER 9

1 The argument had previously appeared in Pigou (1927).

2 This is a necessary implication of the real wage model. So much was that model taken for granted at the time that Pigou had no need to make the point explicitly.

3 This letter is not in the *Collected Writings* of John Maynard Keynes.

NOTES TO CHAPTER 10

1 This postulates a separate factor of production, call it entrepreneurship or entrepreneurial ability, which will only be brought into play by the appropriate reward. If entrepreneurship is treated as a specialised form of 'labour', then 'normal' profits would be zero.

2 There would be zero output at an infinite price, and the proceeds would still be a finite amount. If this is dismissed as a mathematical conceit, one could make a slightly more realistic statement that the firm would employ a few workers to produce a small output, to be sold at a very high price. The firm would have no incentive to expand, since proceeds would be the same – *MR* is zero – while *MC* is positive.

NOTES TO CHAPTER 11

1 Earlier Chancellors seemed primarily worried about inflation. More recently, a classical twist has been given to the exhortations, by urging that excess will cause unemployment. This, of course, implies that higher money wages entail higher real wages, which may, or may not, be the case.

2 Keynes did argue that if, *ceteris paribus*, the level of employment did rise, then, somehow or other, the real wage would have to fall and he gave roundabout examples of how this might happen. Since it was, in any case, a subsidiary issue, it was unfortunate that Keynes retained this classical association

between real wages and employment, for it is quite easy to set up models, consistent with known facts, in which real wages do not fall when there is a general rise in employment. The central point remained, however, that a cut in money wages might well leave real wages unchanged.

3 This is true of the term, but not quite true of the substance. In *The Economic Consequences of Mr Churchill*, which he wrote following the return to the Gold Standard in 1925, Keynes put forward the idea that the Chancellor of the Exchequer would invite trade unions to agree to a uniform cut of 10 per cent in money wages in all industries, including public service. His argument was that, because of the overvaluation of the pound, either money wages would be *forced down*, in a hateful and disastrous way, because of unequal effects on stronger and weaker groups, or they could be reduced by agreement. But this proposal was not followed up. See Keynes, 1972.

4 In a survey of incomes policies in European countries (Boltho, 1982), Faxen challenges the traditional view taken in the United Kingdom and the United States that incomes policy is an additional instrument for controlling inflation – a third instrument of demand management. He notes that smaller countries are sometimes both highly unionised and have centralised systems of wage determination, bipartite or tripartite. In such cases, the primary purpose of incomes policy may be not so much to reduce inflation, as to minimise conflict between the parties in reaching an end on which all are agreed.

5 In Boltho (Ed.) (1982), *op.cit.*

6 This may come as a surprise, especially if one looks only at the last of the series of incomes policies, the one introduced by the Labour government in 1975. That policy began, in its first year, by imposing a uniform lump-sum pay rise limit of £6 a week, with a cut off for any increase at all at £8,500 a year. In the second year a gradual move away from lump-sum payments towards percentage limits on increases began. In an article on 'Incomes Policies and Differentials', in the *National Institute Economic Review*, August 1978, Dean looked for evidence whether, in the incomes policies introduced in the 1970s, differentials were squeezed and relativities distorted. It is worth quoting his conclusion at some length: 'The main conclusion is that we can find little evidence, apart from the highest income groups, that there has been a strong compression of pay brought about directly by incomes policies. The period of the £6 policy, which might have been expected to narrow differentials considerably, had very little effect at the aggregate level, although at company level it may well have been more important ... The end of incomes policy periods is always said to be a period when differentials are restored, but we have also found little evidence of this.'

7 One of the more convincing examples of this *genre* is Henry and Ormerod, (1978).

8 The most fully worked out argument in favour of incomes policy in recent years is that of Meade (1982). In his view, demand management, that is fiscal and monetary policy, would endeavour to keep the money value of GDP growing at an appropriate steady rate. Within that context, the primary purpose of wage fixing would be, not to contain the growth of money wages,

but to 'promote employment'. He recommended some kind of independent arbitral body, or pay commission, to make awards setting rates of pay which would promote employment. We do not ourselves agree with the switch of the objective of incomes policy from establishing pay levels to promoting employment, but we do endorse Meade's observation that an incomes policy will only be acceptable in a humane, compassionate society, if it is accompanied by measures to ensure a socially acceptable distribution of income and wealth.

NOTES TO CHAPTER 12

1 Addressing a conference of economists in 1980, Meade (*Economic Journal*, March, 1981) dismissed the 'clearly foolish crudity of dividing the universe into monetarists and Keynesians', and in no time at all he had run up a taxonomic schema distinguishing at least eighteen non-empty classes of macroeconomists. The twofold distinction I am making here is not that between monetarists and Keynesians, although it may be equally foolhardy. I am distinguishing between those who normally assume that market forces will work to achieve the best possible result, should not be interfered with, and require no assistance; and those who assume that market forces can work, but equally can fail to do so, and that there is a presumption that the system will work better if provided with an accelerator and a brake.

2 In this model, saving, S, is defined as the difference between income and consumption. Thus $S = Y - C$, and from equation (1), therefore, $S = I$, saving equals investment.

3 We need constantly to remind ourselves that the background against which the early debates took place was one in which the general price level in Britain and the United States had been steady or falling (wars apart). By contrast, in the postwar period in nearly all countries nominal incomes and prices have risen in most years. In Britain, in no year since the war has the retail price index not exceeded that of the previous year, with the exception of 1959, when, to the first place of decimals, the index was the same as in 1958. There are no exceptions for nominal wage indexes. When both nominal incomes and prices are rising all the time, we are in a different ball game. At one time the predominant view, derived from the experience of European inflations after the First World War, was that if prices rose sharply, that would create expectations of even greater rises in future, and consumers would spend now rather than wait. The personal saving ratio would fall: in the worst case, there would be a 'flight into goods'. More recently, when we have become long accustomed to inflation, a speeding up of inflation would, so the argument runs, *increase* the saving ratio, as people were obliged to put aside larger amounts in order to maintain the real value of their liquid assets, which was being reduced by the increased inflation. In the inflationary burst of 1978–80, the British saving ratio rose and, as inflation fell back, the ratio also declined. However, the personal saving ratio went on falling after the inflation rate flattened out, and even started to rise again. Whether the

inflation effect on the propensity to save is wholly, or partially, stabilising, is an empirical question, and it may well vary with the historical context.

4 There are two broad categories of transaction, those in which money is exchanged for labour or materials in the production of goods and services, for consumption or for capital equipment, and those where money is exchanged for second-hand assets, be they used cars, old masters or company shares. In the present context, we are concerned with the first category, so that the value of PT is an indicator of national income. P and T are index numbers of the average price and the average quantity of the multiplicity of individual transactions which take place within a given period. We avoid pursuing the many problems which beset the construction of such indexes.

5 'Money', in the present context, denotes a non-interest bearing liquid asset. In the 1930s, when the *General Theory* was written, current accounts in commercial banks did not bear interest, and money was usually taken to mean notes and coin in the hands of the public *plus* current accounts in banks. In recent decades the term 'money' has often been extended to include interest bearing deposit accounts, on the grounds that, for practical purposes, they were highly liquid. More recently still, many current accounts, which previously carried no interest, have begun to do so.

6 That is, whether an increase in monetary demand will elicit a considerable increase in real output.

7 Excess demand will not necessarily lead to open inflation if, as was the case in Britain in the war, there is price control and rationing.

8 They might loosely be described as the Rational Expectations school. Lucas (1976) presented an argument, which has become known as the Lucas Critique, against the use of the then conventionally estimated econometric models for the evaluation of alternative economic policies. Since then, econometric models incorporating REH have been constructed, for example, for Britain by the National Institute of Economic and Social Research.

NOTES TO CHAPTER 13

1 That is, the closeness, or otherwise, of the relationship depends on the accident of the choice of the time period for its measurement.

2 Another rule to displace discretionary demand management was given a brief airing in the early 1970s by the Economic Policy Group of the Department of Applied Economics in Cambridge. The New Cambridge view is expounded in a memorandum of evidence for the Ninth Report of the Expenditure Committee of the House of Commons (HC 328, July 1974). The New Cambridge economists estimated an equation which, they claimed, established a strong link between total private income and total private expenditure, from which they drew two conclusions. In the first place, since exports had not been notably unstable, it followed that the economic fluctuations of recent years must have originated in government policy. Fine-tuning was the cause, and not the solution, of fluctuations of output. Secondly, a change in the budget balance would be followed, up to two years

later, by a corresponding change in the balance of payments on current account. Policy should therefore be to set the budget balance (the PSBR began to appear in policy discussion for the first time in the early 1970s) to secure the desired external balance. This would not, however, bring about full employment: indeed, with existing competitiveness, it would be likely to cause considerable unemployment. The way to overcome this would not be to devalue, which might be ineffective, and in any case cause inflation, but to bring in substantial protection. Already by 1975, however, the New Cambridge equation had 'broken down massively' (Bispham, in *National Institute Economic Review*, November 1975). In recent years the trend in the budget balance has been from deficit into surplus, while the trend in the current account of the balance of payments has been strongly in the opposite direction. Even allowing for the large size of the residual error in balance-of-payments statistics, the evidence would still appear to be against this particular rule.

3 See, for example, Keynes (1971), chapter 4.

4 It is not the only route. A rise in the world price of imported materials will raise costs and be passed through to domestic prices. Brown writes: ' ... the forces of the world market did something towards keeping the larger countries' export prices in line, rather less towards doing so for their unit labour costs'. The evidence suggests that: ' ... the world markets' control over national unit labour cost levels is weak, while its influence over manufactured goods prices is plainly insufficient to destroy the evidence we have seen of, broadly, cost-plus pricing' (Brown, 1985, page 333).

NOTES TO CHAPTER 14

1 As we saw in Chapter 3, page 28, the profile of productivity and output growth in the United States in the postwar period differed from that of Japan and the major economies of Europe.

2 The ideas of the *General Theory* were being absorbed at a time when the economic context was changing rapidly from the demand deficiency of the 1930s to the enormous pressure of demand in the war, which required a battery of physical controls to manage it. It is because of this change in context that the idea of raising the propensity to consume never received so much attention. The best British sources on Keynesian policy are Beveridge (1944) and Institute of Statistics (1944).

3 When there is a spontaneous increase in national income, for example originating in a rise in exports, there will be 'automatic' increases in direct and indirect tax revenues, as well as 'automatic' falls in government expenditure, for example, unemployment benefits. Besides these automatic budgetary effects, there are discretionary changes in tax rates, with corresponding effects on revenues, and in government expenditures.

4 In his study of United States fiscal policy between 1945 and 1959, Holmans concluded that the record of fiscal policy after the Second World War showed that the automatic stabilisers were allowed to work unhampered. As regards discretionary policies, these were cautious, but virtually always in the right

direction. He asks how this can be squared with the generally held 'sound finance' view of United States politicians, especially Republicans. Summing up the experience of the Eisenhower administration, he writes: 'The principle of the balanced budget is not explicitly renounced in times of deflation, but is quietly disregarded'. See Holmans (1961).

5 Measuring the extent to which fiscal policy improves stability is not easy but, if the technical difficulties can be overcome, one is inclined to accept without too much demur that reducing instability is a 'good thing'. However, a few *caveats* should be entered. Firstly, as is discussed on page 194, there could be a conflict between stability of GDP and securing a satisfactory external balance. Secondly, there could be a conflict with other specific aims of policy, such as rearmament. Thirdly, it is conceivable that stability could be improved, but at the expense of growth. Some measures, based on output changes, make the Japanese economy, in the postwar years, very unstable. But what if the growth fluctuations were, in some Schumpeterian way, the expression of entrepreneurial dynamism, which might suffer if booms were nipped in the bud? Finally, governments may use fiscal policy, in a variety of ways, to improve their prospects of winning a forthcoming election. Economists may deplore this, but they should not ignore it.

6 There is a very good account of postwar monetary policies in European countries by Thygesen in *The European Economy* (Boltho, 1982).

7 Bispham (1984) estimated an eventual effect of 19 per centage points.

8 The impetus for higher prices came from the supply side, and it placed many governments in an acute dilemma, especially those heavily dependent on imports of oil. Take, for instance, an oil-importing country, initially at full employment, and with exports and imports in balance. We suppose fixed exchange rates, and zero price elasticity in the demand for oil. When the OPEC price went up, the immediate consequences would be (a) an increase in the value of imports and a corresponding trade deficit, and (b) a rise in the price of oil to domestic users. Consumers might respond to the price rise in a number of ways. Their real incomes would, of course, have fallen. They could, however, (1) maintain their real consumption by reducing their saving ratio to the necessary extent. In this case the personal sector financial deficit would rise to match the external deficit. Domestic output would remain unchanged but, of course, the external deficit remains. Alternatively, (2), consumers could cut their real consumption in line with the higher oil price, so that their saving ratio was maintained. Since the price elasticity for oil has been assumed to be zero, the cut in consumption will fall on non-oil goods, whose output will fall, so that there is the beginning of adjustment. The third possibility (3) is that, in response to the higher oil price, consumers, in their role as wage-earners, would demand, and secure, higher money wages in an attempt to recover the initial loss of real income. In the nature of the case, this rise in money wages will do little more than push up costs and the general price level. If carried far enough, of course, it will push up non-oil prices as much as oil prices, recoup the initial loss in the terms of trade, and restore the initial real internal and external equilibrium.

Insofar as we speak of price rises as inflationary and output losses as deflationary, the impact of the oil-price rise is simultaneously inflationary and deflationary. As the House of Commons Committee on Expenditure pointed out at the time, a better term would be 'contractionary' (*Ninth Report*, HC 238).

So far, we have said nothing of the response of the public sector. Here, also, there are different possibilities. As an analogue of case (1) above, the government could have reduced the public sector's propensity to save, by reducing taxes. Ideally, they would cut indirect taxes so as to offset the effect of higher oil prices on the general price level. In this way, real private income would have remained unchanged and hence domestic activity and employment. The public sector deficit would rise, equal to the external deficit. The real domestic economy would remain as it was, so long as it was possible to finance the external deficit.

Different governments might be expected to react in different ways, as also would consumers in different countries. In the case where the consumers try to maintain real income by pushing up money incomes, we would expect that non-oil prices would be carried upward in the wake of the oil price. Any such inflation of nominal incomes would again present the government with a dilemma – either to accommodate the higher money income by keeping interest rates constant, which would normally entail an increase in the money supply, or else to maintain the nominal money supply unchanged. In our view, this would be more likely to contract demand and output, but monetarist economists would maintain that it would reduce non-oil prices sufficiently to offset the rise in the oil price, and leave the general price level unchanged. We discuss this general question elsewhere (page 146), and merely repeat here that, in our view, the monetarist story of the OPEC price rise is wrong. The different positions in the British case are to be found in the papers and minutes of evidence given to the House of Commons Committee on Expenditure for its Ninth Report, in 1974, already cited.

9 The British government's Medium Term Financial Strategy has provided the framework for its economic policy since 1980. In the *Financial Statement and Budget Report* of 1988–9, it is asserted that: 'Monetary and fiscal policies are designed to keep the growth of money GDP on a downward trend over the medium term. The MTFS is complemented by policies to improve the working of markets and the supply side of the economy'.

10 The British inflation rate was intensified by a singular policy misfortune. In 1972 the Conservative government, under Mr Heath, had introduced a statutory incomes policy: in the second stage of this policy, to start in the autumn of 1973, a clause was introduced to the effect that, for every percentage point rise in the retail price index beyond 7 per cent, a corresponding increase would be allowed in the average wage. This clause was intended to elicit the willing cooperation of trade unions in the policy and, at the time it was invented, the possibility of a 7 point rise in the retail price index within the planning horizon seemed remote. The OPEC oil price rise changed all that and in the event the threshold arrangement was triggered as many as eleven times in some agreements.

11 The slowdown in GDP growth was matched by a slowdown in productivity growth, whose nature is discussed in Chapter 3, pp. 29 *et seq*.

12 It has long been recognised that the nominal budget balance is not a proper

measure of fiscal stance, and that a cyclically-adjusted, or high-employment, or structural budget balance should be calculated. More recently, it has been suggested that further adjustments should be made, for example, for inflation. Eisner and Pieper (1984) have made such adjustments for the United States budget since 1955. They pointed out that in the decade of the 1970s, not only was the nominal budget in deficit, but so also was the high-employment budget. However, when allowance was made, (1) for changes in the value of assets due to interest changes, and (2) for changes in the rate of inflation, there were deficits only in 1970, 1971, 1974 and 1975, the fully adjusted budget being in surplus for the remaining years. Nevertheless, this was a notional surplus. In money terms the debt was rising.

13 The extent to which governments, in adopting monetary targets, were ideologically committed to monetarist doctrine would have to be examined case by case. In the British case it was said by monetarists that Mr Healey's adoption of targets was in 'bad faith', while there was no doubt about the ideological purity of the 1979 Conservative government in its first few years.

14 This was the explanation offered by Mr Nigel Lawson, the British Chancellor of the Exchequer in 1988, when an influx of funds into London pushed the money supply well beyond the target range.

15 A 'weighted full employment balance' changed from -7.02 per cent of GDP in 1967/8 to -1.58 per cent in 1969/70, a swing of 5.5 per cent (see Blackaby et al., 1978, page 187).

16 There was no statutory control of wages, but price control was retained and, under the Price Code, if the pay limit was exceeded, the whole of any pay increase could be disallowed. The White Paper introducing the policy, *Cmnd 6151*, stated that the government might take reserve powers to make it illegal for a particular employer to pay above the limit.

17 See page 202.

18 The simple *ex post* measure of the PSBR, or, alternatively, the net acquisition of financial assets by the government, are the least revealing – since they can increase as a result of a policy decision, or as a consequence of recession. Hence the use of cyclically-adjusted or constant-employment budget surplus or deficit. Further refinement is possible to allow for the differing impact on aggregate demand of various components of revenue and expenditure. See Biswas et al. (1985).

19 Prior to the 1980s, there were a number of liquidity constraints on the personal sector. Central controls limited the capacity of banks to lend to the personal sector. The existence of a cartel of building societies meant that mortgage borrowing was periodically limited by informal rationing schemes, which at times could amount to mortgage 'famine'. There were controls on hire-purchase. During the 1980s most of these constraints were removed. The 'corset' was removed from the banks in 1980 and this was followed by the ending of hire-purchase restrictions. The ending of restriction was followed by the development of new financial instruments. The banks re-entered the mortgage market, and mortgage borrowing both for house purchase, and to acquire cars and other durables, increased. The personal sector built up its liabilities much faster than its assets. In this borrowers

have been encouraged by intensive advertising by lenders of all kinds. Doubts have been expressed by some commentators about the wisdom of such a rapid growth of personal indebtedness. However, our concern here is with the increase of consumers' expenditure as a generator of output and employment. (See Dicks, 1987.)

20 Changes in interest rates have an almost immediate effect on the *index* of retail prices, in the direction opposite to that which the changes are intended to bring about in the medium or longer term. Thus, a 1 per cent rise in the interest rate may raise the mortgage rate by the same amount. But the latter is a component of the housing cost element in the RPI. 1 per cent on the mortgage rate brings about 0.4 per cent on the RPI. For this reason, where trends are concerned, it is better to look at the RPI with the mortgage element removed.

21 The last time there was a trough in output and employment similar to 1981 was 1932. The growth of output from 1932 onwards was faster, and just as steady as the recovery after 1981.

22 Most stops of the 1950s and 1960s were slowdowns. Absolute falls in output occurred twice only, in 1952 (0.7 per cent) and 1958 (0.1 per cent).

NOTES TO CHAPTER 15

1 Measured from peak-to-peak, average UK GDP growth in 1973–9 was 1.5 per cent, and in 1979–88 was 2.1 per cent. From trough to peak, average GDP growth 1981–8 was 3.5 per cent per annum.

2 A full account of this episode, making use of the public records, is now available in Cairncross and Watts (1989), pp. 264 *et seq.* There were many cross-currents involved in framing the April Budget, so that it is over-simplified to see it simply as a case of electoral opportunism overriding sound economic judgement: but that element was an important part of the story.

3 The National Institute estimated the effect as being about ½ per cent of GDP in a full year. It was not made clear what control over wage changes the Chancellor was supposed to have.

NOTES TO CHAPTER 16

1 We do not have figures for manufacturing alone, but the Bank of England *Quarterly Bulletin* gives figures for total (non-bank) outward and inward direct investment. From the *Bulletin* of November, 1989, we learn that outward investment from the United Kingdom in the 1980s (up to 1988) averaged about 2.5 per cent of GDP, compared with 1.2 per cent of GDP for inward flows. The outward flow jumped to over 4 per cent in 1987. These figures cover all industries, except banks, but, on the face of it, one would expect the same sort of effect on employment as in manufacturing. The figures also cover acquisitions and mergers, where the employment argument may be less strong.

2 There is an important argument that the prevention of deterioration in the
   trade balance is not something which can be halted or reversed by a
   reduction of relative prices of British goods and services with the rest of the
   world. One must go deeper to examine all aspects of non-price competition,
   such as the type and quality of British goods, their servicing and delivery
   dates (see, for instance, Greenhalgh, Gregory and Ray, 1990). This is a
   subject where it is wise not to be dogmatic. There is no reason, in principle,
   why price and non-price competition should be in conflict, except for a range
   of luxury goods and services where the demand appears to be increased by
   making them more expensive. Whether, and by how much, a general lowering
   of prices would help the trade balance may vary over time, and needs constant
   empirical re-examination. On the basis of a study of United Kingdom
   engineering products in general and machine tools in particular, Brech and
   Stout (1981) indicated that there might be a positive feedback from product
   inferiority in British exports, through devaluation, to even further product
   inferiority. They stressed, however, that 'no topsy-turvy recommendation'
   would necessarily follow for exchange rate policy. For the time being, we
   shall continue to assume that, when there has been time to adjust, lower
   relative prices will improve, rather than worsen the trade balance.

3 This was most cogently demonstrated by Henderson in a brilliant Treasury
   paper on *The International Economic History of the Inter-War Period*, written in
   1943, and later published in Henderson (1955).

4 For a fuller discussion of the effects of the 1949 devaluation, see the chapter
   on 'Trade and Payments' by the present author in Cairncross (1971).

5 The powers extended to national insurance contributions, but were never
   used.

6 For 1964 as a whole, the current account deficit reached 1¼ per cent of GDP.
   This compares with a figure of over 4 per cent in 1989.

7 'The effects of the devaluation of 1967 on the current balance of payments',
   Economic Journal, Special Issue, March 1972. This estimate was at the lower
   end of the spectrum of a number of estimates made around this time.

8 Some economists estimated the full-employment current account balance in
   1971 to be zero or negative.

9 Britain left the Snake almost immediately after joining.

10 The pound is in ECU – the European Currency Unit – and the Bank of
   England participates in the ECU-creating mechanism. Britain intends to
   join the Exchange Rate Mechanism (ERM) when the conditions are right,
   but up to early 1990 it had not done so.

11 At the time there was intense discussion whether this recourse to the IMF
   was necessary. Cooper (1987) later examined a number of case studies of
   European economies which are often cited to show how powerful are the
   external constraints on macroeconomic policies. He considered, among
   others, the British recourse to the International Monetary Fund in 1976.
   Why, if Britain had 'unlimited access to international capital markets' did it
   go for a loan to the IMF, which imposed restrictions on macroeconomic
   policy? Cooper acknowledged that signs of external constraint in borrowing
   were emerging in some cases, but thinks that they were 'weak signals': the

countries concerned could have borrowed more. His conclusion in the British case was that the British Chancellor, Mr Healey, went to the IMF, not so much because he needed the funds, but to get external pressure and support for domestic retrenchment which he thought necessary anyway. Mr Healey has given his own account of this episode in his memoirs (1989). Commenting on the debate within the Cabinet, he writes: 'Tony Crosland was a more formidable opponent: he argued that the situation was already under control. So in fact it was, but the markets would not believe it'. And, at the end of his record of the incident, he writes: 'Yet, in a sense, the whole affair was unnecessary. The Treasury had grossly overestimated the PSBR, which would have fallen within the IMF's limit without any of the measures they prescribed. Later figures showed that we also managed to eliminate our current account deficit in 1977, before the IMF package had had time to influence it.' The conclusion I would draw here is that Mr Healey was right: the situation was under control, but the market would not believe it.

If I may be permitted to add a personal note, I was in the United States in the autumn of 1975, visiting the economic departments of many universities as well as other institutions. There were many discussions of the prospects for sterling, the most commonly expressed opinion being that, sooner or later, it would fall through the floor. My observation that I thought that the British balance of payments was going to be transformed by North Sea oil was listened to with polite scepticism.

12 About this time the question was put to two econometric models about what the effect would be of a '5 per cent appreciation of sterling'. One model was that of the National Institute, which would have been classified as conventional Keynesian, and the other was one newly developed at the London Business School by Burns and Beenstock, on the basis of the 'monetary theory of the balance of payments', which was also the basis of the Green Paper. Both models showed a slowing down of the rate of inflation in the first five years, but both also showed a worsening of competitiveness, and a worsening in the current balance (apart from J-curve improvement in the first year) over five years (see Major, 1979, page 127).

13 For a comparison of the British recessions and recoveries of the 1980s and the 1930s, see Gregg and Worswick (1988).

NOTES TO CHAPTER 17

1 External transactions may be conveniently classified under four heads: (1) the current account, which consists mainly of payments for exports and imports of goods and services, but also includes the payment, either way, of interest, profits and dividends, and some other items; (2) the long-term capital account, which includes both direct and portfolio investment; (3) the short-term capital account; and (4) reserves, defined according to the international monetary regime in operation. Unless the context requires finer detail, we shall write as though the current balance consists simply of exports *minus* imports of goods and services.

2 There has been an echo of this last point in the contemporary British case, inasmuch as the 'balancing item' which is the statistical discrepancy between the recorded current and capital flows in the balance of payments, was as large as 70 per cent of the current account deficit in both 1988 and 1989.

3 With the capital, many countries also imported, on a temporary or permanent basis, people with technical knowledge to help build up the economy.

4 For a discussion of the importance of the basic balance, see Pain and Westaway (1990).

5 It is, of course, true that when the short-run cost effect of higher mortgage rates on the Retail Price Index is past, higher interest rates should, in the longer run, reduce the money value of GDP, reducing output and/or prices below what they would otherwise have been.

6 These questions are extensively analysed in an issue of *Oxford Review of Economic Policy* (1989) devoted entirely to exchange rates.

7 Will not any improvement in competitiveness, however achieved, invite retaliation? If the improvement originates in a genuine reduction in real costs in the exporting country, then, in theory at least, any losses imposed on the rest of the world could be compensated. But this might not be possible in the case of devaluation. Although, to the consumer in the rest of the world, it might appear to make no difference whether the cut in the price of imports originates in a fall in real costs, or in a change in the exchange rate, the former might be regarded as fair and the latter not. In practice, in anti-dumping legislation, for instance, an effort is made to distinguish fair and unfair competition.

8 Williamson has been discussing schemes of target zones for exchange rates for many years, and has developed refinements of the proposal with various colleagues. The extended zones scheme outlined here was presented in a paper by Edison, Miller and Williamson (1987).

9 By the same token its weakness is that the rate of inflation may be absolutely insensitive to the pressure of demand.

10 As Britton remarks in his introduction to *Policymaking with Macroeconomic Models, op.cit.*, the alternative to numbers based on sophisticated models may be numbers based on crude models!

11 Professor Feldstein, of Harvard University, is currently President of the National Bureau of Economic Research. He was Chairman of the Council of Economic Advisers from October 1982 to July 1984. The views reported here are taken from a shortened version of a lecture delivered in December 1987, and published in the *Journal of Economic Perspectives*, Spring, 1988.

NOTES TO CHAPTER 18

1 Sterling is included in the calculation of the value of the ECU.

2 These figures are taken from Taylor and Artis (1988). We have drawn heavily from this paper in this section.

3 They assumed, sometimes explicitly, sometimes not, that the lower nominal rate would not immediately be cancelled by *pro tanto* higher inflation, so that the real exchange rate would also fall.

4 These figures come from *Historical Statistics of the United States Colonial Times to 1970*, Part 1, page 126.

5 See the *Report of the Study Group on the Role of Public Finance in European Integration* (The MacDougall Report), Commission of the European Communities, Brussels, 1977.

6 This gives a ratio Ireland to Denmark of 1:2.7. The Padoa-Schioppa report gives figures a decade later of 1:1.8 for Ireland to Denmark, and 1:2.8 for Portugal to Denmark.

NOTES TO CHAPTER 19

1 The generalisation is for developed economies. In less developed countries, notably in Latin America, much higher inflation has been tolerated over long periods, without necessarily being accompanied by low unemployment.

2 The political mechanics of any Community agency with significant fiscal leverage are obviously of great importance. Should it be a matter simply of extending the scope of the Commission under present arrangements with the Council of Ministers and a European Parliament with limited powers? Or should it mean creating an elected European executive, related in some way to the elected Parliament? However, our concern is with the economic linkages between the centre and the national economies, and we avoid going into the political structure.

NOTE TO APPENDIX

1 'Compensation' is wages and salaries of employees *plus* employers' contributions to social security and private benefit plans. Also included is an estimate of wages and salaries and supplementary payments for the self-employed. The nominal figures are divided by the 'implicit price deflator' for GDP. There is a convenient source for these figures in the Statistical Tables in the 1990 *Economic Report of the President*, Washington.

LIST OF WORKS CITED

Artis, M. J., Bladen-Hovell, R., Karakitsos, E. and Dwolatzky, B. (1984), 'The effects of economic policy: 1979–82', *National Institute Economic Review*, no. 108, May.

Bank of England (1981), 'Factors underlying the recent recession', Panel Paper no. 15, July.

(1983), 'Monetary trends in the United Kingdom', Panel Paper no. 22, October.

Bean, C. R., Layard, P. R. G. and Nickell, S. J. (1988) (Eds), *The Rise in Unemployment*, Oxford, Blackwell.

Berndt, E. P. and Wood, D. P. (1986), 'Energy price shocks and productivity growth in US and UK manufacturing', *Oxford Review of Economic Policy*, vol. 2, no. 3, Autumn.

Beveridge, W. H. (1909), *Unemployment*, London, Longmans, Green and Co.

(1944), *Full Employment in a Free Society*, London, Allen and Unwin.

Birch, D. (1979), *The Job Generation Process*, MIT Program on Neighborhood and Regional Change, Cambridge, Mass.

Bispham, J. A. (1984), Inflation, recession and recovery, BIS Economic Paper no. 11, February.

Bispham, J. A. and Boltho, A. (1982), Chapter 2 in Boltho, A. (1982) *op. cit.*

Biswas, R., Johns, C. and Savage, D. (1985), 'The measurement of fiscal stance', *National Institute Economic Review*, August.

Blackaby, F. T. *et al.* (1978), *British Economic Policy, 1960–74*, Cambridge University Press.

Blanchflower, D. G. and Oswald, A. J. (1988), 'Profit-related pay: prose discovered?', *Economic Journal*, September.

Boltho, A. (1981), 'British fiscal policy – stabilising or destabilising?' *Oxford Bulletin of Economics and Statistics*, Vol. 43, no. 4, November.

Boltho, A. (Ed.) (1982), *The European Economy*, Oxford University Press.

Boltho, A. and Allsopp, C. (1987), 'The assessment: trade and trade policy', *Oxford Review of Economic Policy*, vol. 3, no. 1.

Brech, M. J. and Stout, D. K. (1981), 'The rate of exchange and non-price competitiveness' in Eltis, W. A. and Sinclair, P. J. N. (Eds), *The Money Supply and the Exchange Rate*, Oxford, Clarendon Press.

Britton, A.J.C. (1986a), *The Trade Cycle in Britain*, Cambridge University Press.

(1986b), 'Employment policy in the public sector', in Hart, P. E. (Ed), (1986).

(Ed.) (1989), *Policymaking with Macroeconomic Models*, Gower.

Brown, A. J. (1972), *The Framework of Regional Economics in the United Kingdom*, Cambridge University Press.

(1983), *Friedman and Schwartz on the United Kingdom*, Bank of England Panel paper no. 22, October.

(1985), *World Inflation since 1950*, Cambridge University Press.

Bruno, M. and Sachs, J. D. (1985), *Economics of World Wide Stagflation*, Oxford, Blackwell.

Bryant, R. *et al.* (1988), *Empirical Macroeconomics for Interdependent Economies*, Washington, Brookings Institution.

Burns, T. (1988), 'The UK Government's Financial Strategy', Chapter 20, Eltis, W. and Sinclair, P. (eds.) (1988) *op. cit.*

Cairncross, A. (ed.) (1971), *Britain's Economic Prospects Reconsidered*, London, George Allen and Unwin.

(1985), *Years of Recovery*, London, Methuen.

Cairncross, A. and Watts, N. (1989), *The Economic Section, 1939–1961*, London, Routledge.

Caves, R. E. *et al.* (1968), *Britain's Economic Prospects*, Washington, Brookings Institution; London, George Allen and Unwin.

Cooper, R. N. (1987), 'External constraints on European growth' in Lawrence, R. Z. and Schultze, C. L. (Eds), *Barriers to European Growth*, Washington, Brookings Institution.

Cross, R. (1988) (ed.), *Unemployment, Hysteresis and the Natural Rate*, Oxford, Blackwell.

Currie, D. and Wren-Lewis, S. W. L. (1989) 'Conflict and cooperation in international macroeconomic policymaking: past performance and future prospects', in Britton, A. (Ed) (1989) *op. cit.*

Daniel, W. W. (1987), *Work Place Industrial Relations and Technical Change*, Policy Studies Institute, Francis Pinter.

Darby, J. and Wren-Lewis, S. (1989), 'Manufacturing productivity in the 1980s', *National Institute Economic Review*, May.

Dean, A. (1978), 'Incomes policies and differentials', *National Institute Economic Review*, August.

Denison, E. F. (1974), *Accounting for United States Economic Growth 1929–1969*, Washington, Brookings Institution.

(1979), *Accounting for Slower Economic Growth*, Washington, Brookings Institution.

(1985), *Trends in American Economic Growth, 1929–1982*, Washington, The Brookings Institution.

Department of Employment (1988), *Employment for the 1990s*, Cmd.540, HMSO.

Dicks, M. J. (1987), 'Financial behaviour of the UK private sector, 1976–85' in *Bank of England Quarterly Bulletin*, May.

Dicks, M. J. and Hatch, N. (1989), 'The relationship between employment and unemployment', Bank of England Discussion Paper, no.39. July.

Dornbusch, R. (1988), 'Doubts about the McKinnon standard', *Journal of Economic Perspectives*, Winter.

Dow, J. C. R. (1988), *A Critique of Monetary Policy*, Oxford, Clarendon Press.

EC Commission (1977), *The Role of Public Finance in European Integration* (Mac-Dougall Report), Brussels, Economic Community.

Edison, H., Miller, M. and Williamson, J. (1987), 'On evaluating and extending the target zone proposal', *Journal of Policy Modelling*, Spring.

Egginton, D. M. (1988), 'Regional labour markets in Great Britain', *Bank of England Quarterly Bulletin*, August.

Eisner, R. and Pieper, P. J. (1984), 'A new view of the Federal debt and budget deficits', *American Economic Review*, March.

Eltis, W. and Sinclair, P. (Eds) (1988), *Keynes and Economic Policy*, London, Macmillan.

Friedman, M. (1968), 'The role of monetary policy', *American Economic Review*, March.

Galbraith, J. K. (1958), *The Affluent Society*, London, Hamish Hamilton.

Gallagher, C. C. and Doyle, J. R. (1986), 'Small firms in net job generation', *British Business*, 17 October.

Greenhalgh, C., Gregory, M. and Ray, A. (1990), *Employment and Structural Change in Britain: Trends and Policy Options*, Employment Institute.

Gregg, P. A. (1990), 'Out for the Count: a new approach to modelling claimant unemployment', National Institute of Economic and Social Research Discussion Paper no. 167, January.

Gregg, P. A. and Worswick, G. D. N. (1988), 'Recession and recovery in Britain: the 1930s and the 1980s', *National Institute Economic Review*, November.

Griliches, Z. (1988), 'Productivity puzzles and R&D: Another non-explanation', *Journal of Economic Perspectives*, Fall.

Hakim, C. (1989), 'Identifying fast growth small firms', *Employment Gazette*, January.

Hansen, B. (1969), *Fiscal Policy in Seven Countries, 1955–1965*, OECD.

Hart, P. E. (1987), 'Small firms and jobs', *National Institute Economic Review*, August.

Hart, P. E. (ed.) (1986), *Unemployment and Labour Market Policies*, Gower.

Healey, D. (1989), *The Time of My Life*, London, Michael Joseph.

Henderson, H. D. (1955), *The Inter-war Years, and Other Papers*, Oxford, The Clarendon Press.

Henry, S. G. B. and Ormerod, P. A. (1978), 'Incomes policy and wage inflation: empirical evidence for the UK, 1961–1977', *National Institute Economic Review*, August.

HM Treasury (1978), *The European Monetary System*, Cmnd 7405, HMSO, November.

HM Treasury (1980), *Financial Statement and Budget Report, 1980–81*, London, HMSO, March.

Historical Statistics of the United States Colonial Times to 1970 (1976), Bureau of the Census, US Government Printing Office.

Holmans, A. E. (1961), *United States Fiscal Policy, 1945–1959*, Oxford University Press.

Hopkin, B. (1984), 'Real wages and unemployment', Bank of England Panel Paper no. 24.

Institute of Statistics (1944), *Economics of Full Employment*, Oxford, Blackwell.

Jackman, R. and Kan, B. (1988), 'Structural unemployment: a reply', *Oxford Bulletin of Economics and Statistics*, February.

Jackman, R. and Layard, R. (1986), 'A wage-tax, worker-subsidy policy, for reducing the natural rate of unemployment', chapter 7 of Beckerman, W. (Ed.), *Wage Rigidity and Unemployment*, Johns Hopkins University Press.

Jackman, R. and Roper, S. (1987), 'Structural unemployment', in *Oxford Bulletin of Economics and Statistics*, February.

Johnson, C. (1988), *Measuring the Economy*, Penguin Books.

Jones, D. T. (1976), 'Output, employment and labour productivity in Europe since 1955', *National Institute Economic Review*, August.

Kaldor, N. (1936), 'Wage subsidies as a remedy for unemployment', *Journal of Political Economy*, December.

(1964), *Essays in Economic Policy*, vol. 1, Duckworth.

Kalecki, M. (1943), 'Political aspects of full employment', *Political Quarterly*, vol. 14.

(1944), 'Three ways to full employment' in *Economics of Full Employment*, Oxford University Institute of Statistics, Blackwell.

Keynes, J. M. (1971), *Tract on Monetary Reform, The Collected Writings of John Maynard Keynes*, Vol. IV, London, Macmillan.

(1972), *Essays in Persuasion, The Collected Writings of John Maynard Keynes*, Vol. IX, London, Macmillan.

(1973), *The General Theory of Employment, Interest and Money. The Collected Writings of John Maynard Keynes*, Vol. VII, London, Macmillan.

Laidler, D. E. W. (1975), Commentary on Milton Friedman, *Unemployment versus Inflation*, Institute of Economic Affairs, Occasional paper no. 44.

Lal, D. (1979), 'Comment', in Major R. L. (Ed) (1979).

Layard, R. (1986), *How to Beat Unemployment*, Oxford University Press.

Layard, P. R. G. and Nickell, S. J. (1980), 'The case for subsidising extra jobs', *Economic Journal*, vol. 90, March.

(1988), 'Unemployment in Britain' in Bean, C. R., Layard, P. R. G. and Nickell, S. J. (Eds).

Leontief, W. and Duchin, F. (1986), *The Future Impact of Automation on Workers*, New York, Oxford University Press.

Lindbeck, A. (1988), 'Swedish industry in a national and international perspective', Skandinaviska Enskilka Banken *Quarterly Review*, 3.

Lucas, R. E. Jr. (1976), Econometric policy evaluation: a critique', in Brunner, K., and Meltzer, A. H. (Eds.), *The Phillips Curve and Labour Markets*, Supplement to the *Journal of Monetary Economics*.

McKinnon, R. I. (1988), 'Monetary and exchange rate policies for international financial stability: a proposal', *Journal of Economic Perspectives*, Winter.

Maddison, A. (1982), *The Phases of Capitalist Development*, Oxford University Press.

Major, R. L. (Ed.) (1979), *Britain's Trade and Exchange Rate Policy*, Heinemann Educational Books.

Mansfield, E. *et al.* (1982), *Technology Transfer, Productivity and Economic Policy*, New York, Norton and Co.

Matthews, D. (1989, 'The British experience of profit-sharing', *The Economic History Review*, Second Series, Vol. XLII, No. 4, November.

Matthews, R. C. O. (Ed.) (1982), *Slower Growth in the Western World*, London, Heinemann.

Matthews, R. C. O., Feinstein, C. H. and Odling-Smee, J. (1982), *British Economic Growth, 1856–1973*, Oxford, Clarendon Press.

Maynard, C. and Van Ryckeghem, W. (1976), *A World of Inflation*, London, Batsford.

Meade, J. E. (1982), *Wage-Fixing*, Volume 1 of *Stagflation*, George Allen and Unwin.

Minford, A. P. L. (1983), *Unemployment: Cause and Cure*, Martin Robertson, second edition, Oxford, Blackwell, 1985.

   (1989), 'A new classical policy programme', in Britton, A. (Ed.), *Policymaking with Macroeconomic Models*, Aldershot, Gower.

Moore, B., Rhodes, J. and Tyler, P. (1986), *The Effects of Government Regional Economic Policy*, Department of Trade and Industry, HMSO.

Nabseth, L. and Ray, G. F. (Eds) (1974), *The Diffusion of New Industrial Processes*, Cambridge University Press.

National Economic Development Office (1976), Cyclical fluctuations in the United Kingdom economy, Discussion paper 3, January.

National Institute of Economic and Social Research (1990), Productivity education and training: Britain and other countries compared, reprints of 15 studies from the *National Institute Economic Review* with a preface by S. J. Prais.

Neild, R. R. (1979), 'Managed trade between industrial countries', in Major, R. L. (Ed.) (1979).

Nickell, S. (1988), 'Why is wage inflation in Britain so high?' in Cross, R. (Ed.) (1988).

Northcott, J. (1986), *Microelectronics in Industry – Promise and Performance*, Policy Studies Institute Research Report.

Nuti, D. M. (1987), 'Codetermination and profit-sharing' in *The New Palgrave Dictionary of Economics*, Vol. 1, Macmillan.

OECD (1977), *Towards Full Employment and Price Stability* (The McCracken Report), June.

Oulton, N. (1987), 'Plant closures and the productivity 'miracle' in manufacturing', *National Institute Economic Review*, August.

Oxford Review of Economic Policy (1989), 'Exchange rates', Vol. 5, no.3, Autumn.

Padoa-Schioppa, T. (1987), *Efficiency, Stability and Equity*, Oxford University Press.

Page, S. A. B. (1987), 'The rise in protection since 1974', *Oxford Review of Economic Policy*, vol. 3, no 1.

Pain, N. and Westaway, P. (1990), 'Why the capital account matters', *National Institute Economic Review*, February.

Pechman, J. A. (1990), 'The future of the income tax', *American Economic Review*, March.

Pencavel, J. (1987), *The Classical Unemployment Hypothesis and International Comparisons of Labour Market Behaviour*, Centre for Economic Policy Research, CEPR Publication no. 110, Stanford University and National Bureau of Economic Research, September.

Phelps Brown, E. H. (1983), *The Origins of Trade Union Power*, Oxford.

Phillips, A. W. (1958), 'The relations between unemployment and the rate of change of money wage rates in the United Kingdom 1861–1957', *Economica N.S.*, vol.25, no. 100, November.

Pigou, A. C. (1927), 'Wage policy and unemployment', *Economic Journal*, September.

(1928), *Economics of Welfare*, 3rd edition, Macmillan.

Prais, S. J. (1976), *The Evolution of Giant Firms in Britain*, Cambridge University Press.

Ray, G. F. (1984), *The Diffusion of Mature Technologies*, Cambridge University Press.

Reddaway, B. (1966), 'Rising prices for ever?', *Lloyds Bank Review*, July.

Ricardo, D. (1821), *Principles of Political Economy and Taxation*, reprinted in Volume 1 of *The Works and Correspondence of David Ricardo*, (1951), edited by Piero Sraffa, Cambridge University Press.

Robinson, J. (1937), *Essays in the Theory of Employment*, London, Macmillan.

Salter, W. E. G. (1960), *Productivity and Technical Change*, Cambridge University Press.

Shepherd, D., Silberston, A. and Strange, R. (1985), *British Manufacturing Investment Overseas*, Methuen.

Simpson, D. R. F., Love, J. H. and Walker, J. (1986), *The Effect of New Technology on Work*, Report by Fraser of Allander Institute, Strathclyde, June.

Sinclair, P. (1981), 'When does technical change destroy jobs?', *Oxford Economic Papers*, March.

Solow, R. M. (1964), *The Nature and Sources of Unemployment in the United States*, Stockholm, Almqvist and Wiksell.

(1985), 'Economic History and Economics', Proceedings of the American Economic Association, *American Economic Review*, May.

(1987) 'Unemployment: getting the questions right', in Bean, Layard and Nickell (Eds) (1987).

Storey, D. J. and Johnson, S. (1987), *Job Generation and Labour Market Change*, London, Macmillan.

Taylor, M. P. and Artis, M. J. (1988), 'What has the European Monetary System achieved?', Bank of England Discussion Paper no. 31.

Tobin, J. (1985), 'High time to return to the 1946 Employment Act', *Challenge*, May/June.

Thygesen, N. (1982), 'Monetary Policy', Chapter 11 in Boltho (Ed.) (1982).

Trinder, C. (1988), 'Special employment measures and employment', *National Institute Economic Review*, February.

UN Economic Commission for Europe (1988), 'Wage rigidity in Western Europe and North America', *Economic Survey of Europe in 1987–1988*, Geneva, April.

Wadhwani, S. and Wall, M. (1990), 'The effects of profit-sharing on employment, wages, stock returns and productivity: evidence from UK microdata', *Economic Journal*, March.

Weitzman, M. L. (1984), *The Share Economy*, Harvard University Press.

Whitley, J. D. and Wilson, R. A. (1987), 'Quantifying the impact of information technology using a macroeconomic model of the United Kingdom' in *Information Technology and Economic Prospects*, Paris, OECD.

Williamson, J. (1988), 'On McKinnon's monetary rule', *Journal of Economic Perspectives*, Winter.

Wood, A. (1988), 'How much unemployment is structural?', *Oxford Bulletin of Economics and Statistics*, February.

Worswick, G. D. N. (1959), 'Mrs Robinson on simple accumulation', *Oxford Economic Papers*, June.

Worswick, G. D. N. (Ed.) (1974), *The Concept and Measurement of Involuntary Unemployment*, Allen and Unwin.

INDEX

THE NATIONAL INSTITUTE OF ECONOMIC
AND SOCIAL RESEARCH
PUBLICATIONS IN PRINT

published by
THE CAMBRIDGE UNIVERSITY PRESS
(available from booksellers, or in case of difficulty from the publishers)

NIESR STUDENTS' EDITION

THE NATIONAL INSTITUTE OF ECONOMIC AND
SOCIAL RESEARCH

publishes regularly

THE NATIONAL INSTITUTE ECONOMIC REVIEW

A quarterly analysis of the general economic situation in the United Kingdom and overseas with forecasts eighteen months ahead. The last issue each year usually contains an assessment of medium-term prospects. There are also in most issues special articles on subjects of interest to academic and business economists.

Annual subscriptions, £55.00 (home) and £75.00 (abroad), also single issues for the current year, £15.00 (home) and £22.00 (abroad), are available direct from NIESR, 2 Dean Trench Street, Smith Square, London, SW1P 3HE.

Subscriptions at the special reduced price of £22.00 p.a. are available to students in the United Kingdom and Irish Republic on application to the Secretary of the Institute.

Back numbers and reprints of issues which have gone out of stock are distributed by Wm. Dawson and Sons Ltd., Cannon House, Park Farm Road, Folkestone. Microfiche copies for the years 1959–88 are available from EP Microform Ltd., Bradford Road, East Ardsley, Wakefield, Yorks.

Published by
HEINEMANN EDUCATIONAL BOOKS
(distributed by Gower Publishing Company and available from booksellers)

DEMAND MANAGEMENT
Edited by MICHAEL POSNER. 1978. pp.256. £18.50 net.

BRITAIN IN EUROPE
Edited by WILLIAM WALLACE. 1980. pp.224. £12.95 (paperback) net.

THE FUTURE OF PAY BARGAINING
Edited by FRANK BLACKABY. 1980. pp.256. £31.00 (hardback), £8.95
(paperback) net.

INDUSTRIAL POLICY AND INNOVATION
Edited by CHARLES CARTER. 1981. pp.250. £26.50 (hardback), £9.95
(paperback) net.

THE CONSTITUTION OF NORTHERN IRELAND
Edited by DAVID WATT. 1981. pp.233. £24.00 (hardback), £10.50 (paperback)
net.

SLOWER GROWTH IN THE WESTERN WORLD
Edited by R. C. O. MATTHEWS. 1982. pp.182. £26.50 (hardback), £10.95
(paperback) net.

NATIONAL INTERESTS AND LOCAL GOVERNMENT
Edited by KEN YOUNG. 1983. pp.180. £25.00 (hardback), £10.95 (paperback)
net.

EMPLOYMENT, OUTPUT AND INFLATION
Edited by A. J. C. BRITTON. 1983. pp.208. £36.00 net.

THE TROUBLED ALLIANCE. ATLANTIC RELATION IN THE 1980s
Edited by LAWRENCE FREEDMAN. 1983. pp.176. £25.00 (hardback), £8.95
(paperback) net.

(Available from Heinemann and from booksellers)
THE UK ECONOMY
By the NIESR. 1990. pp.96. £3.95 net.

Published by
GOWER PUBLISHING COMPANY
(Available from Gower Publishing Company and from booksellers)
ENERGY SELF-SUFFICIENCY FOR THE UK
Edited by ROBERT BELGRAVE and MARGARET CORNELL. 1985. pp.224. £22.50 net.

THE FUTURE OF BRITISH DEFENCE POLICY
Edited by JOHN ROPER. 1985. pp.214. £24.00 net.

ENERGY MANAGEMENT: CAN WE LEARN FROM OTHERS?
By GEORGE F. RAY. 1985. pp.131. £22.50 net.

UNEMPLOYMENT AND LABOUR MARKET POLICIES
Edited by P. E. HART. 1986. pp. 230. £30.00 net.

NEW PRIORITIES IN PUBLIC SPENDING
Edited by M. S. LEVITT. 1987. pp. 136. £26.00 net.

POLICYMAKING WITH MACROECONOMIC MODELS
Edited by A. J. C. BRITTON. 1989. pp. 285. £29.50 net.

HOUSING AND THE NATIONAL ECONOMY
Edited by JOHN ERMISCH. 1990. pp. 158. £29.50 net.